Warning—Disclaimer

HEREWARD CARRINGTON, Ph. D.

To
MY MOTHER
IN LOVING MEMORY

PREFACE

AMERICA has just passed through a great financial crisis—one of the many which occur from time to time, because of badly adjusted financial conditions, and as the result of greed—and we hear much talk of "hard times," and the lack of money wherewith to buy the necessities of life. Now, I believe that such "hard times," and such conditions, could be largely averted if only the people were taught to live correctly : taught how to economise their food, and how to take care of their bodies. There can be no doubt but that much of the waste which occurs throughout the land is due to ignorance of the great laws of life and health ; and if people were only taught how to reduce their food-supply scientifically—and not to expend so much money on their bodies, and especially on their food—there would be but a small amount of suffering compared with that which has existed in the past. Teach the public how to preserve the body in a state of health, upon a small amount of money, and we shall have solved one of the greatest economic factors confronting us to-day. I believe that this may be brought about, in a large part at least, by adopting the principles of nutrition outlined in this book ; and I submit it to the public largely with that idea in mind. But that is only part of my object, none the less. My desire is to help humanity to secure better health—to teach them how to live cheaply and economically ; above all, how to live so as to preserve the highest standard of health, strength and energy. We should thus have a cleaner, a hardier and a happier race of individuals ; and I firmly believe that all true

5

reform—social economic, religious—must come primarily through the body—*i.e.* these reforms can only be effected by first of all reforming the body, and its habits; and when that has been rendered clean and pure, the coveted mental and moral reforms will be found to follow of themselves. External conditions and environment may count for much, but the internal factor counts for much more. The internal personality of the man is what we should aim to reach first of all; and this can be reached most easily and effectually by means of the body—for in that he is most wrapped; with its feelings and emotions he is most closely connected. Reform 'the inner man, and particularly his body, and trust to man to reform his environment. Make men and women what they ought to be, and they will soon reform their external conditions.

I have attempted to deal, in this volume, with the *quality* of foods, as I dealt with their *quantity*, in my former book. In this way, the ground will have been pretty thoroughly covered, from the particular point of view from which I have attacked these problems. I can only hope that, as the result of these two volumes, many persons may find health and a long life, who would otherwise have sunk into a premature grave. If I could feel that I had in any way helped to accomplish this, I should be more than satisfied.

H. C.

CONTENTS

The Natural Food of Man

I

THE NATURAL FOOD OF MAN

THERE can be no doubt that, whatever other function
food may or may not have, it replaces broken-down
tissue. The tissue-wastes of the preceding day are
replenished by the food eaten; so the body remains
about the same in weight, no matter how much exercise
be taken, or how much tissue is broken down. These
tissues are very complex in their nature, and a variety
of food is consequently necessary to restore the tissues
destroyed—food containing a number of elements
(the counterpart of the elements destroyed), being
necessary to offset the waste. Proteid, fats, carbohydrates, and various salts are, therefore, necessary in
the food; and no food that does not contain these constituents, in larger or smaller quantities, can be used by
the body, or can be classed as a true "food." Other
things being equal, therefore, it may be said that *a food
is nutritious and capable of sustaining life in proportion
to its complexity—the best food being one that most nearly
supplies the wastes of the tissues.* If an article of diet
contains only one of the essential elements necessary
for supporting life, the body, if fed upon it, will waste
away and die—no matter *how much* of that food be
eaten. In certain experiments conducted upon dogs,
it was found that, when they were fed upon fat—*e.g.*
they became round, plump, *embonpoint*, and yet died of
inanition! The same would be true of any other single

9

'article of diet. If an animal were fed upon it, he would surely die, sooner or later. Proteids are supposed to supply most of the muscle-forming elements, and a part of the energy expended by the body; fats and carbo-hydrates are supposed to be of use chiefly in supplying heat and energy to the system. The mineral salts that are contained in the foods do not fulfil any definite function, so far as is known; but they are very essential, nevertheless. If a diet lacks these salts entirely, the body wastes away and dies of " saline starvation." It will thus be apparent that foods very rapidly and very forcibly affect the state of the health, and even the life of the individual. Food, it must be remembered, *makes blood*; and the blood is absolutely dependent upon the food supply for its character and composition. If the food be poisonous in character, the blood soon becomes tainted, and the mind, no less than the body, shows the effects of this poisoning process. On any theory we may hold of the nature of mind, and its connection with the body, it is certainly *dependent* upon the body for its manifestation, in this life; and is coloured and influenced by the state of the body, and by the condition of the blood. This I have shown more fully in another place. We shall also see the effects of diet upon the mind, more clearly, as we proceed in the present volume.

From what has been said, it will at all events be apparent that this question of the food supply is a very important one—indeed one of the most important before the world to-day. The first thought, the first instinct, of any animal, is to search for and secure food; self-preservation is the most powerful instinct in the world, and the nutrition of the body occupies first place, as one means of preserving life. In the lower organisms, we see this very clearly; they spend almost the whole of their lives in searching for and devouring food; but as we ascend the scale of evolution, we find less and less space devoted, in the body, to the digestive organs, and more and more to the brain, and instruments of the mind. It would appear, therefore, that the higher we ascend in the scale of evolution, the less proportionate space in the body is devoted to the purely animal processes, and the more to the mental and spiritual sides of man. *As the mentality increases, the need for food decreases:* this is a very significant law—for such I believe it to be. It would seem to indicate that man attained the highest level, so far as his physical or physiological structure was concerned; and that evolution thenceforward tended to develop that side of man which rendered possible the increased mental and spiritual characteristics. However, I shall not dwell too strongly upon that point now.

Although an adequate supply of food is very necessary to all organisms, there is but little danger that anyone in a civilised community would run the risk of starving to death, because of the lack of food. The tendency is all the other way, and most persons eat, not too little, but far too much, food. Even the very poor, and especially the babies of the very poor—eat too often, and too much. This may seem strange, but it becomes more rational and intelligible when we take into account the fact that the human body needs *so little food*, in reality, to supply the wastes of the day, that the very poor, even if they have far less food than the majority, still have too much. The average person eats at least three times more food than his system really requires; and it is due to this very fact, I earnestly believe, that much of the suffering and of the insanity, and many of the diseases, are so constantly with us. In his recently published works, Professor Chittenden has shown with great detail that the average standard " dietary tables " of the physiologists have been far too high; and that the average man can cut down his proteid intake fully one third, without detriment, but, on the contrary, with added benefit to himself.   The majority of persons eat far more than the physiologists have said to be necessary ; and now it has been shown that the physiologists have set the standard three times too high !   It would appear, therefore, that most persons eat more than three times too much proteid ; and the same has been found to hold good of the fats and carbohydrates, in a lesser degree, also.   But while the fats and carbohydrates can be eliminated by the system, or stored up within it, without positive danger, proteid in excess creates an abundance of uric acid, and causes much harm to the system throughout.   It is the excess of proteid that is the chief cause of many of the diseases from which mankind suffers ; and, if health is to be maintained, we must see to it that this great excess is not ingested into the body.   While keeping up the due allowance, we must be careful not to eat those foods which tend to introduce this excess into the system ; and, by avoiding them, it will be seen that we thereby avoid all danger of creating an undue amount of uric acid, and consequently of suffering from the induced diseases.

Now, it is a well-known fact that meat contains a large proportion of protein ; and further, that it has a great tendency to create uric acid in the system, owing to the decaying cell-nuclei that form a large part of its structure.   Meat is by no means a clean article of diet, but on the contrary a very unclean one ; and many foods, supplying an equal amount of proteid matter, are to be preferred, for the reason that they supply less toxic material—which invariably accompanies flesh-meat.   It must be remembered that the tissues of all animals contain a certain amount of poisonous material—simply by reason of the fact that the animal has lived at all—since all animals are constantly creating poisons within their bodies, by the very process of living.   These poisons are being thrown off by the body every minute throughout the day ; and it is because of that fact the animal is enabled to remain alive at all. Were this process of elimination checked for a few hours, death by poisoning would inevitably result—in consequence of the poisons formed by the body itself. All animals, then, create these poisons ; and it would be impossible to find an animal body without them. So that, when we eat the flesh of any animal, we must eat, together with the nutritious portions, these poisons—which are practically inseparable from all animal tissue. That is, whenever we eat meat, we invariably eat, at the same time, a certain quantity of poison—which it is impossible to avoid ! I shall elaborate this idea at considerable length in my chapter on the hygiene of diet. In this place I shall only call attention to that fact—the strongest argument of all, to my mind, for abstaining from flesh ; and shall point out that, if any diet furnishes all the nutritious properties of meat, without these poisons, it is certainly to be preferred, on that account. We shall see, when we come to the chapter devoted to the chemistry of foods, that all the elements contained in meat are also contained in a purer and better form in other substances—grains, some vegetables, and in nuts— and in as large or larger proportions than they are in meat.

It will thus be seen that certain foods are better for us than others—a fact which daily observation confirms. Everyone knows that certain articles of diet are indigestible, others not so much so : that some are nutritious, and others hardly of any food value at all. Some foods are better for us than others, therefore ; and, if we wish to maintain our health, it is obvious that we should eat those foods, and only those foods, as a general thing, which can be shown to be of use and benefit to the body If some foods are thus more wholesome than others, does it not behove everyone interested in the health and care of his body—and especially all those interested in hygiene, or the improvement of the race—to endeavour to ascertain what these foods are, those most natural and best for the human body ; and, having found them, to advise all who wish to maintain their bodies in the highest state of health, to live upon these foods—or at least to make them the staple articles of their diet ?   Believing this to be most certainly true, I shall devote myself, in the present volume, to a careful search through the records and evidences of science, and endeavour to ascertain in what man's natural food consists ; and, having found the food which is indicated by nature as the best and most natural for man, I shall proceed to give my reasons for thinking that this food is the most wholesome, and why it is that all other foods must be more or less harmful to the system.   This done, we shall be in a position to define what foods are " natural " for man, and indicate why it is that they are the most wholesome.

In order to clarify the problem, then, and clear away any misconceptions that may arise in the reader's mind, I shall state here what my conclusions are, and my reasons for thinking them sound. Assuming that there is an " ideal " diet of some sort—that upon which the human race originally lived, and which it should still live upon, if it wishes to maintain the best possible health—I have gone carefully through the various foodstuffs, and, by careful analysis, have shown that all meats are injurious to the body, for the reason that they are not suited to it, by reason of its anatomical structure—and, further, by the facts of experience and hygiene, which clearly indicate that if man eats meat, he suffers in consequence. These arguments will be found in full in the book. I also found that there were many objections to all vegetables, to cereals, grains and flour of all kinds; to soups, to bread and eggs, to butter, milk, cheese, and to all dairy products. Most cookbooks and works devoted to the hygiene of foods have been in the habit of pointing out all the beneficial and *good* qualities of these foods, and saying very little about their *bad* qualities. In this book, I have pointed out all the bad qualities, and have insisted that these so far offset their good qualities as to show them utterly unfitted for human food, and consequently to be discarded from any truly hygienic diet. Thus, by a process of elimination, we are forced to the conclusion that the only foods that are really natural to man, those best suited to his organism, are fruits and nuts—the diet of his anthropoid brethren, and man's own natural diet, as is clearly indicated by his anatomical structure. Fruits and nuts will alone suffice to maintain the human body in the highest state of health; and are the foods which should be adopted, and eaten, by mankind, to the exclusion of all others. From them, he can obtain all the elements necessary for the upbuilding of a healthy body; and from them he can derive the greatest amount of health and strength, and the greatest amount of energy.

Many persons would be willing to concede, I fancy, that man can live without meat—indeed, there is no escaping this conclusion, since thousands of persons are actually doing so. But not very many would be willing to concede, probably, that all breads, grains, and vegetables are to be abandoned as unfit for human food also! They would be unwilling to admit that! And yet I think it can be shown very conclusively that none of these foods are intended for the human being, any more than is the grass of the field. Each *genus* has its own particular food, alloted by nature; and man's food consists—or should consist—of fruit and nuts. Further, these fruits and nuts should be eaten uncooked

—in their original, primitive form. I am convinced that cooking ruins nearly all foods treated in that manner— my arguments for this will be found in full in the chapter on " The Fruitarian Diet."

If this be true, as I most firmly believe it is—it will be seen that practically all other foods are naturally barred out, by the very nature of the case. Certainly no one would care to eat his meat raw ; and all vegetables, with very few exceptions, would also fall under the ban, for but few of them can well be eaten without cooking. Grains, also, are very unappetising, when eaten raw, and it is now well known that but a small amount of their starch is converted properly, in the body, unless the grains are well cooked ; so that all these foods would be eliminated from the diet, and practically nothing left but fruits and nuts ! Although this may seem appalling to the average reader, it is the logical outcome of the theory, and I am cônvinced the right interpreta- tion of the facts. The fruitarian diet is the one best suited for man ; and the one upon which he can live best and longest. I mysèlf have lived upon this fruit and nut diet almost exclusively for several years, and I may perhaps say that I am always in excellent spirits and condition, and a source of constant surprise to my friends in that I seem to possess an untiring energy and ability for work. I say this, not to boast, buf to show that a diet of this character is perfectly compatible with health and strength ; and I believe that almost any person could double his energies, his health, and his self-respect by adopting a diet of this character. For it has a tremendous effèct upon the mental and moral, no less than upon the physical life, as I shall presently endeavour to show.

With the invention of fire, however, many articles of food became edible which had not been edible before. Finding that grains and roots, and certain weeds (vegetables) could be eaten, when cooked, although they were uneatable when raw, man took to cooking his food, and substituting this food for a portion of his original diet—which was probably scarce at the time. In this way, the cooking of food probably originated. It began in the far-off ages, and has been handed down to us—a legacy of barbarism, to which man rigidly clings, in the vain effort to preserve a distinction between himself and other animals—who do not cook their food—because of this fact! •He prides himself that he is the only " cooking animal " ! If man would only learn that it is owing to this very process of cooking that much of the suffering, and many of the ills from which mankind suffers, are due !

Many persons imagine that, if they returned to a primitive diet of this character, they would become as the savages—wild and uncivilised. They " don't want to become like the animals," they will say. They wish to remain " civilised," and not return to a state of savagery and barbarism ! There is no logic in this argument—indeed, no sense. Because a man lives upon fruits and nuts, it is, of course, no reason why he should return to a primitive state, *mentally* ; indeed, there is far less evidence for this than there is that man becomes like the carnivorous animals by eating meat. There *is* evidence for that ! But living upon fruits and nuts has no other effect than to elevate the tone and character of the body ; to increase its energies and to render the mind clearer and more active. If these objectors to the fruitarian diet would only study physiology and human nature before passing any such absurd judgment upon the facts, their arguments would have more force—but then, in that case, they would not raise the arguments at all !' Of course, this whole idea is conclusively proved to be erroneous by the facts in the case.

B

There is one other point I should like to touch upon, though briefly, before passing on to the main argument of the book. The usual position with regard to food, and its functions in the body is this. Food has three functions : (1) The replacement of tissues which have been broken down as the result of the day's work ; (2) the maintenance of the bodily energy ; and (8) the maintenance of the bodily heat. Now, in my former book,[1] I advanced a number of facts tending to show that food has but *one* function—replacing broken-down tissue. It supplies no heat and no energy whatever to the body, at any time, or under any circumstances. Both the heat and the energy are due to another source altogether, and not to the food ingested.[2] I cannot enumerate the arguments in support of this position here ; they will be found in full in the work referred to ; but I would point out that, if this theory were true, it would cause us to modify very largely the views entertained as to the necessary amount of food required by the body. Now, a large percentage of the food eaten is supposed to create heat and energy, or at least liberate it, and is eaten for that express purpose. But if it be true that food has no other function than to supply the body with material for the rebuilding of its structures and tissues, it will be apparent that far *less* food is necessary than is usually thought to be necessary by the physiologists ; and this would account for the enormous differences in quantity said to be

---

[1] " Vitality, Fasting and Nutrition."

[2] At first sight this position seems, of course, absurd, and opposed to the well-known facts of calorimetry : but such is not the case. All the known facts as to the equivalence of energy, heat, work, etc., can be accounted for just as readily on my theory of the relations of food and bodily energy—viz. that the energy is restored by sleep (the nervous system, like an electric motor) and not by combustion, as in the steam engine. As to the equivalence noted, this can be accounted for by assuming that as energy acts upon matter, it wastes ; and this waste is made good by a proportionate amount of food. There is therefore an equivalence, a relation, but it is not that of cause and effect. For the details of this theory, however, see " Vitality, Fasting and Nutrition," pp. 225-303 *et seq.*

necessary by the various physiologists.   The truth of the matter doubtless is, that the *smallest* amount of food is that which is necessary, and all amounts over and above this are passed through the body at an expense of the vital energies, and to the detriment of the vital economy.   However, I shall not dwell unduly upon this point, in this place ; partly because Dr Rabagliati and myself are, as yet, practically alone in our belief that the energy of the body does not come from the food ; and partly because this book is devoted to the *quality* of the various foods, rather than to their *quantity*—as was my former book.   Both—quantity. and quality—are of great interest and importance ; but as I have already said all that is necessary regarding one aspect of this question—that of quantity —I feel that a somewhat detailed discussion of the " quality " of food could not fail to be of interest.   I accordingly turn to this aspect of the problem ; and shall devote the remaining pages of this book to a discussion of the relative qualities and proportions of the various foods.

II

THE ARGUMENT FROM COMPARATIVE ANATOMY

PERHAPS the most important factor of all, in considering this question of man's natural diet, is the anatomical
argument—the argument, that is, which says that
man must or should naturally eat certain foods, for
the reason that he belongs to the class or *genus* of
animals which lives upon that class of foods—and that,
consequently, he should live upon them also. Comparative anatomy affords us one of the most tangible
and at the same time one of the most forceful and
convincing arguments that can be furnished in favour
of man's natural diet (whatever that may prove to
be)—for the reason that its *facts* are so well-attested
that they cannot be gainsaid by anyone who is in
possession of them; and only the *inferences drawn
from these facts* can be disputed—which is a question
that will be considered later. As before stated, this
line of argument is in many ways the most important
with which we shall have to deal; it will tend either
to condemn or to confirm my argument most strongly.
From a scientific standpoint, the study of this subject
is founded upon the fact that the diet of any animal,
in its natural state, is always found to agree both
with its anatomical structure and with its several
digestive processes and general bodily functions. So
clearly is this fact recognised, indeed, by comparative
anatomists and scientists generally, that animals have
been divided, according to their dietetic habits, into
four great classes—herbivorous, frugivorous, carnivorous and omnivorous. There are various sub- and
minor-divisions that can be and in fact are made—
such as the gramnivora, or grain-eaters; the rodentia,

or gnawers; the ruminants, or cud-chewers; and the edentata or creatures without teeth. These sub-divisions need not concern us here, however; and I shall not discuss their anatomical structure or food-habits at any length. Their names sufficiently classify them—in a work of this nature, which deals with *foods*, and is not a natural history. For practical purposes, the gramnivora may be included in the class of frugivora—since most frugivorous animals eat grains to some extent. This understood, we can proceed to a consideration of the facts; and we shall see to which of these classes man belongs.

In order to classify an animal, and place him in his proper division, it is necessary first of all to make a careful examination of his physical structure, and examine his organs in turn and severally, with the utmost care; when, by a comparative study of his organs, and by comparing them with those of other animals, living upon other foods, we shall be enabled to classify man properly—at least, so far as the evidence afforded by comparative anatomy enables us to reach a decisive conclusion one way or the other. There are numerous other facts and arguments to be taken into consideration; but, as said before, the argument drawn from comparative anatomy is the most complete and convincing of all—since that alone practically settles the case for all other animals. Let us, therefore, consider the structure or anatomy of man, from this point of view; and see how far these arguments lead us, and to what class we should naturally assign man, from a study of these facts alone. I shall take up for discussion first of all the teeth.

THE TEETH

The Herbivora.—Let us consider first the teeth of the herbivorous animal. The horse, the ox, and the sheep are typical of this class of animals—living,. as they do, almost entirely upon grass and herbs. The character of their food is peculiar. It is bulky, coarse, and covered with sharp, cutting edges—ill suited for tender mouths and gums. It must be mashed and ground thoroughly between the teeth and in the mouth before it is fit to be swallowed ; and teeth of a peculiar construction and mutual relation are necessary in order properly to perform this function. Just such teeth they possess. There are twenty-four molars, six on each side in each jaw ; and in the lower jaw, in front, eight incisors, or cutting teeth, with none on the upper jaw. In place of any of these teeth on the upper jaw, there is simply a horny plate upon which the long incisors of the lower jaw impinge when the jaws are closed. This renders possible the tearing, grinding motions necessary for biting off and masticating the food upon which these animals live. Not only that. The actual *structure* of their teeth is peculiarly suited to their food and its mastication. Unlike our teeth, they are not covered with enamel, but are composed of alternate layers of enamel and dentine—a soft, bony substance lying between the layers of enamel, and wearing away more rapidly than it does. The result is that there is soon formed a series of jagged edges, which form cutting, grinding surfaces, and are especially adapted for the food which these animals feed upon. No such formation is present in any other class of animals, since their food is different from that of the herbivora. It is a wise provision of nature, precisely adapted to the desired ends.

The Insectivora.—The insect-eaters are more nearly related to the Rodentia than to the Carnivora. The form of teeth varies with the species. The incisors and canines are not especially prominent, but the molars are always serrated with numerous small-pointed eminences, or cusps, adapted to crushing insects. The three leading families of the Insectivora are the moles, the shrew-mice, and the hedgehogs. They are of small size, and are found in all countries, except in South America and Australia.

The Rodentia.—The Rodentia is a peculiar order of animals, characterised by two very long and strong teeth in each jaw, which occupy the place of the incisors and canines in other animals. Back of these there is a toothless space, and then four or five molars, which, when they have a roughened crown, indicate a vegetable, but when pointed, an insectivorous, diet. Their principal foods are grains and seeds of all kinds, and with these, often, fruits, nuts and acorns. To this order belong the families of the squirrel, marmot, all species of mice, the beaver, porcupine, hare, and others.

An especial dietetic subdivision of the Rodentia is the Rhizophaga, or root-eaters, which includes some species of the Marsupials, and of mice. The food often consists exclusively of the roots of the beet, carrot, celery and onion.

The Edentata.—Occasionally, though rarely, animals of this class have rudimentary back teeth. Their food consists of leaves, blossoms, buds, and juicy stalks. Some also devour insects, especially ants. To this order belong the sloth, armadillo, pangolin, and great ant-eater.

The Omnivora.—Omnivorous animals have very distinctive teeth. The canines are markedly developed, forming regular tusks at the side of the mouth. These are used for attack and defence, and also to dig up roots, upon which these animals largely feed. The hog is typical of omnivorous animals of this character, and we all know his disposition no less than his anatomy! Animals of this class can live upon both animal and vegetable food, and *man* is supposed to be included in this category! The great argument brought forward by those who recommend a " mixed " diet (*i.e.* one composed of flesh, vegetables, fruits, roots, grains, etc.), is that man can live on all these foods, and retain life and some degree of health, and that therefore he is omnivorous. We shall come to consider this argument somewhat at length presently. For the moment, it is enough to say that (so far as his teeth are considered, at any rate) man is in no way similar to the hog, or to any omnivorous animal whatever, but totally different from all of them. The most casual glance at the mouth and teeth of the hog should convince us that we are not in *that* class! The other considerations we shall come to later.

The Carnivora.—The next great class that we must consider is the *carnivora.* Their teeth are very distinctive, and their shape and arrangement are entirely different from those of any of the other animals. There are the incisor teeth in front, and molars behind ; but the most distinctive teeth are the canine, which especially distinguish this class of feeders. There are four of these—two in each jaw, placed upon the sides, and they are long, sharp, and pointed. The more nearly the animal is purely carnivorous, the more are these teeth developed, and the less meat the animal eats, the less are they developed. Thus, the feline species, which is perhaps the most typically carnivorous of all, have canine teeth very well developed ; in them, they are most marked. In such animals, the canine teeth are also set considerably apart from other teeth. In the dog, however, the teeth are less prominent than they are in the cat ; his claws, eyes, etc., are also less distinctly carnivorous, and it will be observed that his habits are decidedly less like those of the preying animal than are those of the cat : he sleeps at night instead of in the day-time ; does not adopt the stealthy methods for catching birds, etc., which the cat follows. All this has its significance when it is remembered that dogs are much more easily weaned away from a flesh diet, on to one of milk, bread, biscuits, etc., than are cats, who are very difficult to wean from their carnivorous habits. This, however, is by the way.

In the bear family, again, the carnivorous characteristics are still less marked. The canine teeth are less and the molars and incisors more developed—the latter having a flat but roughened crown. All this indicates a still nearer approach to a vegetable and fruit diet—as is actually the case. The bear, as is well known, is fond of berries, fruits of all kinds, milk and honey.

Man, has, of course, two " eye teeth," which are more or less pointed, and that I do not deny. But these teeth are comparatively so small, when compared with the corresponding canines of the real carnivora, as to be altogether insignificant. When we examine the mouth of a person with normal teeth, we find that the teeth are almost exactly similar in size and shape—so much so, in fact, that any person ignorant of the fact that we have " carnivorous teeth " in our heads (supposedly) cannot pick them out from the others ! He does not experience any such difficulty in selecting the carnivorous teeth of the tiger or the cat ! Strange, is it not ? Even the omnivorous hog has teeth so much larger as to be totally dissimilar to those of man. Man's teeth are so uniform that all traces of his carnivorous nature have entirely disappeared. The only reply that can be made to this criticism is that, although man's carnivorous teeth are considerably smaller than those of the pure carnivora, they are still *there*, none the less, and consequently man is entitled to live upon a *certain amount* of meat—though not to make it his chief or exclusive diet, as do the pure carnivora. The very fact that he has such teeth in his head at all is proof positive, it will be urged, that man should, or at least *can*, without injury, live upon flesh to some extent.   For otherwise how came these teeth into his head ?

The answer to this is very simple.   The gorilla—a typical example of the frugivorous animal—has these teeth much more strongly and markedly developed than man ;   and yet he does not feed upon flesh to any appreciable extent ;   and in fact lives almost entirely upon fruits, nuts, roots, etc.   If we were to argue that man must eat meat, because of the carnivorous teeth in his head, *much more* must we insist that the orang and the gorilla should live upon flesh-food—and yet we know that these animals in their natural state do not eat flesh-foods at all, or only when they cannot obtain their own food in abundance !   *They* are clearly frugivorous by nature ;   and, inasmuch as their eye-teeth are far more developed than are the same teeth in man's head, we must come to the conclusion that man is certainly not adapted to a flesh diet, on account of his teeth or because of them.   He is more certainly frugivorous than the gorilla—were we to judge by the teeth alone !   They are mere rudiments—atrophied relics of bygone ages. Their use has ceased to be.   Orangs and gorillas have some need of their teeth for purposes of cracking nuts, for digging up roots, for attack and defence, and perhaps other purposes in extreme necessity.   But *we* have no need of teeth for any of these reasons, and hence the teeth are not developed in us, to any such great extent.   All reason and analogy, therefore, clearly indicate that our teeth are far more indicative of a frugivorous diet than any animal living.

" I can never mention vegetarianism to a flesh-eating medical gentleman," said Dr Trall,[1] " who does not

[1] " Scientific Basis of Vegetarianism," pp. 25-26.

introduce the teeth argument as the conclusion of the whole matter, as he asks triumphantly, ' What were carnivorous teeth put in our jaws for if not to eat flesh ? '

" I have an answer. They were never put there at all ! If they really exist in particular cases, it must be by some accident. They were no part of the original constitution of humanity. And in truth, they have no existence at all, except in the imaginations of medical men—in medical books and journals, in the public newspapers, and the jaws of carnivorous animals. . . .

" And now I propose to put this matter of teeth to the proof. Hearing may be believing, but seeing is the naked truth. I ask medical men to show their teeth ; to open their jaws and let their teeth be seen. Let us have the light to shine in upon this dark and perplexing question. I appeal from their statements to their faces ; from their books and schools to their own anatomy.

" Is there a person here who believes that, in the anatomy of his teeth, he is only part human ? that he is a compromise of human and brute ? Let him come forward and open his mouth. . . . I think, if we make a careful examination, we shall readily discover that he is, ' toothically considered,' neither perdaceous nor beastial ; that he is, dietetically, neither swinish nor tigerocious ; neither dogmatical nor categorical ; nor is he exactly graminivorous, like the cattle ; he is not even sheepish— but simply, wholly, and exclusively human !

" True, there are some resemblances between the teeth of men, women and children, and the teeth of cats, dogs, lions, tigers, hogs, horses, cattle, crocodiles, and megalosauruses. But there are differences, too ! And the differences are just as significant as are the resemblances. There is a resemblance between a man's face and the countenance of a codfish. There is also a striking difference. There is some resemblance between a man's features—especially if he does not shave —and the features of a bear. There is some resemblance between a woman's hair and a peacock's feathers ; between a man's finger-nails and a vulture's talons ; between his eye-teeth and a serpent's fangs. But, luckily for us, they are not the same, nor precisely alike. Man resembles, more or less, every animal in existence. He differs, too, more or less, from all animals in exist-ence. . . .

"There is one class of scholars who are competent and qualified by their studies to give an opinion on the question of the natural dietetic character of man. I mean naturalists, who have studied comparative ana-tomy with a special reference to this question. And it gives me pleasure to inform medical gentlemen that all of them without a single exception, with the great Cuvier at their head, have testified that the anatomical conformation of the human being, teeth included, is strictly frugivorous.

"There are indeed specimens of the human family who very closely resemble carnivorous animals, not only in their teeth, but also in their expressions of face and habits of eating—the Kalmuck Tartars, for example. But it is precisely because they have for many genera-tions fed on the grossest animal food and offal, that their forms and features became coarse, brutal and re-volting. No such example can be found in any nation or tribe whose dietetic habits have long been wholly or even chiefly vegetarian. I repeat, if these persistent advocates of a flesh-diet based on the anatomical argu-ment will but come forward and let us look into the interior of their countenances, we will show them that they are much better than they supposed themselves to be. We will prove that they are higher in the scale of being than they have given themselves credit for. They have been altogether too modest in their preten-sions. In consequence of a little mistake in the anatomy of their masticators, they have humbled themselves quite unnecessarily. Instead of ranking themselves high above the highest, of the animal kingdom, and close on to the borders of the angel kingdom, where God placed them, they have degraded themselves to the level of the scavengers. . . ."

Further, it is interesting in this connection to note that anthropoid apes, as soon as they are deprived of their natural food and their natural life, soon become diseased and die. Says Dr Hartmann :

"Anthropoids when kept in confinement suffer from caries of the teeth, and jaws, from chronic and acute bronchial catarrhs, from inflammation and consumption of the lungs, from inflammation of the liver, from pericardial dropsy, from parasites of the skin and intestine, etc."[1]

This is interesting as an illustration of the effects of perverted living upon apes ; and suggests that man cannot depart from his natural food to any great extent, either, without dire consequences to himself. The thousands of sick and dying in every part of the country, the well-filled hospitals and overflowing graveyards unfortunately prove this to be the case !

Moreover, the eye-teeth of the anthropoid apes are of a totally different character from the canine teeth of the carnivora. The former are small and stout, and somewhat triangular ; while the latter are long, round and slender. It is a noteworthy fact that the anthropoid eye-tooth is rough and cartilaginous at the point of contact between the external tooth and the gum, while that of the carnivora at the same point is smooth and sharp. The eye-tooth of the anthropoids is adapted for use in cracking nuts and the like, while those of the carnivora are exclusively employed in seizing and tearing flesh. Professor Nicholson, in his "Manual of Zoology," pp. 604-605, says of the anthropoid apes :

"The canine teeth of the males are long, strong and pointed, but this is not the case with the females. The structure, therefore, of the canine teeth is to be regarded in the light of a sexual peculiarity, and not as having any connection with the nature of the food."

[1] "Anthropoid Apes," p. 284.

The teeth of man are inferior in strength to those of the anthropoid apes, but the cause of this is to be sought not so much in their original character as in the fact that they have been weakened and degenerated by the use of cooked food for thousands of years.

It may perhaps be objected that anthropoid apes, which have been cited as typical frugivorous animals, are not so much so as I have contended ; that, while their *chief* food is doubtless fruits and nuts, they do occasionally feed upon all kinds of substances—roots, insects, small animals when they can catch them, etc. Thus Professor Robert Hartmann in his " Anthropoid Apes " p. 255 says :

" Although they are for the most part content with vegetable diet, gibbons sometimes eat animal food, such as lizards ; and Bennet saw a siamang seize and devour one of these animals whole. . . . They do not, however, display the keenness of scent and quickness of sight which distinguish some animals of a lower order ; such as canine beasts of prey and ruminants manifest in many different ways " (p. 256).

Now, it will be noticed in the above connection that (1) these apes are, by reason of their peculiar anatomical and physiological construction, incapable of competing with the carnivora for food of that character—and hence naturally disqualified to live upon it ; and (2) these animals do not *naturally* live upon this food by choice, when other and, to them, more natural food is forthcoming. Only in the last stages of hunger do they resort to food of this nature, which they are obviously driven to by extremity, and are disqualified to eat by reason of their peculiar construction. An animal can be driven to eat anything if he is hungry enough. That does not prove that what he eats is his natural food, nevertheless ! Instinct, and other considerations, must determine that.

The Frugivora.—The orang and the gorilla are perhaps the best examples of this class of animals. Some bats and kangaroos may be included in it also. Animals belonging to this class have thirty-two teeth—sixteen in each jaw; four incisors or cutting teeth; two pointed teeth, known as cuspids, four small molars, known as bicuspids, and six molars. The eye-teeth project somewhat beyond the others and fit into a blank space in the lower row, the other teeth articulating uniformly. I have referred to the uses of this large eye-tooth elsewhere (p. 29).

The Teeth of Man.—Now when we come to consider the teeth of man, we are at once struck by the fact that they correspond, in almost every particular, with the teeth of the gorilla and other frugivorous animals; and the fact they they do not at all resemble or correspond to the teeth of any other animal! To the teeth of the herbivora, the carnivora, the omnivora, etc., they bear but the slightest resemblance, while they agree in almost every respect with the teeth of frugivorous animals. If we compare the teeth of man with those of the orang, the gorilla, or other frugivorous animal, we find that the number, the arrangement, the structure, the nature, and the size of the teeth are almost identical; while they bear but the smallest resemblances to the teeth of any other animal or *genera*. The complete absence of intervening spaces between the human teeth characterises man as the highest and purest example of the frugivorous animal. Man possesses no long, canine tooth, capable of catching and holding a captured prey; he possesses no tusks, like the omnivorous animals, and in every other way bears no resemblance whatever to any other animal—while his teeth do bear the very greatest and most detailed resemblance to the teeth of the apes and frugivorous animals generally. Bearing all these facts in mind, then, we surely can have no hesitation in classifying man as a frugivorous animal—so far as his teeth are concerned.   Considered from that point of view, man must be classed with the pure frugivora.

Not only in the number and structure of the teeth, but also in the manner of masticating the food—in the movements of the teeth and jaws themselves—there is a distinct resemblance between man and the apes and other frugivora, and a radical distinction between him and all other animals.   In herbivorous animals the jaws have three distinct motions—a vertical, or up-and-down motion ;   lateral or sidewise ;   and forward and backward.   These movements are frequent and free, the result being that food eaten by these animals undergoes a thorough grinding process well suited to the nature of their food.   In the carnivorous animals, on the other hand, the movements of the jaws are in one direction only—they open and shut " like a pair of scissors," as one author said, and are well adapted for tearing and biting off food that is to be swallowed more or less *en masse*, to be acted upon by the powerful gastric juices of the stomach.   No such limited action is the case with man.   With him also the jaws can move in three directions—as in the case of the herbivora—but the extent of such motion is much more limited.   In other words, the jaws of man are adapted to a diet necessitating more or less grinding, and he may be classed with the herbivora on that account.   Whatever might be said, however, by way of associating man with the herbivora, he is certainly as distinct as possible from the carnivora, and resembles other animals far more than he resembles them.   He is certainly *not* carnivorous, whatever else he may be !

Having thus passed in review the evidence presented by the teeth for the naturally frugivorous nature of man, we must now turn and examine the evidence afforded by the other organs of the body ; and see how far comparative anatomy affords proof of the nature of man's diet—as derived from a study of the other portions of his bodily frame. I shall review these in turn. First let us consider the *extremities*.

The Extremities.—According to Huxley, there are three great divisions in the animal kingdom, as regards the extremities—viz. those which possess hoofs, those possessing claws, and those possessing hands. To the first division belong the herbivora and the omnivora. Almost all animals possessing claws are carnivorous, while animals possessing hands are almost invariably frugivorous. To this rule there are very few exceptions. Since man certainly belongs to the class possessed of hands, he is certainly frugivorous by nature. The reason for this becomes apparent when we stop to consider the habits of the various animals. The herbivora have no need for hands ; they have merely to walk about the grassy plains, and partake of what nature has offered to them in abundance. The carnivorous animal, on the other hand, takes his food by violence—suddenly springing upon some defenceless and unresisting animal, and tearing it to pieces with its sharp teeth and claws. For this reason they are developed to the size and extent we see—capable of inflicting such terrible injuries. And here I would again call attention to what I said before—as to the carnivorous traits and characteristics of the cat as compared with those of the dog. The teeth and claws are far more developed in the former than in the latter. In man, of course, his teeth and claws are entirely unfitted for any such office. The soft, yielding nails are absolutely unlike the long, sharp claws of the carnivora ; nothing could be more dissimilar. But if we compare the hands and extremities of man with those of other frugivorous animals, there is

c

a very close similarity between them. The reason for this is that man (like the apes) can and should go out into the open fields and forests and pick his food off the trees. The human hand is eminently adapted to this end and for this purpose; but is quite *un*adapted for any such purposes as the claws of the carnivora are adapted for. I may remark here, incidentally, that all carnivorous animals *drink by lapping up the water* or other liquid with their tongues; while man, and all vegetarian animals, *drink by suction*—by drawing up the fluid directly into the mouth. This is a very distinguishing characteristic, to which there are few if any exceptions. Needless to say, since man drinks by suction, he is eminently a vegetarian animal, and is quite distinct from the carnivora in *this* respect, as in all others.

The Alimentary Canal.—"One of the most interesting comparisons," says Dr Kellogg,[1] "which has been made by comparative anatomists is the length of the alimentary canal. This is very short in the carnivora, and long in the herbivora. When compared to the length of the body of the different classes of animals, the proportion is found to be as follows:—In the carnivora, the alimentary canal is three times the length of the body; in the herbivora, as the sheep, thirty times the length of the body; in the monkey, twelve times; in the omnivora ten times; in man, as in the frugivora, twelve times. Here, as before, we see that anatomy places man strictly in the frugivorous class. Some writers have made the amusing blunder of making the proportionate length of the alimentary canal in man 1 to 6, instead of 1 to 12, by doubling the height through measuring him while standing erect. This measurement is evidently wrong, for it includes the length of the lower extremities, or hind legs, whereas in other animals the measurement is made from the tip of the nose to the end of the backbone. In omnivorous

[1] " Shall We Slay to Eat ? " pp. 28-29.

animals, the alimentary canal is shorter than in the apes and in man, thus affiliating this class more nearly with the carnivora than with the herbivora.

"A curious fact had recently been observed by Kuttner, as related by him in an article published in Virchow's *Archives*. This author has made extensive anatomical researches respecting the lengths of the small intestine in different classes of persons. He finds that in the vegetarian peasants of Russia, the small intestine measures from twenty to twenty-seven feet in length, while among Germans, who use meat in various forms quite freely, the length of the small intestine varies between seventeen and nineteen feet. The author attributes the difference in these two classes of persons to the difference in diet. Of course differences of this sort must be the influence of the diet exerted through many generations. This observation would seem to suggest that the special anatomical characteristic of the carnivorous class of animals is due to the modifying influence of their diet, acting through thousands of years. If the length of the intestine in man may be shortened by the use of flesh, with other foods, for a few hundred years, more extensive modifications may easily result from the longer experience of animals that subsist upon an exclusively carnivorous diet." [1]

---

[1] I would point out, in this connection, however, that, apart from this possible shortening of the small intestine, *no anatomical changes whatever* have resulted from a partially carnivorous diet for the hundreds of years that have preceded us, and upon which man still largely subsists. Doubtless this is partly due to the fact that much *other* food was always eaten with the meat consumed ; and also the fact that the poorer classes—the peasantry, etc.—were unable to purchase large quantities of meat at any time—and hence to eat it. With them it was always an occasional luxury, rather than a steady article of diet. The interesting fact is, however, that, in spite of these hundreds of years of abuse, the human alimentary tract still maintains all the characteristics of the frugivorous animal, and in no way resembles the carnivorous alimentary tract ! Had our hundreds of years of flesh-eating enabled us to subsist upon such a diet with impunity—or even adapted the human body to the diet in any degree—as is frequently contended—then our alimentary tract would indicate that fact by its evolutionary modifications. As this is not the case, however, what becomes of the argument that meat is a necessary article of diet, because man has subsisted largely upon it for hundreds of years ?

The Stomach.—The position and form of the *stomach* are also of significance. In the carnivora, it is only a small roundish sack, exceedingly simple in structure ; while in the vegetable feeders it is oblong, lies transversely across the abdomen, and is more or less complicated with ringlike convolutions — according to the nature of the food. This appears conspicuously in the primates, which include man, in the Rodentia, Edentata, Marsupials, and, above all, in the Ruminants. In the latter, it presents a series of from four to seven wide, adjoining and communicating sacks.

At a first superficial glance at the exteriors of the stomachs of the carnivora and that of man, we apparently perceive a far closer resemblance than between man's stomach and that of a herbivorous animal. In one sense, there can be no question that there is a closer similarity ; in another sense, it is not so. In man this organ is simple, but is divided into a cardiac and pyloric portion—thus occupying, as in many other anatomical respects, a middle line between the carnivorous and herbivorous mammalia. The inner surface of the stomach is covered with *rugæ*, or wrinkles, formed by the mucous membrane, which lines the whole intestinal canal, and which forms valvular folds ; while in the carnivora the stomach is a simple globular sac, without these corrugations. As Dr Trall observed [1]:

" Some may imagine, at a first glance, a closer resemblance between the human stomach and the lion's than between the human and that of the sheep. But when they are viewed in relation to their proper food, their closer resemblance will vanish at once. It should be particularly observed that, so far as mere bulk is concerned, there is a greater similarity between the food of frugivorous animals and carnivorous animals than between frugivorous and herbivorous. The digestion and assimilation of coarse herbage, as grass, leaves, etc.,

[1] " Fruits and Farinacea," pp. 82-83.

requires a more complicated digestive apparatus than grains, roots, etc., and these more so than flesh and blood. The structure of the stomach, therefore, in such cases, seems precisely adapted to the food we assume Nature intended for it." [1]

The Liver.—Dr John Smith, in calling attention to the many distinctions between the bodily structure of man and that of the carnivora, pointed out the following differences among others :—

" In the carnivora and rodentia, which present the most complex form of liver among the mammalia, there are five distinct parts ; a central or principal lobe, corresponding with the principal part of the liver in man ; a right lateral lobe, with a lobular appendage, corresponding to the 'lobulus Spigelii' and the 'lobus caudatus,' and a small lobe or lobule on the left side. Through the whole animal series, however, the magnitude of the liver varies in inverse ratio to the lungs.

" In man, the liver is much less developed than the same organ in many other mammalia ; and presents, as rudimentary indications, certain organs which are in other animals fully developed. Europeans, and the inhabitants of Northern climes, who partake more of animal food, have the liver much larger, and its secretions more copious, than the inhabitants of warm climates. Perhaps this, in some measure, depends upon the amount of non-azotised articles taken along with the flesh of animals, by which means the system is supplied with more carbon than is needed. So that the enlarged liver is attributable to gross living on mixed diet, rather than to an exclusively animal diet."

This author also says elsewhere (p. 79) :

" The temporal and masseter muscles, by which the motion of the lower jaw is effected, are of immense size in carnivorous animals. The temporal muscle occupies the whole side of the scull, and fills the space beneath the zygomatic arch, the span and spring of

[1] " Fruits and Farinacea," p. 84.

which are generally an index of the volume of this muscle ; while the extent and strength of the arch indicate the development of the masseter muscle.   On the contrary, the pterygoid muscles, which aid the lateral movement of the jaw, are extremely small.   The zygoma is of great size and strength in the carnivora ; consisting of a long process of the masseter bone, over-laid by the usual process of the temporal bone, which is equally strong.   The arch extends not only back-ward but upward, by the bending down of the ex-tremity ;   the line of anterior declination falling pre-cisely on the centre of the carnassière tooth—the point in which the force of the jaws is concentrated, and where it is most required for cutting, tearing, and crush-ing their food.   In ruminants, the zygomatic arch is short, and the temporal muscles are small ; but the masseter muscle on each side extends beyond the arch, and is attached to the greater part of the side of the maxillary bone.   The pterygoid fossa is ample, and its muscles are largely developed.   The arch is small in man, the temporal muscles moderate, and the force of the jaws comparatively weak."

The Placenta.—Let us now turn to another im-portant distinction between the carnivorous and non-carnivorous animals.   Of these, perhaps the most im-portant is the character of the *placenta*—one of the most distinguishing marks or characteristics of any species of animal.   This subject has been so well and ably summed up by Professor Schlickeysen, in his " Fruit and Bread " (pp. 48-57), that I cannot do better than quote the main portion of the argument, as stated by this learned and able author.   He says :

" We now come to consider the peculiar structure, form and size of the placenta, as well as the exact method by which, through it, in different species of animals, the nourishment is effected.   One of the most striking differences presented in placental animals relates to the method of union between the mother and the fœtus. There are two very distinct types of the placenta, and, according to Professor Huxley, no transitional forms between them are known to exist. These types are designated as follows :—

1. The non-deciduate placenta of the Herbivora.

2. The deciduate placenta, of which there are two kinds :

> (a) The zonary deciduate placenta of the Carnivora.
>
> (b) The discoidal deciduate placenta of the Frugivora.

"The deciduate placenta is a distinct structure, developed from the wall of the uterus, but separated from it at parturition, and constituting what is known as the 'after birth'; of this the human placenta is regarded by Huxley as the most perfect example; while, of the non-deciduate placenta, that of the pig and horse are the typical representatives. The word ' decidua ' signifies ' that which is thrown off.'

"*The Non-Deciduate Placenta.*—This form is thus described by Professor Huxley: 'No decidua is developed. The elevations and depressions of the un-impregnated uterus simply acquire a greater size and vascularity during pregnancy, and cohere closely to the chorionic villi, which do not become restricted to one spot, but are developed from all parts of the chorion, except at its poles, and remain persistent in the broad zone thus formed throughout fœtal life. The cohesion of the fœtal and maternal placentæ, however, is over-come by slight maceration; and at parturition the fœtal villi are simply drawn out, like fingers from a glove, no vascular substance of the mother being thrown off.' To this class belong all the ruminants and Ungulata (hoofed quadrupeds); the camel, sheep, goat and deer; the ant-eater, armadillo, sloth, swine, tapir, rhinoceros, river-horse, sea-cow, whale, and others.

"*The Zonary Deciduate Placenta.*—A zonary placenta surrounds the chorion, in the form of a broad zone, leaving the poles free. This form characterises all the land and sea carnivora, and thus includes the cat, hyena, puma, leopard, tiger, lion, fox and wolf; the dog and bear, the seal, sea-otter and walrus. It includes, also, certain extinct species, as the mastadon and dinotherium, which, although not wholly carnivorous, were, to judge from their teeth, partially so. The elephant, the only living species of these ancient animals, is also of this class.

"*The Discoidal Deciduate Placenta.*—The discoidal placenta is a highly developed vascular structure, lying on one side of the fœtus, in the form of a round disc; leaving the greater part of the chorion free. It is thus united only on one side, at one circular point, with the mucous membrane of the uterus, from which, as already mentioned, it is separated at parturition. The orders of the animals characterised by this form of placenta are the rodentia, ant-eaters, bats, and various species of apes, and man. All these are very closely united by homologous anatomical forms. The human placenta does not differ, in its general character, from that of the others, and there is no good reason for separating man from his placental classification."

Relations between placental forms and Individual Characteristics.—From our entire knowledge of the development of races and of individuals, we may conclude, upon the basis of Huxley's classification, that an intimate relation exists between the form and character of the placenta and the entire nature of the individual. We find among the non-deciduata, besides the toothless sloths, only the Ungulata, or hoofed quadrupeds, and others developed from them. The arrangement of their teeth, as of their entire digestive apparatus, marks them as belonging to a single family—namely, the herbivora.

The zonary placenta characterises a very large family of animals whose peculiarities are distinctly marked, especially with regard to their teeth and digestive apparatus. These belong to the widely diffused and numerous orders of the carnivora. But the most interesting and important group, with reference to our present study, is that characterised by the discoidal placenta; for, since it includes man and the fruit-eating apes, it gives occasion for the comparison between these and other placental animals from the standpoint of dietetics.

We observe here at once that the majority of animals having a discoidal placenta subsist chiefly upon fruits and grains, and that the typical representatives of this class, namely, those whose plactental formation is most distinctly discoidal, are also the most exclusively frugivorous.

Here, as elsewhere in nature, an exact line cannot be drawn. Transitional forms exist everywhere, and to this the placenta is no exception. The most striking accordance, however, exists between the placenta of man and that of the tailless apes—namely, the gorilla, orang, chimpanzee and gibbon. Between other discoidal species, the differentiation, though minute, is clearly marked; but between man and these apes the resemblance is so exact as to stamp them plainly as members of the same family.

The completely developed placenta is in the form of a circular disc, about eight inches broad, one inch thick, and weighing about two pounds. Its manner of development is identical in the human subject and that of the above-named anthropoid apes. Its exact formation is thus described by Huxley:

" From the commencement of gestation, the superficial substance of the mucous membrane of the human uterus undergoes a rapid growth and textural modification, becoming converted into the so-called decidua. While the ovum is yet small, this decidua is departable into three portions: The *decidua vera*, which lines the general cavity of the uterus; the *decidua reflexa*, which immediately invests the ovum; and the *decidua serotina*, a layer of especial thickness, developed in contiguity with those chorionic villi which persist and become converted into the fœtal placenta. The *decidua reflexa* may be regarded as an outgrowth of the *decidua vera* ;. the *decidua serotina* as a special development of a part of the *decidua vera*. At first, the villi of the chorion are loosely implanted into corresponding impressions of the *decidua* ; but, eventually, the chorionic part of the placenta becomes closely united with and bound to the uterine *decidua*, so that the fœtal and maternal structures form one inseparable mass."

The fœtus thus united to the mother is nourished by means of numerous arterial and venous trunks, which traverse the deeper substance of the uterine mucous membrane, in the region of the placenta. These are connected with the placenta by means of the umbilical cord, which consists of two arteries and two veins. The length of this cord is greater in the case of man and the anthropoid apes than in any other animals, reaching in them a length of about two feet. The strict accordance which thus appears between the placental structure of man and the ape indicates, upon the basis of Huxley's principles of classification, the same physiological functions *and the same dietetic character*. There exists a complete similarity between the corresponding organs in each :   Their extremities end in hands and feet. Their teeth and digestive apparatus indicates a frugivorous diet. Their breasts and manner of nursing suggest the same tender care of the new-born creature ; while the brain and mental capacity are also of a like character—differing only in degree ; indeed, the difference between the ape and animals of the next lower grade is much greater than between the ape and man ; there being in the latter case really no essential anatomical or physiological differences.

The fact that man has four cuspid teeth affords no evidence whatever that he is either partially or wholly carnivorous as regards his dietary. If in diet he is naturally omnivorous, his teeth should have the structure and arrangement of those of omnivorous animals—as exhibited in the hog, for example.

That the cuspid teeth do not indicate a flesh dietary, either in whole or in part, is shown by the presence of the so-called cuspids in purely herbivorous animals—as in the stag, the camel and the so-called " bridle-teeth " of the horse.

I am convinced that no animals were created to eat flesh, but that so-called carnivorous animals were originally nut-eating animals (see p. 55). The squirrel eats birds as well as nuts, which closely resemble meat in composition. This view readily explains the close resemblance in many particulars existing between the human digestive apparatus and that of the so-called carnivorous animals. It is reasonable to suppose that these nut-eating animals were at some remote time forced by starvation to slay, and eat, by the failure of their ordinary food supply—just as the horses of the Norwegian coast have been known to plunge into the sea and catch fish, when driven to this extremity by starvation. Suppose the carnivorous animal's natural diet to be nuts, in the absence of his normal food he would find nothing else so closely resembling his ordinary food as the flesh of animals, since the two have about the same proteid percentages.

Dr Kellogg, in his excellent little book, entitled " Shall We Slay to Eat ? " (pp. 80-82), sums up a number of remarkable facts in favour of a fruitarian diet, or at least in favour of a non-flesh diet, as follows :—

" In carnivorous, herbivorous and omnivorous animals, the mammary glands are located upon the abdomen, while in the higher apes and man they are located on the chest. This is an interesting anatomical fact to which there is no exception.

" In carnivorous animals the colon is smooth and non-sacculated. In the higher apes and man the colon is sacculated. In herbivorous animals the colon is sacculated, as in man." (The great importance and significance of this fact will be apparent presently, when we come to consider the physiological arguments against flesh-eating.)

" In carnivorous animals the tongue is very rough, producing a rasping sensation when coming in contact with the flesh. In the higher apes and man the tongue is smooth.

" In carnivorous animals the skin is not provided with perspiratory ducts—hence the skin does not perspire in the dog, the cat, and allied animals. In the ape, the skin is provided with millions of these glands, and in man they are so numerous that if spread out, their walls would cover a surface of eleven thousand square feet. In the pig, an omnivorous animal, only the snout sweats. In horses, cows and other vegetable-eating animals, the whole skin sweats, as it does in man." (The great importance of this fact will be apparent when we come to consider the physiological arguments against a flesh-diet : see p. 55.)

" Carnivorous, herbivorous and omnivorous animals are all supplied with an extension of the backbone— a tail. In the higher apes, as well as in man, the tail is wanting.

" Carnivorous, herbivorous and omnivorous animals go on all fours, and their eyes look on either side, while many of the higher apes walk nearly or entirely upright, as does man, and their eyes look forward.[1]

" Carnivorous animals have claws, herbivorous and omnivorous have hoofs, while apes and men have flat nails, not found in any other animal. Carnivorous,

[1] Dr Woods Hutchison and other writers upon the subject have contended that all flesh-eating animals have their eyes set in the front of their heads, and all herbivora on the side. Because man's eyes are set in the front of his head, it is contended, therefore he is carnivorous ! This argument is completely disproved by the fact (among others) that the higher apes, which, in a state of nature, are pure frugivora, have their eyes set in the front of their heads—as has man. This is consequently no argument whatever in favour of a flesh diet.

herbivorous and omnivorous animals are all quadrupeds, or four-footed, while the higher apes and man are provided with two hands and two feet. The hinder or lower extremities of the ape are sometimes erroneously called hands ; according to Dr Huxley, they are, from both bony and muscular structure, properly classified as feet, and not as hands.

" In carnivorous animals, the salivary glands are small, and the saliva which they secrete has little effect upon starch, while in the apes and man the glands are well developed and the saliva is active " (see pp. 47-48).

In addition to all the facts that have been pointed out, there are others of lesser interest, but all of which, nevertheless, go to confirm the fact that man is closely related to the apes, and consequently intended for a fruitarian diet, and that he is in no wise related to the carnivora or *their* diet. Metchnikoff has summarised many of these facts, extending the work of Darwin, Huxley, Hæckel, etc. These other, minor, facts might perhaps be summarised as follows :—

There is an exact agreement between the skeleton of man and the higher apes—all the bones corresponding, each to each, while there is a great dissimilarity between man and any other animal whatever. The nerves, the viscera, the spleen, the liver, the lungs, the brain, the skin, nails and hair—all present the closest possible analogy and similarities. The eyes are strikingly similar, while the chemical and microscopical character of the blood is also very similar in man and the higher apes. This fact is of especial importance and significance, when we bear in mind that only apes and men are subject to certain blood diseases—to which all other animals are impervious. In structure, as in habits, man and the apes are in many respects remarkably alike, and proportionately dissimilar to all other animals.

CHAPTER III

" AFTER structure—function ! " Having seen in the last chapter that man is constructed throughout for a diet composed entirely of fruits, nuts, grains, and other non-flesh foods, we now turn to a consideration of the functions of the various organs of the body—the chemical composition of the organic tissues, secretions, etc.—in order to see if these will further bear us out in our argument. There can be no question that the most important argument of all, on this subject of diet, is the argument based upon comparative anatomy—since that argument places man in his right class immediately, and in a manner that cannot be evaded by any amount of argument. But other aspects of the question are also of importance, and afford strong proof of the natural character of man's diet. The next argument we should consider, therefore, is the physiological, and we shall first of all consider the *secretions*.

The Saliva.—The differences between the saliva of man and that of any of the carnivora is striking. In man, this secretion is *alkaline*—though only slightly so, in a healthy man. Nevertheless, that is its normal reaction, and to this there is no exception. In the carnivora, on the other hand, the reaction is *acid*, and because of this fact is capable of dissolving the food more or less whole, and without the long process of mastication necessary for the herbivora and frugivora. The saliva in the human being effects many chemical changes in the food—notable among these being the conversion of starch. Were man intended to live on flesh, the saliva would be acid also—instead of alkaline as it is.

The Gastric Juice.—Dr Schlickeysen says of this : [1]

" A leading element of the gastric juice is lactic acid. This excites a slight fermentation of the chyme, and thus exerts an influence upon the digestion of vegetable, but not upon that of animal, food. It is far too weak to act upon the fibres of animal flesh. All fats are insoluble in water, spirits of wine, and acids. Flesh, when eaten by man, tends to undergo a process of decay in the stomach, causing a scrofulous poisoning of the blood. In this unnatural action lies the cause of many complaints and disturbances of the system : as bad breath, heartburn, eructions and vomiting. In the case of the carnivora, the gastric juice exerts a decomposing influence upon flesh, and causes its assimilation and excretion. Since the pancreatic juice of the duodenum, into which the chyme passes from the stomach, bears a close resemblance to the saliva, it follows that the chyme here, also, can have only a slightly acid property, which it indeed can only have when it is of a vegetable character. Bile, which is here poured into the intestines, has only a slight alkaline reaction, and its use seems to be limited to the prevention of decay; which, however, can only occur in the case of flesh-food ; so that the effort of nature to maintain flesh-food in its proper condition by the secretion of bile must be excessive, and must eventually cause an excitement and weakening of the whole organism."

And Dr Kellogg has pointed out [2] :

" Another property possessed in a high degree by the gastric juice of carnivorous animals is its antiseptic or germicidal quality. When exposed to the conditions of warmth and moisture, flesh, whether that of mammals, birds or fish, readily decomposes or decays, giving rise

[1] " Fruit and Bread," pp. 108-109.
[2] " Shall We Slay to Eat ? " p. 35.

to poisonous substances of the most offensive character. The gastric juice of the dog is capable of preventing this putrefactive change while the food is undergoing the process of stomach digestion. That such changes occur later, however, while the food residue is lying in the colon previous to expulsion from the body, is evidenced by the extraordinarily offensive character of the fæcal matters of this class of animals."

In man, this secretion is very weak, comparatively speaking, and hence of small value in preventing such putrefactive changes as those mentioned above. Take any piece of meat, and expose it for some considerable period to an environment of heat and moisture, and see the result! Putrefaction soon occurs—except where the meat is " embalmed " or preserved by powerful chemicals—thus rendering it unfit for human food. But it will be seen that just such conditions prevail in the human alimentary tract as are most suitable for the speedy and deadly decomposition of the food eaten; and, in the case of flesh-foods, the resulting products are poisonous in the last degree. The gastric juice of the human stomach being so far weaker than that of the carnivorous animal, the flesh is far less completely acted upon and digested in the stomach—much more work being passed on to the intestines, in consequence. Now comes in a most important factor. The bowel of the carnivorous animal is, as we have seen, *short*, (three times the length of the body) when compared to the frugivora, whose alimentary tract is about twelve times the length of the body. That is, the digestive tract in man is, roughly, about four times as long as in the carnivorous animal. The result of this is that any food eaten would take, *ceteris paribus*, four times as long to pass through the tube in the one case as in the other. This fact alone is sufficient to condemn the use of flesh-foods in any form for frugivorous animals, since the less active antiseptic and germicidal properties of the gastric juice in these animals render unsafe the long retention of such easily decomposable substances as flesh.

But more than that, and worse still; the character of the internal structure of the tract is not alike in the two cases! In the carnivora, this is smooth, and offers but few impediments to the free passage of the food through it. In man, on the contrary, as with the higher apes and the herbivora, the intestine is corrugated or sacculated—this being for the express purpose of retaining the food as long as possible in the intestine, and until all possible nutriment has been abstracted from it. This is admirably suited to such foods as the herbivora and frugivora enjoy, but is quite *unsuited* for flesh-foods of all kinds—being, in fact, the worst possible receptacle for such foods. The intestine, in the carnivora, is suited for its particular food—it is short and smooth, and well adapted to dissolve the food quickly and pass it out of the system as rapidly as possible; while in frugivora, on the other hand, the intestine is adapted to retain the food a much longer time—the sacculated surface retaining the food as long as possible. The result of this is that, when flesh-foods are eaten, disastrous results are sure to follow.

As previously shown, the *liver* is much larger, proportionately, in the carnivora; and not only is this the case, but the amount of bile secreted is far greater in the carnivora than in man. It has been found, by careful experiments upon dogs, that the quantity of bile might increase fifty per cent., and even more, under a purely meat diet; but rapidly decreased when the quantity and proportion of the meat was reduced. Thus it appears that the use of a meat diet requires a far greater degree of activity on the part of the liver than any other diet. This is amply provided for in the carnivora by the increased size and power of that organ,

D

but in man and the frugivora such is not the case, and the result is that if meat be eaten by man, the liver is called upon to do an extra amount of work, and this may ultimately result in its premature breakdown.

The *kidneys* also are greatly affected by the diet. It is now well known that uric acid is created in large quantities by a flesh diet—the measured excretions showing that from three to ten times as much uric acid is secreted when flesh is eaten as when no meat is ingested ; and when we bear in mind the exceedingly disastrous effects of uric acid upon the system, and what a powerful disease-producing agency it is, I think that we must conclude that this symptom is strongly suggestive, and strongly indicative of the fact that man cannot eat meat without running grave chances of diseasing and ruining his organism.

The Excretions.—There is also a marked difference in the excretory products of the various animals. While, in the carnivora, the action of the urine is acid, it is alkaline in the herbivora (or should be). In man it is frequently acid—though this varies with the nature of the food. Thus, if the diet be largely one of flesh, the urine will become far more acid, and will also become very offensive ; the perspiration will also be tainted, and very noticeable to those with a keen sense of smell, and who do not eat meat themselves ! This has frequently been observed, and may account for the fact that flesh-eating animals will always eat a horse or a sheep in preference to man, if it be possible. Doubtless, their keen sense of smell detects the fact that man is (usually) largely carnivorous in his habits, and their instinct teaches them that the flesh of the purely herbivorous animal is for this reason superior to that of man. Has anyone thought why it is that a cat will kill a mouse, *and eat it,* while a dog will kill a cat, but will *not* eat it ? It is because the mouse is a vegetarian animal, and the cat is a carnivorous animal. Instinct teaches the cat that the tissues of the mouse's body are more or less pure and inoffensive—owing to the nature of the diet; while the same instinct teaches the dog that the cat's body is impure and more or less poisonous, for the reason that *its* flesh is tainted and full of poisons, because of its diet. If any animal lives upon flesh, that animal's body is bound to be tainted more or less in consequence; and those animals which prey upon others know that fact, by reason of their sense of smell and instinct. This is a remarkable and most instructive fact; a rule which will rarely be found to fail. Its significance and interpretation is obvious. Professor Schlickeysen also informs us that " the overloading of the blood with flesh-food causes, in order to effect their decomposition, an excessive consumption of oxygen, and hence the difficulty of breathing, and asthmatical affections of many flesh-eaters, and their excessive excretion of carbonic acid." I have referred to some of these poisons, formed within the system, and the harm they must doubtless exert upon the organism, elsewhere.

In addition to all these arguments, there are other forcible reasons for considering man as one of the non-flesh-eating animals—which reasons may be included in this chapter. The *habits* of any animal are distinctive; and they, collectively, indicate man's position—though this argument must always be confirmatory, and not proof in itself. For instance, all naturally carnivorous animals sleep in the daytime, and prowl about in search of their prey at night; while with the vegetarian animals (man included) this is not the case. The manner of eating, and especially of drinking, is also highly characteristic—all carnivorous animals *lapping* their liquids —while the herbivora and frugivora drink—as I have previously pointed out. The peculiar mode of functioning of various organs might also be pointed out and insisted upon. But one of the most striking arguments is that based upon the anatomical structure of the *skin*. As before stated, this perspires, in the case of all vegetarian animals, while the glands are atrophied and inactive in all carnivora. Let us now consider the significance of this fact.

" Recent researches show us that uric acid arises from the decay of cell nuclei. That portion of uric acid which has its origin in the digestive organs is, like other alloxanic bases, changed into urea—or rather should be. But a diseased liver (or a healthy one which is overworked, owing to an excessive ingestion of food containing cell nuclei, and therefore an excessive amount of uric acid) is unable to transform all the uric acid formed into urea. The quantity of uric acid arising from the normal decay of the tissue is small ; in fever, when there is a more rapid decay of cells, the quantity of uric acid and other related alloxanic bodies is considerably increased. The greater the quantity of useless bodymaterial, and the worse (more dysæmic) it is in quality, the greater is the danger of a more rapid decay of cells, and a precipitation of uric acid and related products taking place. . . . The uric acid, passing through the liver, may perhaps be transformed into urea by a special action of the cells ; but the uric acid drawn directly from the digestive canal, and that formed directly from the assimilated food or from the body-material, has to be oxidised, in order to be excreted in the innocuous form of urea. An organism possessed of the faculty of oxidation is protected against a precipitation of uric acid, but in a dysæmic organism, the faculty of transforming uric acid into urea is lessened. . . . It is a fact well worth considering that the urine of carnivorous animals—*e.g.* dog and cat—is often quite free from uric acid, while human urine varies in this respect according to the food taken : if vegetable food alone is consumed, the urine will contain, like the urine of herbivorous animals, only traces of uric acid (from ·2 to ·7 grammes in 24 hours) ; but if a large proportion of flesh-food be taken, the urine will contain 2 grammes or more. Man is the only creature which suffers from the uric acid diathesis ; is it not likely that this arises from a wrong choice of food ?

" Now, if the excretion of the uric acid always took place easily, we should not have much trouble about its formation, but it is this excretion which constitutes the difficulty. Uric acid and the acid salts of the uric acid dissolve with difficulty in cold water ; but more easily in warm ; still, one gramme of uric acid requires from 7 to 8 litres of water at the temperature of the body for its solution. The acid urate of soda dissolves in 1100 parts of cold and 124 parts of boiling water. The ammonia salts and the salts of the alkaline earths do not dissolve nearly so easily.

" The ' warm water ' which keeps the uric acid and the uric acid salts dissolved in the body is the blood and tissue fluids. Serious disturbances must take place if this fluid becomes cooler or diminished in quantity ; for a deposit of crystalline uric acid would occur in the body.

" A person who has to daily excrete 2 grammes of uric acid, is constantly liable to this precipitation, as he may at any time lose large quantities of water through perspiration. It is, therefore, undoubtedly safer to have the uric acid combined with soda, as an acid urate ; but where is soda to be obtained if it is absent from the blood, owing to dysæmia ?

" The more acid the urine is, the more easily will a precipitation of the uric acid occur in the organism— for instance, in the kidneys or bladder. The urine of a person eating flesh contains a large amount of uric acid, as we have seen before ; it is also strongly acid in re-action, whereas the urine of herbivorous animals is generally alkaline in reaction. . . .

" A very acid urine rich in uric acid is also produced by salt meat and salt fish, because in the process of salting, the basic salts (basic alkaline phosphates and carbonates) pass into the pickle water and neutral common salt takes their place. Russian physicians have told me that in certain parts of Russia, where the people eat a great deal of salt fish, urine stones are frequent. . . . Now, if we wish to prevent by the use of alkalies the formation of uric acid sediments, or gradually to dissolve such concretions as have already formed in the bladder, it is certainly more rational to prescribe a diet of fruits and potatoes than to order alkaline mineral waters—which, when taken constantly, may produce all sorts of disturbances.

" If, then, it is true that our ordinary diet consists chiefly of foods rich in albumen and phosphoric acid but poor in soda, and that in consequence of this a tendency towards the accumulation of uric acid in the body is pretty generally found, the very slightest extra strain on the system will be sufficient to cause a precipitation of uric acid and uric acid salts in the body. This result is very often brought about by a chronic acid catarrh of the stomach, which in its turn depends upon dysæmia, and is in 95 out of 100 cases the predecessor of gout. The fermentation acids, especially oxybutyric acid (which is found in the urine both in acid catarrh of the stomach and in diabetes mellitus), combine with some of the alkalies of the blood, and thus lessen its alkalescence (basic character); and as catarrh of the bowels and periodic diarrhœas are frequently associated with acid catarrh of the stomach, these bases may be even directly excreted in the stools, and thus the quantity of alkalies in the blood be further diminished.

" Now we find that men consuming vegetable food form only small quantities of uric acid, herbivorous animals as well as carnivorous hardly any, but men living on flesh-food very large quantities, we must come to the conclusion that *men cannot properly manage flesh-food.* The organism of the flesh-eating animal has the faculty of completely digesting flesh-food, whereas the organism of man is unable to accomplish this. Consequently man cannot be classed as carnivorous and cannot eat flesh unpunished. . . .

" To illustrate this further, we may mention another important point here. Carnivorous animals have atrophied, inactive sweat glands, whilst man and herbivorous animals possess well-developed sweat glands. There is no doubt, therefore, that *the herbivora must have preceded the carnivora in point of time*—the carrion feeders being the connecting link between them.[1] The carnivora have retained the sweat glands as atrophied (rudimentary) organs, and as a sign of their origin, but have given up the habit of sweating, or, in other words, have adapted their skin to the changed conditions of feeding. An animal whose food contains large quantities of urea as well as of creatin, creatinin, xanthin, hypoxanthin, guanin, etc. (the early stages of uric acid), and thus increases the quantity of urea and uric acid already present in the body, must take care always to keep these substances in solution. But the urea and uric acid can only be dissolved in comparatively large quantities of warm water (blood). Such an animal must, therefore, be exempt from the possibility of suddenly losing a large part of its blood and tissue fluid by sweating—or else a precipitation of the above substance will take place. Nor should an organism allow of any sudden cooling down of portions of the skin—such as might be caused by evaporation of the sweat, or else a precipitation would again take place. In a word, such an animal must not be subject to sweating, or else it would be troubled with acute and chronic rheumatism, gout, etc. . . .

" Now as man *is* subject to sweating, it is evident that he was not intended to live on flesh, but on vegetables, or rather on fruits, for he was never meant to live on cereals. . . . Man may eat a limited amount of meat and cereals without doing himself much harm ; but he must always remember that they ought never to form his principal food.

" As soon as it is really understood that we were never intended to live on flesh and cereals, the uric acid diathesis as a trouble of mankind will disappear. We

---

[1] This is most interesting. It shows conclusively that at one time there were *no* carnivora on this globe : they merely developed through countless ages, as the result of deprivation and lack of their proper and natural food.

must, of course, not forget to restrict the consumption of common salt and to use such vegetable foods as are rich in food salts, and not those which are rich in albumen; for a diet consisting of bread, pulses, and cereals, and potatoes will tend to produce gout just as much as a diet consisting of flesh, fish and *caviare*. . ." [1]

It is only by reason of the excessive functioning of the liver that we are not soon poisoned, as the result of such food, and when this organ is constantly over-taxed, as it often is, for a lifetime, it is apparent that it must sooner or later break down, and be ruined from overwork.

[1] " Natural Hygiene," by H. Lahmann, M.D., pp. 76-85.

IV

HAVING seen in the preceding chapters that man is adapted by nature of his constitution to live upon vegetable foods (meaning by this latter term not only vegetables, but fruits and nuts as well), we must next turn to a consideration of the question as to whether these foods would supply all the necessary elements for the nutrition of the human body. The bodily tissues being in a constant state of flux—worn-out particles of the body being continuously thrown off by means of the various eliminating organs, and fresh material constantly taking their place and being built into living tissue—it is obvious that the nature of this material supplied to the body should be of the best in quality ; and that best adapted to maintain its structural integrity. If certain elements are lacking in the food material supplied, these elements will be lacking throughout every stage of the process of digestion, and the tissues ultimately become impoverished because of the lack of them. The chief reason why we eat meat (apart from mere custom), is that it contains a fairly large percentage of proteid—that material from which the muscles are largely built, and which physiologists have lately come to believe is one of the true sources of the bodily energy. Meat being a highly concentrated article of food, and, as before said, containing a large percentage of this proteid, it has always been considered necessary that more or less of it should be consumed in the course of the day in order to offset or replace the wastes necessitated by physical exercise and other causes. Professor Russell H. Chittenden,

57

in speaking of the value of proteid in the human body says :

" The organic substance of all organs and tissues, whether of animals or plants, is made up principally of proteid matter. . . . Proteid substances occupy, therefore, a peculiar position in the nutrition of man and of animals in general. They constitute a class of essential food-stuffs without which life is impossible. For tissue building, and for the renewal of tissues and organs, or their component cells, proteid or albuminous food-stuffs are an absolute requirement. The vital part of all tissue is proteid, and only proteid food can serve for its growth or renewal ; hence, no matter how generous the supply of carbohydrates and fats, without some admixture of proteid food, the body will weaken and undergo ' nitrogen starvation. . . .' It is thus quite clear that the true proteid foods are tissue builders in the broadest sense of the term, and it is equally evident that they are absolutely essential to life, since no other kind nor form of food-stuff can take their place in supplying the needs of the body. Every living cell, whether of heart, muscle, brain or nerve requires its due allowance of proteid material to maintain its physiological rhythm. No other food-stuff stands in such intimate relationship to the vital processes ; and, so far as we know at present, any form of true proteid, whether animal or vegetable, will serve the purpose." [1]

It will be seen from the above, therefore, that proteid is doubtless the most essential element in our diet ; and a lack of proteid material in the food ensures more disastrous consequences to the organism than any other single deviation from a normal diet. Meat, as we have said, contains a large percentage of proteid, and, this being the case, it is evident that, if we are to discard it as an article of diet, we must replace it by other foods which contain an equal amount of proteid, or must

[1] " The Nutrition of Man," pp. 4-5.

eat a proportionate bulk of foods which contain proteid, in order to maintain that physiological equilibrium
which ensures health.

The simplest, and in fact the *only* way to settle this
question, therefore, is to compare the chemical analyses
of the various food-stuffs, and see if any non-flesh foods
contain as much proteid as meat does. If they do, and
if it can be shown, further, that their proteid is as
easily assimilable and as nutritious as animal proteid,
then the case will have been won—for the reason that
there will no longer be any grounds for defending flesh-
eating, upon the basis that that is the only article of
diet capable of supplying the body with the requisite
amount of proteid. I shall take these chemical analyses
from the latest official bulletins—those issued under
the supervision of the U. S. Department of Agriculture,
and corrected up to 1908. The bulletin from which I
quote these tables is entitled " The Chemical Composition of American Food Materials," and is written
jointly by Professors W. O. Atwater and A. P. Bryant.
These authors first of all define what they mean by the
" composition of food materials," as follows :—

COMPOSITION OF FOOD MATERIALS

" Ordinary food materials, such as meat, fish, eggs,
potatoes, wheat, etc., consist of :

" *Refuse.*—As the bones of meat and fish, shells of
shellfish, skin of potatoes, bran of wheat, etc.

" *Edible portion.*—As the flesh of meat and fish, the
white and yolk of eggs, wheat flour, etc. This edible
portion consists of water (usually incorporated in the
tissue and not visible as such), and nutritive ingredients
or nutrients.

" The principal kinds of nutritive ingredients are
protein, fats, carbohydrates, and ash or mineral
matters.

" The water and refuse of various foods and the salt of

salted meat and fish are called non-nutrients. In comparing the values of different food materials for nourishment they are left out of account.

"*Protein.*—This term is used to include nominally the total nitrogenous substance of animal and vegetable food materials, exclusive of the so-called nitrogenous fats. Actually it is employed, in common usage, to designate the product of the total nitrogen by an empirical factor, generally 6·25.

"This total nitrogenous substance consists of a great variety of chemical compounds, which are conveniently divided into two principal classes, proteids and non-proteids.

"The term proteid, as here employed, includes (1) the simple proteids—*e.g.* albuminoids, globulins, and their derivations, such as acid and alkali albumins, coagulated proteids, proteoses, and peptones ; (2) the so-called combined or compound proteids ; and (8) the so-called gelatinoids (sometimes called " glutinoids ") which are characteristic of animal connective tissue.

"The term albuminoids has long been used by European and American chemists and physiologists as a collective designation for the substances of the first two groups, though many apply it to all three of these groups. Of late a number of investigators and writers have employed it as a special designation for compounds of the third class.[1]

"The term non-proteid is here used synonymously with non-albuminoid, and includes nitrogenous animal and vegetable compounds of simpler constitution than the proteids. The most important animal compounds of this class are the so-called " nitrogenous extractives " of muscular and connective tissue, such as creatin, creatinin, xanthin, hypoxanthin, and allied cleavage products of the proteids. To some of these the term " meat bases " has been applied. The latter, with certain mineral salts (potassium phosphates, etc.), are the most important constituents of beef tea and many commercial " meat extracts."

"The non-proteid nitrogenous compounds in vegetable

[1] U. S. Dept. Agr., Office of Experimental Stations Bul. 65, p. 118.

foods consist of amids and amido acids, of which aspara-
gin and aspartic acid are familiar examples.

" The ideal method of analysis of food materials would
involve quantitative determinations of the amounts of
each of the several kinds or groups of nitrogenous compounds. This, however, is seldom attempted. The
common practice is to multiply the percentage of nitrogen by the factor 6·25 and take the product as repre-
senting the total nitrogenous substance For many
materials, animal and vegetable, this factor would be
nearly correct for the proteids, which contain, on the
average, not far from 16 per cent. of nitrogen, although
the nitrogen content of the individual proteids is quite
varied.   The variations in the nitrogen of the non-proteids are wider and they contain, on the average, more
than 16 per cent. of nitrogen.   It is evident, therefore,
that the computation of the total nitrogenous substance
in this way is by no means correct.   In the flesh of meats
and fish, which contain very little of carbohydrates, the
nitrogenous substance is frequently estimated by difference—i.e. by subtracting the ether extract and ash from
the total water-free substance.   While this method is
not always correct, it is oftentimes more nearly so than
the determination by use of the usual factor.

" The distinction between protein and proteids is thus
very sharp.   The latter are definite chemical compounds
while the former is an entirely arbitrary term used to
designate a group which is commonly assumed to include
all of the nitrogenous matter of the food except the
nitrogenous fats.

" In the tables herewith the common usage is followed,
by which the protein is given as estimated by factor,
i.e., total nitrogen multiplied by 6·25.   In the analyses
of meats and fish, however, the figures for protein ' by
difference ' are also given.   Where the proteid and
non-proteid nitrogenous matter have been estimated
in a food material the proportions are indicated in a
footnote.

" Fats.—Under fats is included the total ether extract.
Familar examples of fat are fat of meat, fat of milk
(butter), oil of corn, olive oil, etc.   The ingredients of

the ' ether extract ' of animal and vegetable foods and feeding stuffs, which it is customary to group roughly as fats, include with the true fats various other substances, as fatty acids, lecithins (nitrogenous fats), and chlorophylls.

" *Carbohydrates*.—Carbohydrates are usually determined by difference. They include sugars, starches, cellulose, gums, woody fibre, etc. In many instances separate determinations of one or more of these groups have been made. The determinations of ' fibre ' in vegetable foods, *i.e.*, substances allied to carbohydrates but insoluble in dilute acid and alkali, and somewhat similar to woody fibre, are given in a separate column. The figures in parenthesis in the crude-fibre column show the number of analyses in which the fibre was determined. The figures for ' total carbohydrates ' include the fibre, as well as sugars, starches, etc. Where the sugars or starches have been determined separately footnotes are added giving the average results.

" *Ash or Mineral Matters*.—Under this head are included phosphates, sulphates, chlorides, and other salts of potassium, sodium, magnesium, and other metallic elements. Where analyses of the mineral matters have been found they are added in the form of footnotes. These results usually give the percentage composition of the ash as produced by incineration rather than the proportions in which the different mineral ingredients occur in the food material.

" *Fuel Value*.—By fuel value is meant the number of calories of heat equivalent to the energy which it is assumed the body would be able to obtain from one pound of a given food material, provided the nutrients of the latter were completely digested. The fuel values of the different food materials are calculated by use of the factors of Rubner, which allow 4·1 calories for a gram of protein, the same for a gram of carbohydrates, and 9.8 calories per gram of fats. These amounts correspond to 18·6 calories of energy for each hundredth of a pound of protein and of carbohydrates, and 42·2 calories for each hundredth of a pound of fat in the given food material. In the following table the fuel value per pound has been calculated by use of these factors. In these calculations the values of protein by factor have been used in all cases with the exception of salt cod and hens' eggs, in which the value of protein by difference was used."

I now present a few extracts from these lengthy tables of the chemical composition of food materials—mentioning, first, some typical meats, then fishes, vegetables, grains, flours, etc., dairy products, fruits, nuts, and various sundries.   I take but a few of each, in order to show the typical proteid value of the various foods, without making these tables too long ; and the reader can readily see, by referring to the column of proteid percentage, that many articles of diet contain a far *larger* percentage of proteid than the best meats!   I present the tables, however, before discussing this question at greater length.

[TABLES

Food Materials.	Number of analyses.	Refuse.	Water.	Protein. N × 6.25.	Protein. By difference.	Fat.	Total carbohydrates.	Ash.	Fuel value per pound.
		P. ct.	P. ct.	P. ct.	P. ct.	P. ct.	P. ct.	P. ct.	Cals.

ANIMAL FOOD.

BEEF, FRESH.

Food Materials.	Number of analyses.	Refuse.	Water.	Protein. N × 6.25.	Protein. By difference.	Fat.	Total carbohydrates.	Ash.	Fuel value per pound.
Loin, lean: Edible portion .....Minimum	12	..	64.6	13.4	13.1	11.4	..	.7	735
Maximum	12	..	74.7	24.2	23.1	15.0	..	1.1	1000
Average.	12	..	67.0	19.7	19.3	12.7	..	1.0	900
As purchased...................Min.	11	6.7	52.1	11.9	11.6	10.0	..	.6	650
Max.	11	21.0	66.2	20.8	19.8	13.0	..	1.0	865
Avge.	11	13.1	58.2	17.1	16.7	11.1	..	.9	785
Loin, medium fat: Edible portion...Min.	32	..	56.5	16.6	16.6	16.1	..	.5	1040
Max.	32	..	68.3	22.0	22.0	23.7	..	2.2	1355
Avge.	32	..	60.6	18.5	18.2	20.2	..	1.0	1190
As purchased...................Min.	32	4.1	44.4	8.5	8.5	13.7	..	.4	860
Max.	32	25.6	58.1	19.3	19.1	22.7	..	1.9	1300
Avge.	32	13.3	52.5	16.1	15.6	17.5	..	.9	1040
Loin, fat: Edible portion..........Min.	6	..	52.1	16.0	15.8	25.1	..	.8	1380
Max.	6	..	56.9	18.7	17.8	29.6	..	1.0	1575
Avge.	6	..	54.7	17.5	16.8	27.6	..	.9	1490
As purchased...................Min.	6	5.9	44.3	14.1	13.8	23.6	..	.7	1295
Max.	6	15.0	53.6	16.5	16.1	25.9	..	.9	1400
Avge.	6	10.2	49.2	15.7	15.0	24.6	..	.8	1305
Loin, all analyses: Edible portion.......	56	..	61.3	19.0	18.6	19.1	..	1.0	1155
As purchased.......	55	13.3	52.9	16.4	16.0	16.9	..	.9	1020
Ribs, lean: Edible portion..........Min.	6	..	66.0	16.5	16.9	9.8	..	.8	790
Max.	6	..	69.5	20.9	20.8	14.0	..	1.1	955
Avge.	6	..	67.9	19.6	19.1	12.0	..	1.0	870
As purchased...................Min.	6	12.8	46.7	12.1	12.4	6.8	..	.6	555
Max.	6	32.6	60.7	17.5	17.1	11.0	..	.9	750
Avge.	6	22.6	52.6	15.2	14.6	9.3	..	.7	675
Ribs, medium fat: Edible portion...Min.	15	..	49.9	16.2	15.9	18.0	..	.7	1110
Max.	15	..	63.0	18.8	18.1	32.9	..	1.1	1700
Avge.	15	..	55.5	17.5	17.0	25.6	..	.9	1450
As purchased...................Min.	15	16.3	40.2	12.2	12.0	12.8	..	.4	1790
Max.	15	28.7	49.9	14.9	14.6	26.5	..	.9	1870
Avge.	15	20.8	43.8	13.9	13.5	21.2	..	.7	1155
Ribs, fat: Edible portion..........Min.	9	..	47.4	12.0	13.3	33.9	..	.6	1730
Max.	9	..	51.7	16.8	16.5	36.8	..	.9	1845
Avge.	9	..	48.5	15.0	15.2	35.6	..	.7	1780
As purchased...................Min.	8	14.3	34.3	11.4	10.4	26.8	..	.5	1325
Max.	8	22.0	47.8	16.0	15.6	39.9	..	.7	1790
Avge.	8	16.8	39.6	12.7	12.4	30.6	..	.6	1525

BEEF, COOKED.

Food Materials.	Number of analyses.	Refuse.	Water.	Protein. N × 6.25.	Protein. By difference.	Fat.	Total carbohydrates.	Ash.	Fuel value per pound.
Cut not given, boiled, as purchased........	1	..	39.1	26.2	26.1	34.9	..	.9	2005
Scraps, as purchased...............Min.	2	..	4.5	16.3	19.0	27.7	..	.7	1660
Max.	2	..	41.9	26.4	24.2	75.8	..	6.2	3500
Avge.	2	..	23.2	21.4	21.6	51.7	..	3.5	2580
Roast, as purchased...............Min.	7	..	38.7	16.1	14.5	19.6	..	.7	1210
Max.	7	..	59.5	29.0	29.7	41.4	..	2.7	2030
Avge.	7	..	48.2	22.3	21.9	29.6	..	1.3	1620
Pressed, as purchased................	1	..	44.1	23.6	26.7	27.7.	..	1.5	1610
Round steak, fat removed, as purchased Min.	18	..	53.5	19.4	20.3	3.3	..	1.1	615
Max.	18	..	72.3	34.1	34.1	16.9	..	3.1	1170
Avge.	18	..	63.0	27.6	27.5	7.7	..	1.8	840
Sirloin steak, baked, as purchased........	1	..	63.7	23.9	24.7	10.2	..	1.4	875
Loin steak, tenderloin, broiled: Edible portion......................Min.	6	..	42.7	19.8	21.6	11.8	..	1.0	925
Max.	6	..	64.5	26.7	26.6	35.7	..	1.4	1875
Avge.	6	..	54.8	23.5	23.6	20.4	..	1.2	1300
Sandwich meat, as purchased.......Min.	3	..	56.3	27.1	27.2	8.0	..	2.5	870
Max.	3	..	61.2	28.6	28.8	13.6	..	3.1	1075
Avge.	3	..	58.3	28.0	27.9	11.0	..	2.8	985
Corned beef, all analyses: Edible portion..	10	..	53.6	15.6	15.3	26.2	..	4.9	1395
As purchased..	10	8.4	49.2	14.3	14.0	23.8	..	4.6	1271
Spiced beef, rolled, as purchased..........	1	..	30.0	12.0	11.8	51.4	..	6.8	2390
Tongues, pickled: Edible portion....Min.	2	..	50.9	8.3	8.0	15.3	..	3.1	800
Max.	2	..	73.6	17.3	17.0	25.8	..	6.3	1410
Avge.	2	..	62.3	12.8	12.5	20.5	..	4.7	1105
As purchased...................Min.	2	2.1	45.8	8.2	7.8	15.0	..	3.1	785
Max.	2	10.0	72.0	15.6	15.3	23.3	..	5.6	1275
Avge.	2	6.0	58.9	11.9	11.6	19.2	..	4.3	1080
Tripe, as purchased...............Min.	4	..	84.0	7.1	7.2	.9	0.4	.1	185
Max.	4	..	91.1	18.6	18.3	1.3	.5	.4	335
Avge.	4	..	86.5	11.7	11.8	1.2	.2	.3	270

Food Materials.	Number of analyses.	Refuse.	Water.	Protein.		Fat.	Total carbo-hydrates.	Ash.	Fuel value per pound.
				N x 6.25.	By differ-ence.				
		P.ct.	P.ct.	P.ct.	P.ct.	P.ct.	P.ct.	P.ct.	Cals.
VEAL, FRESH.									
Leg, all analyses: Edible portion........	19	..	71.7	20.7	20.5	6.7	..	1.1	670
As purchased..............	18	11.7	63.4	18.3	18.1	5.8	..	1.0	585
Leg, cutlets: Edible portion....... Min.	3	..	67.3	20.1	20.1	3.3	..	1.0	515
Max.	3	..	75.4	20.5	21.1	10.6	..	1.2	830
Avge.	3	..	70.7	20.3	20.5	7.7	..	1.1	705
As purchased.............. Min.	3	2.1	64.3	19.6	19.6	6.3	..	.9	505
Max.	3	4.5	73.8	21.1	20.2	10.1	..	1.2	790
Avge.	3	3.4	68.3	20.1	19.8	7.5	..	1.0	690
LAMB, FRESH.									
Breast or chuck: Edible portion.........	1	..	56.2	19.1	19.2	23.6	..	1.0	1350
As purchased	1	19.1	45.5	15.4	15.5	19.1	..	.8	1090
Leg, hind, medium fat: Edible ptn... Min.	2	..	68.1	18.7	18.1	15.3	..	1.1	1010
Max.	2	..	64.7	19.7	18.9	17.6	..	1.2	1090
Avge.	2	..	63.9	19.2	18.5	16.5	..	1.1	1055
As purchased.............. Min.	2	17.0	52.4	15.5	15.0	12.6	..	.9	830
Max.	2	17.7	53.3	16.2	15.5	14.4	..	1.0	905
Avge.	2	17.4	52.9	15.9	15.2	13.6	..	.9	870
Leg, hind, fat: Edible portion........	1	..	54.6	18.3	17.1	27.4	..	.9	1495
As purchased	1	13.4	47.3	15.8	14.8	23.7	..	.8	1295
Leg, hind, very fat: Edible portion.......	1	..	51.8	17.6	17.2	30.1	..	.9	1595
As purchased	1	7.0	48.2	16.4	16.0	28.0	..	.8	1485
Leg, hind, all analyses: Edible portion....	4	..	58.6	18.6	17.8	22.6	..	1.0	1300
As purchased	4	13.8	50.3	16.0	15.3	19.7	..	.9	1130
LAMB, COOKED.									
Chops, broiled: Edible portion...... Min.	4	..	43.4	19.2	19.2	24.3	..	1.1	1495
Max.	4	..	50.4	25.2	23.6	34.7	..	1.7	1860
Avge.	4	..	47.6	21.7	21.2	29.9	..	1.3	1665
As purchased..............	1	13.5	40.1	18.4	18.5	28.7	..	1.2	1470
Cut not given, as purchased..............	1	..	47.1	23.7	22.1	29.4	..	1.4	1680
Leg, roast..............	1	..	57.1	19.7	19.4	12.7	..	.8	900
Leg, hind, lean: Edible portion...... Min.	3	..	66.6	19.3	18.5	11.9	..	1.0	875
Max.	3	..	68.3	20.2	19.6	13.0	..	1.2	920
Avge.	3	..	67.4	19.8	19.1	12.4	..	1.1	890
As purchased.............. Min.	3	8.4	51.0	14.7	14.1	9.3	..	.8	665
Max.	3	23.7	65.0	19.5	19.0	11.5	..	1.1	850
Avge.	3	16.8	56.1	16.5	15.9	10.3	..	.9	740
Leg, hind, medium fat: Edible ptn... Min.	11	..	58.4	17.4	17.3	14.6	..	.9	955
Max.	11	..	65.3	19.4	19.0	22.5	..	1.0	1295
Avge.	11	..	62.8	19.5	18.2	18.0	..	1.0	1105
As purchased.............. Min.	11	9.8	48.0	13.8	13.4	11.0	..	.7	730
Max.	11	26.0	56.7	17.5	17.1	19.3	..	.9	1105
Avge.	11	18.4	51.2	15.1	14.9	14.7	..	.8	900
Leg, hind, fat: Edible portion.............	1	..	55.0	17.3	17.0	27.1	..	.9	1465
As purchased	1	12.4	48.2	15.2	14.8	23.8	..	.8	1290
Leg, hind, all analyses: Edible portion....	15	..	63.2	18.7	18.3	17.5	..	1.0	1085
As purchased	15	17.7	51.9	15.4	15.1	14.5	..	.8	900
Hind quarter—as purchased......... Min.	10	9.8	36.5	11.9	11.6	17.7	..	0.6	1020
Max.	10	22.4	50.0	15.7	14.7	41.5	..	.8	1975
Avge.	10	17.2	45.4	13.8	13.5	23.2	..	.7	1235
Side, including tallow: Edible ptn... Min.	25	..	47.2	14.5	14.0	14.7	..	.7	965
Max.	25	..	55.9	18.9	18.4	38.0	..	1.0	1860
Avge.	25	..	54.2	16.3	16.0	28.9	..	.9	1520
As purchased .... Min.	25	13.0	40.7	12.2	11.7	11.2	..	.6	730
Max.	25	22.8	55.2	14.9	14.4	33.1	..	.8	1625
Avge.	25	18.1	45.4	13.0	12.7	23.1	..	.7	1215
Side, not including tallow: Edible portion Min.	10	..	38.8	12.6	12.3	23.3	..	.7	1295
Max.	10	..	58.8	17.4	17.4	48.2	..	.9	2265
Avge.	10	..	53.6	16.2	15.8	29.8	..	.8	1560
As purchased.............. Min.	10	12.9	33.8	11.0	10.7	18.1	..	.6	1005
Max.	10	22.7	47.3	14.7	13.8	42.0	..	.8	1975
Avge.	10	19.3	43.3	13.0	12.7	24.0	..	.7	1255
MUTTON, COOKED.									
Mutton, leg roast: Edible portion... Min.	2	..	50.8	23.3	23.2	20.5	..	1.2	1380
Max.	2	..	51.0	27.8	27.4	24.6	..	1.3	1470
Avge.	2	..	50.9	25.0	25.3	22.6	..	1.2	1420

Food Materials.	Number of analyses.	Refuse.	Water.	Protein.		Fat.	Total carbohydrates.	Ash.	Fuel value per pound.
				N x 6.25.	By difference.				
		P. ct.	P. ct.	P. ct.	P. ct.	P. ct.	P. ct.	P. ct.	Cals.
PORK, FRESH.									
Ham, fresh, lean: Edible portion...Min.	2	..	55.6	19.8	18.8	13.0	..	1.0	103?
Max.	2	..	64.4	30.2	30.2	15.8	..	1.6	111?
Avge.	2	..	60.0	25.0	24.3	14.4	..	1.3	107?
As purchased...Min.	2	..	55.6	19.4	18.5	13.0	..	.9	101?
Max.	2	1.8	63.3	30.2	29.8	15.5	..	1.6	111?
Avge.	2	.9	59.4	24.8	24.2	14.2	..	1.3	106?
Ham, fresh, medium fat: Edible ptn.Min.	10	..	37.3	9.9	12.8	21.2	..	.6	1225?
Max.	10	..	60.3	20.3	22.0	39.4	..	1.3	2020?
Avge.	10	..	53.9	15.3	16.4	28.9	..	.8	1505?
As purchased...Min.	10	4.6	34.1	8.7	11.3	19.4	..	.6	1120
Max.	10	14.2	54.7	18.5	20.0	36.0	..	1.2	1890
Avge.	10	10.7	48.0	13.5	14.6	25.9	..	.8	1345
Ham, fresh, fat: Edible portion....Min.	5	..	30.4	10.7	8.0	43.8	..	.5	2030
Max.	5	..	44.3	14.2	12.1	61.1	..	.8	2825
Avge.	5	..	38.7	12.4	10.6	50.0	..	.7	2345
As purchased...Min.	5	9.7	25.9	9.5	6.8	37.8	..	.4	1790
Max.	5	16.8	40.0	12.2	10.4	52.2	..	.7	2410
Avge.	5	13.2	33.6	10.7	9.2	43.5	..	.5	2035
Ham, fresh, average all analyses: Edible portion...	17	..	50.1	15.7	15.6	33.4	..	.9	1700
As purchased...	17	10.3	45.1	14.3	14.1	29.7	..	.8	1520
Ham, luncheon, cooked: Edbl. ptn.Min.	2	..	47.8	19.5	22.8	19.4	..	5.0	1290
Max.	2	..	50.5	25.5	25.1	22.7	..	6.7	1320
Avge.	2	..	49.2	22.5	24.0	21.0	..	5.8	1305
As purchased...Min.	2	1.5	46.5	19.0	22.2	19.1	..	4.9	1270
Max.	2	2.8	49.7	25.1	24.8	22.0	..	6.5	1280
Avge.	2	2.1	48.1	22.1	23.5	20.6	..	5.7	1280
POULTRY AND GAME, COOKED.									
Capon: Edible portion...	1	..	59.9	27.0	27.3	11.5	..	1.3	985
As purchased...	1	10.4	53.6	24.2	24.5	10.3	..	1.2	885
Capon, with stuffing: Edible portion...	1	..	62.1	21.8	..	10.9	3.8	1.4	935
As purchased...	1	7.7	57.2	20.1	..	10.3	3.5	1.2	875
Chicken, fricasseed: Edible portion...	1	..	67.5	17.6	..	11.5	2.4	1.0	855
Turkey, roast: Edible portion...	1	..	52.0	27.8	28.6	18.4	..	1.2	1295
Turkey, roast, light and dark meat and stuffing: Edible portion...	1	..	65.0	..	17.1	10.8	5.5	1.6	870
FISH, FRESH.									
Bass, striped, whole: Edible portion.Min.	6	..	75.8	17.1	16.9	1.6	..	0.9	405
Max.	6	..	79.6	19.5	19.3	4.6	..	1.4	530
Avge.	6	..	77.7	18.6	18.3	2.8	..	1.2	465
As purchased...Min.	5	48.6	32.5	7.4	7.2	.7	..	.5	175
Max.	5	57.1	39.7	9.8	9.7	1.6	..	.6	255
Avge.	5	55.0	35.1	8.4	8.3	1.1	..	.5	200
Cod, whole; Edible portion...	5	..	80.7	15.5	14.9	.8	..	1.0	300
Max.	5	..	83.5	18.3	17.6	.5	..	1.4	370
Avge.	5	..	82.6	16.5	15.8	.4	..	1.2	325
As purchased...Min.	2	48.5	35.1	8.0	7.7	.1	..	.6	155
Max.	2	66.5	42.3	8.7	8.3	.8	..	.6	175
Avge.	2	52.5	38.7	8.4	8.0	.2	..	.6	165
Salmon, whole; Edible portion...Min.	6	..	60.1	19.4	19.1	10.2	..	1.1	790
Max.	6	..	69.5	25.2	24.5	15.0	..	1.6	1035
Avge.	6	..	64.6	22.0	21.2	12.8	..	1.4	960
SHELLFISH, ETC., FRESH.									
Lobster, whole: Edible portion...Min.	5	..	68.6	11.6	..	1.5	..	1.6	345
Max.	5	..	84.3	25.4	..	2.5	0.9	4.0	555
Avge.	5	..	79.2	16.4	..	1.8	.4	2.2	390
As purchased...Min.	5	44.0	18.0	4.4	..	.5	..	.6	115
Max.	5	73.7	47.2	6.7	..	.9	.4	1.0	165
Avge.	5	61.7	30.7	5.9	..	.7	.2	.8	140
Mussels, in shell: Edible portion...	1	..	84.2	8.7	..	1.1	4.1	1.9	285
As purchased...	1	46.7	44.9	4.6	..	.6	2.2	1.0	150
Oysters, in shell: Edible portion...Min.	34	..	81.7	4.2	..	.6	1.8	1.2	135
Max.	34	..	91.4	10.0	..	1.9	6.7	2.8	370
Avge.	34	..	86.9	6.2	..	1.2	3.7	2.0	235
As purchased...Min.	34	74.0	10.7	.7	..	.1	.2	.2	15
Max.	34	88.3	23.1	1.8	..	.4	1.3	.6	65
Avge.	34	81.4	16.1	1.2	..	.2	.7	.4	45

Food Materials.	Number of analyses.	Refuse.	Water.	Protein.		Fat.	Total carbo-hydrates.	Ash.	Fuel value per pound
				N x 6.25.	By differ-ence.				
		P. ct.	P. ct.	P. ct.	P. ct.	P. ct.	P. ct.	P. ct.	Cals
Oysters, solids, as purchased........Min.	9	..	82.2	4.5	..	.5	1.5	.7	1
Max.	9	..	92.4	7.3	..	1.8	6.2	2.5	3
Avge.	9	..	88.3	6.0	..	1.3	3.3	1.1	2
Scallops, as purchased............Min.	2	..	77.8	14.5	..	..	1.1	1.3	30
Max.	2	..	82.8	15.1	..	.3	5.6	1.5	38
Avge.	2	..	80.3	14.8	..	.1	3.4	1.4	34
Terrapin : Edible portion................	1	..	74.5	21.2	21.0	3.5	..	1.0	54
As purchased........................	1	75.4	18.3	5.2	5.2	.9	..	.2	13
Turtle, green, whole : Edible portion......	1	..	79.8	19.8	18.5	.5	..	1.2	39
As purchased........................	1	76.0	19.2	4.7	4.4	.1	..	.3	9
EGGS.									
Hens', uncooked : Edible portion....Min.	60	..	67.2	11.6	11.4	8.6	..	.6	66
Max.	60	..	75.8	16.0	17.4	15.1	..	1.6	91
Avge.	60	..	73.7	13.4	14.8	10.5	..	1.0	72
As purchased........................	..	11.2	65.5	11.9	13.1	9.3	..	.9	63
Hens', boiled : Edible portion......Min.	19	..	68.6	10.0	10.3	9.1	..	.6	57
Max.	19	..	79.9	15.6	16.8	14.7	..	1.1	88
Avge.	19	..	73.2	13.2	14.0	12.0	..	.8	76
As purchased........................	..	11.2	65.0	11.7	12.4	10.7	..	.7	68
Hens', boiled whites : Edible portion.Min.	11	..	83.1	11.6	12.3	..	..	0.4	2
Max.	11	..	87.1	14.8	15.4	0.3	..	1.0	29
Avge.	11	..	86.2	12.3	13.0	..	..	.6	25
Hens', boiled yolks : Edible portion..Min.	11	..	48.4	15.3	15.5	32.2	..	1.0	1685
Max.	11	..	50.2	16.8	18.0	34.4	..	1.4	1745
Avge.	11	..	49.5	15.7	16.1	33.3	..	1.1	1705
DAIRY PRODUCTS, AS PURCHASED.									
Butter.....................	..	..	11.0	1.0	..	85.0	4.8	3.0	3605
Buttermilk................	..	..	91.0	3.0	..	.5	4.8	.7	165
Cheese, American, pale.......	1	..	31.6	28.8	..	35.9	6.3	3.4	2055
Cheese, American, red........	1	..	28.6	..	29.6	38.3	..	3.5	2165
Cheese, Bondon.............	1	..	56.2	15.4	..	20.8	1.6	7.0	1195
Cheese, California flat........	4	..	34.0	24.3	..	33.4	4.5	3.8	1945
Cheese, Cheddar............	6	..	27.4	27.7	..	36.8	4.1	4.0	2145
Cheese, Cheshire............	1	..	37.1	26.9	..	30.7	6.9	4.4	1810
Cheese, cottage............Min.	2	..	67.0	16.1	..	.4	3.7	1.6	435
Max.	2	..	77.0	25.7	..	1.6	4.9	2.0	585
Avge.	2	..	72.0	20.9	..	1.0	4.3	1.8	510
Cheese, Crown brand cream.......	1	..	31.4	5.2	..	58.0	2.2	3.2	2585
Cheese, Dutch.............Min.	2	..	27.6	..	29.6	16.3	..	8.7	1240
Max.	2	..	42.7	..	44.7	19.0	..	11.4	1630
Avge.	2	..	35.2	..	37.1	17.7	..	10.0	1435
Cheese, Fromage de Brie........	1	..	60.2	15.9	..	21.0	1.4	1.5	1210
Cheese, full cream..........Min.	25	..	27.0	17.9	..	24.5	1.2	2.5	1790
Max.	25	..	44.1	37.0	..	44.6	4.0	4.9	2430
Avge.	25	..	34.2	25.9	..	33.7	2.4	3.8	1950
Cheese, imitation full cream, Ohio........	1	..	37.9	..	25.9	31.7	..	4.5	1820
Cheese, imitation old English..............	1	..	20.7	30.1	..	42.7	1.3	5.2	2385
Cheese, Limburger............	1	..	42.1	23.0	..	29.4	.4	5.1	1675
Cheese, Neuchatel..........Min.	2	..	42.7	15.1	..	22.3	.2	2.3	1275
Max.	2	..	57.2	22.3	..	32.5	2.9	2.5	1790
Avge.	2	..	50.0	18.7	..	27.4	1.5	2.4	1530
Cream.....................	..	..	74.0	2.5	..	18.5	4.5	.5	910
Koumiss..................Min.	8	..	88.3	2.6	..	1.7	5.1	.4	215
Max.	8	..	90.0	3.0	..	2.4	5.9	.4	255
Avge.	8	..	89.3	2.8	..	2.1	5.4	.4	240
Milk, condensed, sweetened........Min.	24	..	21.6	6.0	..	.4	44.4	1.5	1270
Max.	24	..	37.3	10.5	..	10.6	56.9	2.1	1650
Avge.	24	..	26.9	8.8	..	8.8	54.1	1.9	1520
Milk, condensed, unsweetened, "eva-porated cream.................Min.	6	..	66.3	8.6	..	7.8	10.4	1.5	740
Max.	6	..	69.6	10.5	..	10.4	12.2	2.1	835
Avge.	6	..	68.2	9.6	..	9.3	11.2	1.7	780
Milk, skimmed................	..	..	90.5	3.4	..	.3	5.1	.7	170
Milk, whole...................	..	..	87.0	3.3	..	4.0	5.0	6.7	325
Whey.....................	..	..	93.0	1.0	..	.3	5.0	.7	125

Food Materials.	Number of analyses.	Refuse.	Water.	Protein.	Fat.	Total carbohydrates (including fibre).	Fibre (number of determinations in pars.).	Ash.	Fuel value per pound.
VEGETABLE FOOD.—FLOURS, MEALS, ETC.		P. ct.	P. ct.	P. ct.	P. ct.	P. ct.	P. ct.	P. ct.	Cals.
Barley, granulated.................... 1	1	..	10.9	7.5	0.9	79.8	0.7	0.9	1680
Barley meal and flour............. Min.	3	..	9.9	9.0	1.5	70.4	5.9	1.6	1535
Max.	3	..	13.6	12.7	3.2	74.5	7.0	3.8	1680
Avge.	3	..	11.9	10.5	2.2	72.8	6.5	2.6	1640
Barley, pearled ....·.............. Min.	3	..	9.8	7.0	.7	77.3	..	.6	1635
Max.	3	..	12.9	10.1	1.5	78.1	..	1.6	1675
Avge.	3	..	11.5	8.5	1.1	77.8	.3	1.1	1650
Buckwheat flour................. Min.	17	..	11.2	3.9	.5	71.6	.2	.5	1560
Max.	17	..	17.6	10.4	2.3	81.5	.7	1.8	1650
Avge.	17	..	13.6	6.4	1.2	77.9	.4	.9	1620
Corn flour..................... Min.	3	..	12.0	5.9	1.0	76.9	.6	.5	1630
Max.	3	..	13.0	8.5	1.8	79.6	1.2	.8	1665
Avge.	3	..	12.6	7.1	1.3	78.4	.9	.6	1645
Corn meal, granular .... Min.	19	..	8.8	6.7	1.0	68.4	..	.5	1550
Max.	19	..	17.9	11.6	5.3	80.6	..	1.9	1720
Avge.	19	..	12.5	9.2	1.9	75.4	1.0	1.0	1655
Corn meal, unbolted : Edible portion Min.	7	..	10.9	7.8	4.5	71.9	..	1.2	1720
Max.	7	..	12.4	9.3	5.2	75.4	..	1.4	1740
Avge.	7	..	11.6	8.4	4.7	74.0	..	1.3	1730
As purchased.................... Min.	7	4.2	9.2	6.5	3.5	55.7	..	1.0	1305
Max.	7	24.1	10.8	8.0	4.5	72.2	..	1.8	1670
Avge.	7	10.9	10.3	7.5	4.2	65.9	..	1.2	1545
Pop corn...................... Min.	2	..	4.1	10.3	4.7	78.6	1.3	1.3	1870
Max.	2	..	4.4	11.1	5.4	78.7	1.4	1.4	1880
Avge.	2	..	4.3	10.7	5.0	78.7	1.4	1.3	1875
Oatmeal...................... Min.	16	..	2.0	12.9	6.0	63.8	.6	1.5	1810
Max.	16	..	8.8	20.8	8.8	70.2	1.2	2.2	1875
Avge.	16	..	7.3	16.1	7.2	67.5	.9	1.9	1860
Oatmeal, boiled................. 1	1	..	84.5	2.8	.5	11.5	..	.7	285
Oatmeal gruel................. Min.	2	..	87.5	0.9	0.2	2.9	..	0.3	80
Max.	2	..	95.7	1.6	.5	9.6	..	.8	230
Avge.	2	..	91.6	1.2	.4	6.3	..	.5	155
Oatmeal water .... Min.	2	..	94.0	.4	.1	1.3	..	.1	35
Max.	2	..	98.1	.9	.1	4.5	..	.5	105
Avge.	2	..	96.0	.7	.1	2.9	..	.3	70
Oats, other preparations : Rolled oats									
Min.	20	.·	5.5	13.6	5.6	62.8	1.2	1.6	1755
Max.	20	..	11.2	19.1	8.8	70.8	1.4	4.7	1885
Avge.	20	..	7.7	16.7	7.3	66.2	2.3	2.1	1850
Miscellaneous.................. Min.	26	..	6.4	13.7	6.1	63.9	.6	1.3	1830
Max.	26	..	9.2	18.4	8.2	70.5	1.7	1.9	1890
Avge.	26	..	7.9	16.3	7.3	66.8	.9	1.7	1855
All analyses, average................	46	..	7.8	16.5	7.3	66.5	1.0	1.9	1850
Rice........................ Min.	21	..	9.1	5.9	.1	75.4	.1	.2	1600
Max.	21	..	14.0	11.3	.7	81.9	.4	.5	1680
Avge.	21	..	12.3	8.0	.3	79.0	.2	.4	1630
Rice, boiled..........·........ Min.	3	..	52.7	1.6	..	15.5	..	.1	330
Max.	3	..	82.7	5.0	.1	41.9	..	.3	575
Avge.	3	..	72.5	2.8	.1	24.4	..	.2	510
Rice, flaked.................. Min.	2	..	9.4	7.5	.3	81.4	.1	.3	1680
Max.	2	..	9.7	8.3	.5	82.2	.2	.4	1690
Avge.	2	..	9.5	7.9	.4	81.9	.2	.3	1685
Rice flour.................. Min.	4	..	3.7	4.7	1.7	58.3	9.1	6.6	1635
Max.	4	..	10.9	12.0	10.4	79.2	26.3	10.7	1765
Avge.	4	..	8.5	8.6	6.1	68.0	16.1	8.8	1680
Rye flour...............·..... Min.	8	..	11.9	4.9	.2	77.6	.4	.6	1615
Max.	8	..	13.6	8.8	1.3	80.2	.5	.9	1660
Avge.	8	..	12.9	6.8	.9	78.7	.4	.7	1630
Rye meal...................... 1	1	..	11.4	13.6	2.0	71.5	1.8	1.5	1665
Wheat flour, California fine........ Min.	3	..	12.4	7.2	1.2	73.9	..	.4	1590
Max.	3	..	15.6	8.8	1.6	77.8	..	.5	1660
Avge.	3	..	13.8	7.9	1.4	76.4	..	.5	1625
Wheat flour, entire wheat...··...... Min.	9	..	6.4	12.2	1.5	69.5	.5	.6	1635
Max.	9	..	13.1	14.6	2.1	77.0	1.2	1.5	1760
Avge.	9	..	11.4	13.8	1.8	71.9	.9	1.0	1675
Wheat flour, gluten............. Min.	5	..	10.5	12.8	1.1	69.6	..	.5	1635
Max.	5	..	13.0	15.0	2.4	72.8	.6	1.3	1690
Avge.	5	..	12.0	14.2	1.8	71.1	.6	.9	1665
Wheat flour, Graham............. Min.	13	..	9.9	8.5	1.5	66.0	1.8	1.0	1615
Max.	13	..	13.7	17.7	3.6	75.8	2.0	2.7	1710
Avge.	13	..	11.3	13.3	2.2	71.4	1.9	1.8	1670
Wheat flour, prepared (self-raising).. Min.	29	..	8.0	8.0	1.2	67.4	.4	1.5	1560
Max.	29	..	13.0	12.3	2.2	78.6	.5	7.1	1730
Avge.	29	..	10.8	10.2	1.2	73.0	.4	4.8	1800

68

Food Materials.	Number of analyses.	Refuse.	Water.	Protein.	Fat.	Total carbo-hydrates (in-cluding fibre).	Fibre (number of determina-tions in pars.).	Ash.	Fuel value per pound.
VEGETABLES.		P. ct.	P. ct.	P. ct.	P. ct.	P. ct.	P. ct.	P. ct.	Cals.
Beans, dried, as purchased.........Min.	11	..	9.6	19.9	1.4	57.2	3.2	2.7	1540
Max.	11	..	15.5	28.6	3.1	63.5	7.2	4.4	1690
Avge.	11	..	12.6	22.5	1.8	59.6	4.4	3.5	1605
Beans, frijoles (N. Mexico), as puchsd.Min.	4	..	6.3	20.9	1.0	60.7	..	4.0	1625
Max.	4	..	9.9	24.4	1.5	66.9	..	4.4	1695
Avge.	4	..	7.5	21.9	1.3	65.1	..	4.2	1675
Beans, Lima, dried, as purchased.....Min.	4	..	8.3	12.8	.6	61.6	..	3.6	1600
Max.	4	..	12.2	24.5	1.9	70.1	..	4.7	1645
Avge.	4	..	10.4	18.1	1.5	65.9	..	4.1	1625
Lentils, dried, as purchased.........Min.	3	..	6.4	24.5	.7	58.6	..	3.2	1595
Max.	3	..	10.7	26.6	1.5	59.8	..	8.6	1635
Avge.	3	..	8.4	25.7	1.0	59.2	..	5.7	1620
Peas, dried, as purchased...........Min.	8	..	6.9	20.4	.8	58.0	1.2	2.2	1570
Max.	8	..	15.0	28.0	1.3	67.4	7.9	4.3	1670
Avge.	8	..	9.5	24.6	1.0	62.0	4.5	2.9	1655
Cowpeas, dried, as purchased.......Min.	13	..	10.0	19.3	1.1	53.1	3.4	2.9	1450
Max.	13	..	20.9	23.0	1.6	65.4	5.0	3.8	1650
Avge.	13	..	13.0	21.4	1.4	60.8	4.1	3.4	1590
Potatoes, raw or fresh : Edible ptn....Min.	136	..	67.8	1.1	..	13.5	0.2	0.5	285
Max.	136	..	84.0	3.0	0.2	27.4	.9	1.9	570
Avge.	136	..	78.3	2.2	.1	18.4	.4	1.0	385
As purchased........................	..	20.0	62.6	1.9	.1	14.7	..	.8	310
Potatoes, evaporated, as purchased...Min.	3	..	4.8	7.3	.4	79.5	..	2.7	1640
Max.	3	..	8.7	9.5	.4	82.2	..	3.6	1725
Avge.	3	..	7.1	8.5	.4	80.9	..	3.1	1680
Potatoes, cooked, boiled, as puchsd.... Min.	11	..	69.7	1.8	.0	16.1	..	.7	340
Max.	11	..	81.0	3.1	.4	28.5	..	1.4	545
Avge.	11	..	75.5	2.5	.1	20.9	.6	1.0	440
FRUITS, BERRIES, ETC., FRESH.									
Apples : Edible portion............Min.	29	..	77.3	.1	.1	8.8	0.9	.2	175
Max.	29	..	90.9	.8	1.4	21.3	1.4	.6	420
Avge.	29	..	84.6	.4	.5	14.2	1.2	.3	290
As purchased........................	..	25.0	63.3	.3	.3	10.8	..	.3	220
Apricots : Edible portion, average.........	11	..	85.0	1.1	..	13.4	..	.5	270
As purchased........................	..	6.0	79.9	1.0	..	12.6	..	.5	255
Bananas, yellow ; Edible portion....Min.	6	..	66.3	1.0	.0	16.3	..	.5	330
Max.	6	..	81.6	1.6	1.4	29.8	..	1.1	640
Avge.	6	..	75.3	1.3	.6	22.0	1.0	.8	460
As purchased........................	..	35.0	48.9	.8	.4	14.3	..	.6	300
Blackberries, as purchased..........Min.	9	..	78.4	.9	.5	7.5	..	.4	245
Max.	9	..	88.9	1.5	2.9	16.7	..	.9	455
Avge.	9	..	86.3	1.3	1.0	10.9	2.5	.5	270
Cherries : Edible portion...........Min.	16	..	76.9	.7	.8	11.4	..	.5	320
Max.	16	..	86.1	1.1	.8	20.6	..	1.0	430
Avge.	16	..	80.9	1.0	.8	16.7	.2	.6	365
As purchased........................	..	5.0	76.8	.9	.8	15.9	..	.6	345
Cranberries, as purchased...........Min.	3	..	87.6	.4	.4	9.3	1.2	.2	200
Max.	3	..	89.5	.5	.9	10.9	1.7	.2	245
Avge.	3	..	88.9	.4	.6	9.9	1.5	.2	215
Currants, as purchased..............	1	..	85.0	1.5	..	12.8	..	.7	265
Figs, fresh, as purchased, average.........	28	..	79.1	1.5	..	18.8	..	.6	380
Grapes : Edible portion, average.........	5	..	77.4	1.3	1.6	19.2	4.3	.5	450
As purchased........................	..	25.0	58.0	1.0	1.2	14.4	..	.4	335
Huckleberries : Edible portion..........	1	..	81.9	.6	.6	16.6	..	.3	345
Blueberries, as purchased...........Min.	3	..	84.9	0.4	0.4	12.2	..	0.2	200
Max.	3	..	86.4	.8	.9	13.8	..	.5	280
Avge.	3	..	85.6	.6	.6	12.8	..	.4	275
Cherries, as purchased..............	1	..	77.2	1.1	.1	21.1	..	.5	415
Cherry jelly : 1st quality, as purchased....	1	..	21.0	1.1	..	77.2	..	.7	1455
Cherry jelly : 2nd quality, as purchased....	1	..	38.4	1.2	..	59.8	..	.6	1135
Figs, stewed, as purchased..........	1	..	56.5	1.2	.3	40.9	..	1.1	785
Grape butter, as purchased....+..........	1	..	36.7	1.2	.1	58.5	..	3.5	1115
Marmalade (orange peel), as purchased....	1	..	14.5	.6	.1	84.5	..	.3	1585
Peaches, as purchased.............Min.	3	..	81.4	.5	..	5.3	..	.3	115
Max.	3	..	93.7	.9	.2	17.3	..	.4	340
Avge.	3	..	88.1	.7	.1	10.8	..	.3	220
Pears, as purchased...............Min.	4	..	79.6	..	.1	15.6	..	.2	300
Max.	4	..	83.6	.5	.9	19.5	..	.3	400
Avge.	4	..	81.1	.3	.8	18.0	..	.3	355

Food Materials.	Number of analyses.	Refuse.	Water.	Protein.	Fat.	Total carbohydrates (including fibre).	Fibre (number of determinations in pars.).	Ash.	Fuel value per pound.
		P.ct.	P.ct.	P.ct.	P.ct.	P.ct.	P.ct.	P.ct.	Cal.
Pineapples, as purchased............	1	..	61.8	.4	.7	36.4	..	.7	71
Prune sauce, as purchased..........	1	..	76.6	.5	.1	22.3	..	.5	43
Strawberries, stewed, as purchased........	1	..	74.8	.7	...	24.0	..	.5	46
Tomato preserves, as purchased..........	1	..	40.9	.7	.1	57.6	..	.7	104

NUTS.

Food Materials.	Number of analyses.	Refuse.	Water.	Protein.	Fat.	Total carbohydrates (including fibre).	Fibre (number of determinations in pars.).	Ash.	Fuel value per pound.
Almonds: Edible portion.........Min.	11	..	2.0	16.6	48.9	12.8	1.6	1.6	287
Max.	11	..	5.3	25.3	60.0	21.4	2.5	2.5	314
Avge.	11	..	4.8	21.0	54.9	17.3	2.0	2.0	303
As purchased....................	..	45.0	2.7	11.5	30.2	9.5	..	1.1	166
Beechnuts: Edible portion............	1	..	4.0	21.9	57.4	13.2	..	3.5	307
As purchased....................	1	40.8	2.3	13.0	34.0	7.8	..	2.1	182
" Biotes " (acorns): Edible portion.......	1	..	4.1	8.1	37.4	48.0	..	2.4	262
As purchased....................	1	35.6	2.6	5.2	24.1	30.9	..	1.6	169
Brazil nuts: Edible portion..........	1	..	5.3	17.0	66.8	7.0	..	3.9	320
As purchased....................	1	49.6	2.6	8.6	33.7	3.5	..	2.0	162
Butternuts: Edible portion..........	1	..	4.4	27.9	61.2	3.5	..	2.9	316
As purchased....................	1	86.4	.6	3.8	8.3	.5	..	.4	43
Chestnuts, fresh: Edible portion....Min.	9	..	29.2	4.1	2.0	36.9	1.4	.7	89
Max.	9	..	53.8	8.0	10.8	54.0	2.5	1.8	144
Avge.	9	..	45.0	6.2	5.4	42.1	1.8	1.3	112
As purchased....................	9	16.0	37.8	5.2	4.5	35.4	..	1.1	94
Chestnuts, dried: Edible portion....Min.	8	..	4.8	8.2	3.9	65.7	2.4	1.5	181
Max.	8	..	6.6	13.5	15.3	80.3	3.0	2.9	204
Avge.	8	..	5.9	10.7	7.0	74.2	2.7	2.2	187
As purchased....................	8	24.0	4.5	8.1	5.3	56.4	..	1.7	142
Cocoanuts: Edible portion..........	1	..	14.1	5.7	50.6	27.9	..	1.7	276
As purchased....................	1	48.8	7.2	2.9	25.9	14.3	..	.9	141
Cocoanut without milk, as purchased.....	1	37.3	8.9	3.6	31.7	17.5	..	1.0	173
Cocoanut milk as purchased..........	1	..	92.7	.4	1.5	4.6	..	.8	15
Cocoanut, prepared, as purchased....Min.	2	..	2.8	6.0	51.0	24.1	..	1.2	299
Max.	2	..	4.3	6.5	63.7	39.0	..	1.4	325
Avge.	2	..	3.5	6.3	57.4	31.5	..	1.3	312
Filberts: Edible portion............	1	..	3.7	15.6	65.3	13.0	..	2.4	329
As purchased....................	1	52.1	1.8	7.5	31.3	6.2	..	1.1	157
Hickory nuts: Edible portion..........	1	..	3.7	15.4	67.4	11.4	..	2.1	334
As purchased....................	1	62.2	1.4	5.8	25.5	4.3	..	.8	126
Lichi nuts: Edible portion..........	1	..	17.9	2.9	.2	77.5	..	1.5	150
As purchased....................	1	41.6	10.5	1.7	.1	45.2	..	.9	87
Peanuts: Edible Portion..........Min.	4	..	4.9	19.5	32.3	15.3	2.0	1.9	241
Max.	4	..	13.2	29.1	48.8	40.4	3.0	2.4	286
Avge.	4	..	9.2	25.8	38.6	24.4	2.5	2.0	256
As purchased....................	..	24.5	6.9	19.5	29.1	18.5	..	1.5	193
Peanut butter, as purchased..........	2	..	2.1	29.3	46.5	17.1	..	5.0	282
Pecans, polished: Edible portion.........	1	..	3.0	11.0	71.2	13.3	..	1.5	345
As purchased....................	1	53.2	1.4	5.2	33.3	6.2	..	.7	162
Pecans, unpolished: Edible portion.......	1	..	2.7	9.6	70.5	15.3	..	1.9	343
As purchased....................	1	46.3	1.5	5.1	37.9	8.2	..	1.0	184
Pine nuts: Pignolias, edible portion......	1	..	6.4	33.9	49.4	6.9	..	3.4	284
Pinjones: Edible portion..........	1	..	3.8	6.5	60.7	26.2	..	2.8	317
As purchased....................	1	41.7	2.2	3.8	35.4	15.3	..	1.6	185
Piñon: Edible portion..........	1	..	3.4	14.6	61.9	17.3	..	2.8	320
As purchased....................	1	40.6	2.0	8.7	36.8	10.2	..	1.7	190
Sabine pine nut: Edible portion.......	1	..	5.1	28.1	53.7	8.4	..	4.7	294
As purchased....................	1	77.0	1.2	6.5	12.3	1.9	..	1.1	67
Pistachios: 1st quality, shelled, edible portion........	1	..	4.2	22.3	54.0	16.3	..	3.2	299
Pistachios: 2nd quality, shelled, edible ptn.	1	..	4.3	22.8	54.9	14.9	..	3.0	302
Walnuts, California: Edible portion........	1	..	2.5	18.4	64.4	13.0	1.4	1.7	330
As purchased................	1	73.1	.7	4.9	17.3	3.5	..	.6	88
Walnuts, California, black: Edbl.ptn.Min.	2	..	2.5	24.9	54.7	7.4	1.6	1.8	307
Max.	2	..	2.5	30.3	57.8	16.1	1.8	2.0	314
Avge.	2	..	2.5	27.6	56.3	11.7	1.7	1.9	310
As purchased....................	..	74.1	.6	7.2	14.6	3.0	..	.5	80
Walnuts, California, soft shell: Edible portion.................... Min.	4	..	2.5	14.3	60.0	14.5	1.4	1.2	319
Max.	4	..	2.5	20.4	67.0	19.1	3.2	1.6	337
Avge.	4	..	2.5	16.6	63.4	16.1	2.6	1.4	328
As purchased....................	..	56.1	1.0	6.9	26.6	6.8	..	.6	137
" Malted nuts," as purchased..........	1	..	2.6	23.7	27.6	43.9	..	2.2	224

Food Materials.	Number of analyses.	Refuse.	Water.	Protein.	Fat.	Total carbo-hydrates (in-cluding fibre).	Fibre (number of determina-tions in pars.).	Ash.	Fuel value per pound.
MISCELLANEOUS.		*P. ct.*	*P. ct.*	*P. ct.*	*P. ct.*	*P. ct.*	*P. ct.*	*P. ct.*	*Cal.*
Chocolate, as purchased............Min.	2	..	1.5	12.5	47.1	26.8	..	1.1	272
Max.	2	..	10.3	13.4	50.2	33.8	..	3.3	299
Avge.	2	..	5.9	12.9	48.7	30.3	..	2.2	286
Cocoa, as purchased...............Min.	3	..	3.2	20.6	27.1	35.3	..	5.4	223
Max.	3	..	5.4	22.7	31.5	40.6	..	8.9	237
Avge.	3	..	4.6	21.6	28.9	37.7	..	7.2	232
Cereal coffee infusion (1 part boiled in 20 parts water).........................	5	..	98.2	0.2	..	1.4	..	0.2	3
Yeast, compressed, as purchased.........	1	..	65.1	11.7	.4	21.0	..	1.8	62
UNCLASSIFIED FOOD MATERIALS.									
ANIMAL AND VEGETABLE.									
Soups, home-made.									
Beef soup, as purchased............Min.	2	..	92.3	2.7	..	0.3	..	1.1	11(
Max.	2	..	93.5	6.2	..	.5	2.2	1.2	13
Avge.	2	..	92.9	4.4	..	.4	1.1	1.2	12
Bean soup, as purchased.................	1	..	84.3	3.2	..	1.4	9.4	1.7	29.
Chicken soup, as purchased.............	1	..	84.3	10.5	..	.8	2.4	2.0	27.
Clam chowder, as purchased........Min.	2	..	81.6	.7	..	.5	2.5	.6	8(
Max.	2	..	96.7	2.9	..	1.1	11.0	3.4	30:
Avge.	2	..	88.7	1.8	..	.8	6.7	2.0	19:
Meat stew, as purchased............Min.	5	..	82.6	3.7	..	2.0	4.3	1.0	25.
Max.	5	..	87.6	5.6	..	6.4	7.9	1.3	44.
Avge.	5	..	84.5	4.6	..	4.3	5.5	1.1	37(

In the above selections from Atwater and Bryant's tables, I have chosen, in every case, the *best parts* or cuts of the meat, and those meats which are supposedly most nutritious, to balance against my selected list of vegetables, etc—containing the highest percentage of protein. If the tables be examined carefully, the following astonishing facts will be brought to light :—That while in lean ribs of beef (considering only the edible portion) we find that the protein percentage is but 19·6, with a fuel value per pound of 870 ; that while cooked mutton contains a protein percentage of 25·0, with a fuel value of 1420 cal. per pound, almonds (nuts) contain a protein percentage of 21·0, with a fuel value of 3030 ! Again, we find a protein percentage of 27·9, with a fuel value of 3165 for butter-nuts ; a protein percentage of 25·8, with a fuel value of 2560 for pea-nuts ; a protein value of 27·6 and a fuel value of 3105 for black walnuts ; and a protein value of 16·6 and a fuel value of 3285 for California walnuts (to mention but a few instances). The protein percentage of ribs of beef is but 17·8 ! Even cocoa, as purchased, contains a far greater protein percentage and a higher fuel value than the choicest portions of almost all meats—for it contains a protein percentage of 21·6 and a fuel value of 2320 ! This is to be compared, be it observed, with, say, a protein percentage of 17·8 and a fuel value of 1330 for ribs of beef—this being the average for all analyses. Many meats fall far below beef and mutton, which have been cited as standard and sample meats—while only the lean and edible portions have been used for purposes of calculation. Were we to compare the protein percentages and fuel values of other meats, and especially game and fish, we should find that they fall far below, not only nuts, but also grains and the legumes, in both protein percentage and fuel values. For instance, we find that fricasseed chicken, taking the edible portion only, contains a protein percentage of 17·6 and a fuel value per pound of but 885 ; that the edible portion of bass contains but 18·6 protein, with a fuel value of 465 ; that cod contains but 16.5 protein percentage, with a fuel value of 325, as against a protein percentage of 22·5 with a fuel value of 1600 for dried beans—against a protein percentage of 25·7, and a fuel value of 1620 of dried lentils, and as against 24·6 protein percentage, and a fuel value of 1655 for dried peas ! The comparison is astonishing. Even evaporated potatoes contain an average of 8·5 protein percentage, with a fuel value of 1680, as against a protein percentage of 6·2 with a fuel value of 285 for oysters ; and a protein percentage of 4·6, with a fuel value of 150 for mussels ! Hens' eggs contain a large proportionate percentage of protein ; the average being 13·4, with a fuel value of 720 ; but this must be balanced against a protein percentage of 28·8 for American cheese, with a fuel value of 2055 ; or a protein percentage of 25·9 with a fuel value of 1950 for cream cheese.

As against the figures just quoted, let me cite two or three analyses of meat soups, which have frequently been administered to invalids under the idea that they are " strengthening " and " heating "—thus supporting or maintaining the temperature and the energy of the sick person.   Apart from the fundamental error contained in this theory—that we *do* derive our strength and the heat of the body from the food eaten (which I have endeavoured to prove incorrect in my " Vitality, Fasting and Nutrition," pp. 225-303 ; 332-350 ; 448-459 ; etc.), there is the direct evidence afforded by the chemical analysis of these articles of diet.   As opposed to an average of more than 20·0 protein percentage, and a fuel value averaging more than 1600 calories, we find for beef soup, as purchased, a protein percentage of 3·2 and a fuel value of 295 ;   a protein percentage of 1·8, and a fuel value of 195, for clam chowder ;   and a protein percentage of 4·6 and a fuel value of 370 for ordinary meat stew !   Quite apart, therefore, from the argument based upon the fact that all meat juices and extracts contain, in addition to the nutritious principles, a large amount of poisonous or toxic material, we have here direct evidence of the fact that these meat soups, so generally administered to invalids, are totally lacking both in high protein value and in fuel value ;   and when we consider that, in addition to all this, they contain a large amount of poisonous matter in solution, it will be seen how false is the doctrine of administering soups of this character to patients, under the impression that we are helping them to sustain their bodily heat, their energies and their strength !

Let us now make another short list of comparisons. Fresh ham, medium fat, average edible portion, contains 15·3 protein percentage, with a fuel value of 1505; dried cow peas, on the other hand, have a protein percentage of 21·4, with a fuel value of 1590.   Leg of

veal averages a protein percentage of 20·7, with a fuel
value of 670 ; as against a protein percentage of 18·1,
and a fuel value of 1625 for lima beans ; leg of lamb,
medium fat, edible portion only, averages 19·2 protein
percentage, with a fuel value of 1055 ; compared with
a protein percentage of 33·9 and a fuel value of 2845 for
pignolia-nuts. Again, we compare a protein percentage
of 28·9, and a fuel value of 875, for sirloin steak, with a
protein percentage of 29·8, and a fuel value of 2825
for pea-nut butter, as purchased ! If we compare all the
analyses of loin of beef, we find the average for the edible
portion to be 19·0 protein percentage, and a fuel value
of 1155 ; while the protein percentage of this same
article of diet, as purchased, would be but 16.4, with a
fuel value of 1020, as against a protein percentage of
28·1, and a fuel value of 2945 for Sabine pine-nuts ; even
"malted nuts" contain a protein percentage of 22·7,
with a fuel value of 2240—this being far ahead of all but
a few meats. And many of the grains are equal, both
in protein percentage and in fuel value, to many of the
best meats. Thus, rolled oats contain a protein percentage of 16·7, and a fuel value of 1850 ; gluten wheat
flour, a protein percentage of 14·2, with a fuel value of
1665 ; while, turning to the vegetables, we find a protein
percentage of more than 20 per cent. (often running up
as high as 25) and a fuel value averaging 1600 calories
per pound, for all the bean and pea family. Practically
all the nuts contain a far larger percentage of protein
than any meats, while even such articles of food as
chocolate and yeast, contain an equal amount (12·9
and 11·7) ! It will be seen from the above tables, therefore, that so far as protein is concerned, the same amount
may be extracted from an equal amount of other foods,
and even a far greater amount of protein from a lesser
quantity of other foods. This being the case, it becomes
obvious how absurd it is to talk of the necessity of meat

as an article of diet, because of the large amount of protein it contains. But since, as we have seen, the chief object (if not the *only* one) for our eating meat at all is to obtain this protein in what has always been thought to be a " readily digestible and condensed " form, it will be seen that there is no basis whatever for this belief, and that it is, in fact, totally disproved by the direct evidence in the case. We can obtain all the protein we need from an equal or lesser quantity of food of non-animal origin.

Let us now briefly examine the other constituents of food, in order to see if the requisite amount of fats, carbohydrates, salts, etc., are supplied. As before stated, our chief reason for eating meat at all is that it is supposed to contain a larger percentage of protein than any other article of diet ; but we have seen that this is not the case It is generally conceded by all those who defend a " mixed," or partly flesh diet, that vegetable foods and fruits will supply all the fats and carbohydrates needed by the system—the percentage of protein being always the point in dispute.

However, in order to make this perfectly plain to the reader, I shall adduce a few examples of the various food-stuffs, in order that it can be seen at once that all these other constituents of food are likewise contained, in far greater quantities than they are in meat, in almost all other articles of diet. A few examples will render this clear.

First of all, let us take the fats. In the edible portion of very fat beef we have a percentage of 32·3 and 27·6 per cent. fat on the edible portion of fat loin of beef. We find a percentage of 35·6 fat on fat ribs of beef. But when beef is cooked, as it must be before eating, we find the amount of this fat greatly reduced. Thus, sirloin steak contains but 10·2 per cent. of fat ; the edible portion of tenderloin averages 20·4 per cent. ; roast beef averages 28·6 per cent. ; veal contains an average of but 7·7 per cent., for the edible portion ; fat leg of lamb, edible portion, 27·4 per cent. ; but when it is cooked, there is here, as in all other cases, a great reduction in the percentage of fat—there remaining but 12·7 per cent. in roast leg of lamb. The percentage in mutton is somewhat higher, being 22·6 per cent., as cooked. Ham, of course, contains a large amount of fat ; fresh ham, edible portions, medium fat, averaging 28·9 per cent., the total average for fresh ham being 33·4 per cent. When ham is cooked, however, there is the invariable reduction in the percentage, being especially noticeable in this case—the average of luncheon ham, cooked, being but 21·0 per cent. Poultry and game contain a smaller percentage of fat than most meats. Capon, chicken, and roast turkey average from 10 per cent. to 11 per cent. in fat. All fresh fish and shellfish contain very much less fat, from 1 per cent. to 2 per cent. on the average. Eggs contain about half the percentage contained in meat, as a rule, the average being 10·5 per cent. for the edible portion. There is a great disproportion, however, between the white and the yolk of the egg ; there being but ·2 per cent. of fat in the edible portion of the white, while 33·3 per cent. of the edible portion of the yolk is fat.

Now, when we turn to dairy products and to the vegetable kingdom for our fats, we find that a very large amount of fat is contained in a number of articles of diet—far greater than in any of the fattest meats. Thus, butter contains 85 per cent. fat ; American cheese, 38·8 per cent. fat ; California cheese, 38·4 per cent. fat ; cheddar cheese, 36·8 per cent. ; cream cheese, 58·0 per cent. ; full cream cheese averages 38·7 per cent. ; old English cheese, 42·7 per cent. ; etc. Cream, on the other hand, contains less than we should suppose, being but 18·5 per cent. fat, and milk only 4·0 per cent. fat.

Our great source of fats, however—leaving out all dairy products, which, it might be claimed, are indirectly derived from the animal kingdom—is nuts. The great value of these articles of food will become apparent to us when we see that not only are they at the head of the list in protein percentage and in fuel value, but also in the percentage of their fats. Thus we find almonds average 54·9 per cent. fat; beech-nuts, edible portion, 57·4 per cent.; Brazil-nuts, edible portion, 66·8 per cent. fat; butter-nuts, 61·2 per cent. fat; cocoanuts, 50·6 per cent. fat; filberts, 65·3 per cent.; hickory-nuts, 67·4 per cent.; pea-nuts, 38·6 per cent.; pea-nut butter, 46·5 per cent.; pecans, 71·2 per cent.; pine-nuts, 60·7 per cent.; California walnuts, 64·4 per cent.; black California walnuts, 58·3 per cent.; soft-shell walnuts, 68·4 per cent. Chocolate also contains 48·7 per cent. fat. If now we compare with these figures those " highly nutritious " invalid foods, meat soups, etc., we find the fat percentages to run as follows :—Beef soup, ·4 per cent. fat; chicken, ·8 per cent.; clam chowder, ·8 per cent.; and meat stew, averaging 4·8 per cent. fat.

Let us now compare the relative percentages of carbohydrates. In the majority of meats these are so very low that it might almost be said they contain no carbohydrates at all. In the above tables from Atwater and Bryant's analysis, it will be seen that no figures at all appear in the column for carbohydrate percentages. With the single exception of tripe, which contains an average of ·2 per cent., no mention is made of a percentage of carbohydrates in any of the meats. Hens' eggs also contain practically none. Poultry and game, when cooked, average from 2 per cent. to 5 per cent.; fish contain practically none, while shellfish range from 1 per cent. to 3 per cent. This is all the carbohydrates that the animal kingdom affords us !

Turning now to dairy products, we find that various cheeses furnish from 2 per cent. to 4 per cent. carbohydrates ; milk averages 5 per cent., but condensed, unsweetened milk, or evaporated cream, average 11·2 per cent. It will be seen, therefore, that dairy products, coming as they do, indirectly from the animal kingdom, furnish a comparatively small percentage of carbohydrates.

Let us now turn to the vegetable kingdom, including the grains, and see the relative percentage obtained from them. Taking first the flours and the meals, we find : barley, granulated, contains 79·8 per cent. carbohydrates ; buckwheat flour, 77·9 per cent. ; corn flour, 78·4 per cent. ; corn meal, 75·4 per cent. ; oat meal, 67·5 per cent. ; rolled oats, average 66·2 per cent. ; rice, average 79 per cent. ; flaked rice, 81·9 per cent. ; entire wheat flour, 71·9 per cent. ; dried beans, 59·6 per cent. ; beans, frijoles, 65·1 per cent. ; lima beans, 65·9 per cent. ; dried peas, 62·0 per cent. ; cow peas, 60·8 per cent. ; potatoes, 18·4 per cent ; evaporated potatoes, 80·9 per cent.

Turning to fruits, we find that some of them contain quite a large percentage of carbohydrates — from 10 per cent., in the case of blackberries, cranberries and peaches, to 22 per cent. in the case of bananas. Other fruits in their fresh condition˝ range between these. Certain nuts also contain a large percentage of carbohydrates. Thus, almonds contain an average of 17·8 per cent. ; chestnuts, an average of 42·1 per cent. ; dried chestnuts, 74·2 per cent. ; cocoanuts, 27·9 per cent. ; Lichi-nuts, 77·5 per cent. ; pea-nuts, average, 24·4 per cent. ; malted nuts, 43·9 per cent. Chocolate also contains 80·8 per cent. ; cocoa averages

37·7 per cent.; and yeast, 21 per cent. Again in comparing with these figures our " nourishing invalid's food," beef soups, etc., we find that meat stew contains an average of 5·5 per cent. carbohydrates; clam chowder, 6·7 per cent.; chicken soup, 2·4 per cent.; beef soup, an average of 1·1 per cent.! It is to be noticed in this connection that bean soup contains a percentage of 9·4 per cent. carbohydrates.

Turning now to the column marked " ash " in the various tables, we find that all meats contain an average of about 1 per cent. Corn beef, pickled tongue, etc., cannot be fairly included in the list, because of the mineral salts injected into the tissues of the animal. But in all other cases 1 per cent. will be found a most liberal allowance for this ash. It will be remembered that our authors classified under the heading of " mineral matters," all phosphates, sulphates, chlorides, salts of potassium, sodium, etc., These are very essential articles of diet, though the part they play in digestive processes is not yet fully understood. They must be considered, however, valuable portions of all food-stuffs; and, other things being equal, the larger percentage of salts contained in organic compound (not as separate mineral elements) the better. Now, when we come to compare the articles of food derived from the vegetable world, with animal products, we find a very much larger percentage of all mineral matters, in these foods. A few references will make this clear. Rolled oats contain 2·1 per cent.; rice flour, 8·8 per cent.; wheat flour, 4·8 per cent.; dried beans, 3·5 per cent.; dried lentils, 5·7 per cent.; evaporated potatoes, 3·1 per cent.; almonds, 2 per cent.; beech-nuts, 3·5 per cent.; Brazil-nuts, 3·9 per cent.; butter-nuts, 2·9 per cent.; chestnuts, 2·2 per cent.; pea-nuts, 2 per cent.; pignolia nuts, 3·3 per cent.; Sabine pine-nuts, 4·7 per cent.; pistachio-nuts,

3·2 per cent. Most fruits contain a small percentage of mineral matter, averaging perhaps, ·5 per cent. Chocolate contains 2·2 per cent. and cocoa, 7·2 per cent. These percentages might, however, be vitiated by the fact that foreign ingredients are used in the preparation of these foods. Beef soups, etc., average from 1 per cent. to 2 per cent.

In thus giving the total percentage of ash contained in any food, however, it must not be forgotten that this is but a crude and imperfect method of arriving at a just estimate of the value of that food, so far as its ash percentage is concerned. Although the percentage of mineral matters contained in the various foods is very small, the part they play in the economy is exceedingly important—altogether disproportionate to the relatively small quantity of this matter. It is well known that if we feed animals (or, for that matter, human beings), upon certain foods, lacking in salts, these individuals will ultimately die of " saline starvation "—no matter how much food may have been eaten, or how well proportioned the proteids, fats and carbohydrates. This is an astonishing fact. These mineral elements, contained in organic compound, must not be confused, however, with the same elements in *inorganic* form—in which condition they are quite unusable by the system. This is a question, however, into which I do not desire to enter now. It is very necessary, however, to point out and insist upon this fact—that giving the total percentage of ash constitutents or mineral matter, in any given article of food, is of small value to us when attempting to balance a diet, unless we know *in what* this percentage of mineral matter consists. That is, 1·7 per cent. ash of a given food may be composed of five different mineral elements (in organic form) and the proportion of each would vary largely. It is quite possible, therefore, for there to be a larger percentage of any one mineral element in a certain food, containing a lesser *total* ash percentage than in one containing a greater ash percentage   That is, supposing there to be two articles of diet, one containing 1·5 per cent. and the other 2 per cent. of ash.   The article of food containing the 1·5 per cent. of salts might contain 1 per cent. of potash, while the article containing 2 per cent. of total ash would contain but ·5 per cent. of potash.   It would be seen from this that an article of food containing less total ash percentage might contain relatively more of a certain element; and if we wish to obtain and supply to the system certain organic salts, it will only be necessary for us to pick out those articles of diet which contain the largest percentage of the required salt, and supply it to the body, as food, for a longer or shorter period In this manner saline starvation, and the many ills that result indirectly from it, may be avoided.   It will be evident from the above, therefore, that any tables, giving the *total* ash percentage of the various foods are practically valueless, so long as they do not carry the analysis a step further, and tell us in what this total percentage consists.   Only in this manner can any definite results be obtained; but it will be evident, at all events, that any of the articles of diet containing such organic salts would be preferable to meats, so far as this aspect of the problem is concerned—since meats contain practically none.   It will be of interest to consider, briefly, this question of the relative proportion of each organic salt in the total ash percentage.

So far as I have been able to discover, only two authors have paid particular attention to this question of minute ash percentages: Dr H. Lahmann, in Germany, and Mr Otto Carqué, in America.   Both of these authors have gone to considerable trouble

F

to obtain exact figures upon this question.[1] Let us consider Dr Lahmann's argument first : Taking milk (of the human species) as the standard with which to compare analyses of all foods—since it is to be supposed that this would contain all organic salts as well as proteid, fats and carbohydrates in exactly the right proportion for the upbuilding of the healthy human body—he found, by comparison, that the quantities of soda and lime contained in our ordinary food are far below the quantities necessary to maintain a healthy existence, whereas the quantities of potash, iron and phosphoric acid are generally too high. Although his conclusions may not be accepted in full, it is evident that some of them, at least, are correct ; and one of the most important conclusions to be drawn from his argument is that, generally speaking, anæmia has nothing to do with want of iron in the blood. It is due to other causes—principally over-feeding, as I have endeavoured to show in my " Vitality, Fasting and Nutrition," pp. 604-605.

Dr Lahmann shows us that we may replace any quantity of meat or lentils, as well as bread and flour, by fruits or green vegetables, and that the amount of lime and other bone-forming salts will be increased thereby. As a general thing it may be said that there

---

[1] In a letter to Mr Carqué, on this subject, Dr Wiley writes :

UNITED STATES DEPARTMENT OF AGRICULTURE
Bureau of Chemistry
Washington, D. C.

Mr OTTO CARQUÉ,   .   1st August 1904.
    765 N. Clark St., Chicago, Ill.

Dear Sir.—I regret to say that no one in this country has undertaken a complete analysis of all the mineral constituents of foods. An analysis usually relates to the nutritive value and general composition, but does not give, as a rule, the composition of the ash.

I think it is highly desirable that the composition of ash be carefully studied and hope that some chemist will take that matter up in the near future. Respectfully,

(Signed) H. W. Wiley, Chief.

is a superabundance of potash in vegetable food. A large number of diseases were found to be due to a disproportion of thé organic salts—this argument running throughout Dr Lahmann's book. The following table will show clearly the percentage of the various mineral salts in food-stuffs, and will prove conclusively that certain salts, lacking in the human system, can never be supplied by any amount of meat ; and, further, that a number of these salts cannot be supplied in proper quantities by any other articles of food than *fruits*. These, and these alone, contain many salts in solution which the system needs. I shall, however, consider this question at greater length when I come to discuss the value of the fruitarian dietary. For the moment, let us turn our attention to the tables of ash percentages.

Now, if we compare the figures in the following tables, we find that in practically every case the quantity of any given food-salt is greater in all fruits, and practically in every other article of diet than it is in meat. Taking potassium, for example, we find that meat averages (out of the total percentage of mineral matter) 41·30 per cent., while blueberries average 57·1 per cent. ; and olives, 80·9 per cent. If we compare the quantity of sodium, we find that meat contains 3·6 per cent. ; while apples contain 26·1 per cent. ; strawberries, 28·5 per cent. ; dried figs, 26·2 per cent. As some of these, however, are percentages of smaller *total* ash percentages, the disproportion is not so great as would at first appear, though it is evident that the fruits contain much more, even allowing for this. Making the same reservations, we find that while meat contains, of iron, an average of ·7 per cent., strawberries contain 5·9 per cent. ; gooseberries 4·56 per cent. ; prunes, 2·5 per cent. ; while spinach contains 3·35 per cent. ; asparagus, 3·4 per cent. ; and lettuce, 5·2 per cent.

Composition of Food Products — PER CENT.
Composition of Mineral Matter — AS GIVEN IN THE 5th COLUMN. PER CENT.

	I Water	II Protein (Albumen)	III Fat	IV Carbo-Hydrates (Sugar, Starch)	V Mineral Matter	Potassium (K₂ o)	Sodium (Na₂ o)	Calcium (Ca o)	Magnesium (Mg o)	Iron (Fe₂ o₃)	Phosphorus (P₂ o₅)	Sulphur (S o₃)	Silicon (Si o₂)	Chlorine (Cl)
Human Milk	87.02	2.36	3.94	6.23	0.45	33.80	9.12	16.70	2.16	0.22	22.66	0.95	0.02	18.38
Cow's Milk	87.20	3.55	3.70	4.88	0.71	24.67	9.70	22.05	3.05	0.55	28.45	0.30	0.04	14.28
Meat (Average)	72.00	20.00	5.00	0.40	1.10	41.30	3.60	2.80	3.21	0.70	42.50	1.60	1.10	3.85
Blood of the Ox	80.80	18.10	0.20	0.03	0.85	7.60	45.00	10.90	0.60	9.40	5.25	3.05	0.8	34.40
Eggs	73.70	12.55	12.10	0.55	1.10	17.40	22.90	10.90	1.10	0.40	37.60	0.30	0.30	9.00
Sealfish	81.00	17.10	0.34	….	1.60	21.80	14.90	15.20	3.90	….	38.16	….	….	11.40
Fruits.														
Apples	84.80	0.40	….	13.00	0.50	35.70	26.10	4.10	8.75	1.40	13.70	6.10	4.30	….
Strawberries	87.70	0.50	….	7.70	0.80	21.10	28.50	14.20	….	5.90	13.80	3.15	12.05	1.70
Gooseberries	85.70	0.50	….	8.40	0.40	38.65	9.90	12.20	5.85	4.56	19.70	5.90	2.60	0.75
Prunes	81.20	0.80	….	11.05	0.71	48.50	9.05	11.50	3.60	2.50	16.00	3.20	3.15	0.40
Peaches	83.00	0.40	….	11.80	0.30	54.70	8.50	8.00	5.20	1.00	15.20	5.70	1.50	….
Blueberries	78.40	0.80	….	5.90	1.00	57.10	5.16	8.00	6.10	1.10	17.40	3.10	0.90	….
Cherries	79.80	0.70	….	12.00	0.70	51.85	2.20	7.50	5.50	2.00	16.00	5.10	9.00	1.35
Grapes	78.20	0.60	….	16.30	0.50	56.20	1.40	10.80	4.20	0.40	15.60	5.60	2.75	1.52
German Prunes	84.90	0.40	….	8.20	0.66	59.20	0.50	10.00	5.50	3.20	15.10	3.70	2.40	….
Dried Figs	31.20	1.34	1.45	65.90	2.86	28.36	26.27	18.91	9.21	1.46	1.30	6.75	5.93	2.70
Olives	30.07	5.24	51.90	….	2.34	80.90	7.53	7.46	0.18	0.92	1.33	1.05	0.65	0.18
Nuts.														
Walnuts	4.70	16.40	62.90	7.90	2.03	31.10	2.25	9.60	13.00	1.32	43.70			
Chestnuts, Dried	7.30	10.86	2.90	73.80	3.00	56.70	7.12	3.87	7.47	0.14	18.10	3.80	1.50	0.50
Almonds	6.00	23.50	53.00	7.80	3.10	28.00	0.20	3.86	17.66	0.50	43.60	0.37	….	….
Cocoanuts	46.60	5.50	35.90	8.10	1.00	43.90	8.40	4.60	9.40	….	17.00	5.09	0.50	13.40
Beechnuts	9.09	21.70	42.50	19.20	3.86	17.15	5.20	18.40	14.15	1.00	30.50	2.45	2.70	2.44

Composition of Food Products
PER CENT.

Composition of Mineral Matter
AS GIVEN IN THE 5th COLUMN. PER CENT.

	Water	Protein (Albumen)	Fat	Carbo-Hydrates (Sugar, Starch)	Mineral Matter	Potassium (K₂O)	Sodium (Na₂O)	Calcium (CaO)	Magnesium (MgO)	Iron (Fe₂O₃)	Phosphorus (P₂O₅)	Sulphur (SO₃)	Silicon (SiO₂)	Chlorine (Cl)
	I	II	III	IV	V									
Vegetables.														
Spinach	88.50	3.50	0.60	4.44	2.10	16.60	35.30	11.90	6.40	3.35	10.25	6.90	4.50	6.30
Savoy-Cabbage	87.10	3.30	0.70	6.00	1.64	27.50	10.20	21.40	3.60	1.70	14.75	8.20	4.78	7.90
Red-Cabbage	90.06	1.83	0.20	5.86	0.77	22.10	12.10	27.90	4.44	0.10	3.90	15.30	0.50	13.65
Onions	76.00	1.70	0.10	10.80	0.70	34.00	2.50	22.90	4.65	2.30	17.35	5.68	8.50	2.40
Carrots	87.05	1.00	0.20	9.40	0.90	36.90	21.20	11.30	4.40	1.00	12.80	36.45	2.40	4.60
Horse Radish	76.70	2.70	0.35	16.00	1.50	30.76	4.00	8.20	2.90	1.94	7.70	30.80	12.70	0.90
Asparagus	93.75	1.80	0.15	2.60	0.54	24.00	17.10	10.85	4.30	3.40	18.60	6.20	10.10	5.90
Radishes	93.30	1.20	0.15	3.80	0.74	32.00	21.15	14.00	3.10	2.80	10.90	6.50	0.90	9.15
Cauliflower	90.90	2.50	0.30	4.55	0.83	44.30	5.90	5.60	3.70	1.00	20.20	13.00	3.70	3.40
Cucumbers	95.60	1.20	0.10	2.30	0.44	41.20	10.00	7.30	4.15	1.40	20.00	6.90	8.00	6.60
Lettuce	94.30	1.40	0.30	2.20	1.03	37.60	7.50	14.70	6.20	5.20	9.20	3.80	8.10	7.65
Potatoes	75.09	2.08	0.15	21.00	1.10	60.01	3.00	2.60	4.93	1.10	16.90	6.53	2.00	3.50
Leguosae & Cereals.														
Lentils	12.35	25.70	1.90	53.30	3.04	34.80	13.50	6.30	2.50	2.00	36.30	...	...	4.63
Peas	15.00	22.85	1.80	52.40	2.58	43.10	1.00	4.80	8.00	0.80	35.90	3.40	0.90	1.60
Beans	14.76	24.30	1.60	49.00	3.26	41.50	1.10	5.00	7.15	0.50	38.90	3.40	0.65	1.80
Whole Wheat	13.40	13.60	1.90	69.10	2.00	31.20	2.10	3.25	12.10	1.30	47.20	0.40	2.00	0.30
Superfine Flour	12.60	10.20	0.90	74.70	0.50	34.40	0.80	7.50	7.70	0.60	49.40	...	...	...
Rye	15.06	11.50	1.80	67.80	1.81	32.10	1.50	2.90	11.22	1.20	47.70	1.30	1.40	0.50
Barley	13.80	11.10	2.20	64.90	2.70	16.30	4.10	0.70	12.50	1.70	32.80	3.00	28.70	...
Oats	12.40	10.40	5.20	57.80	3.02	17.90	1.70	3.60	7.10	1.20	25.60	1.80	39.20	0.90
Corn	13.10	9.85	4.60	68.50	1.51	29.80	1.10	2.20	15.50	0.80	45.60	0.80	2.10	1.90
Rice, *Unpolished*	13.10	7.85	0.88	76.50	1.00	25.00	4.20	3.70	11.10	1.40	53.76	0.50	2.60	0.10

It is evident that, making all allowances for a smaller total ash percentage, these articles of diet contain a far greater percentage of iron than does meat, and the same is true of practically all other salts, as can be seen by referring to the tables. It is evident, therefore, that other food-stuffs, and particularly fruits, will supply us with more mineral matter than will the best of meats, and are to be preferred in consequence.

It will not be necessary for us to compare the columns headed "Refuse" and "Water," since these are practically the same in all food-stuffs, on the average, and they do not effect, appreciably, the food-value of any article of diet.

There remains only one valid objection to my argument, and that is based upon the supposed fact that a larger percentage of animal proteid is appropriated by the system than is the case in vegetable foods. That is, given a certain quantity of animal and vegetable foods, both containing an equal amount of proteid, more will be appropriated from the animal than from the vegetable food-stuffs. A great many writers, such as Miss Leppel, in England, have taken this ground. But I would point out, first of all, that, even if it were true, it would not invalidate the argument in the least, for the reason that a far larger percentage of proteid is contained in a smaller amount of non-flesh food, such as nuts ; and for that reason it would be easy enough to supply the system with the same amount of proteid from an equal, or even a lesser, bulk of food—even granting the validity of the argument. But I dispute the fact itself. Professor Russell H. Chittenden, of Yale University, one of the most famous physiologists in America, and director of the Sheffield Scientific School, writes in his " Nutrition of Man " as follows :—

" In the digestion of proteid food-stuffs by the combined action of gastric and pancreatic juice in the alimentary tract, a large proportion of the proteid is destined to undergo complete conversion into animo-acids; and, from these fragments, the body, by ·a process of synthesis, can construct its own peculiar type of proteid. This latter suggestion is worthy of a moment's further consideration; as is well known, every species of animal has its own peculiar type of proteid, adapted to its particular needs. The proteids of one species directly injected into the blood of another species are incapable of serving as nutriment to the body, and frequently act as poison. . . . The availability or digestibility of food can be determined only by physiological experiment. By making a comparison, for a definite period of time, of the amount of the different food ingredients, and the amount that passes unchanged through the intestines, an estimate of its digestibility can be made. . . . In a general way it may be stated that with animal foods, such as meats, eggs, and milk, about 97 per cent. of the contained proteid is digested, and thereby rendered available to the body. With ordinary vegetables, on the other hand, as they are usually prepared for consumption, only about 85 per cent. of the proteid is made available. With a mixed diet, with a variable admixture of animal and vegetable foods, it is usually considered that about 92 per cent. of the proteid contained therein will undergo digestion."

At first sight, it would appear that this runs counter to the argument that has been advanced; but we must take into account the fact that Professor Chittenden is here speaking only of vegetable proteid, and has made no mention of *nuts*; and, as we have seen from the tables, nuts contain a far larger percentage of protein than meats. When we take into consideration the small disproportion in the percentage assimilated, and find that when meat is mixed with other articles of food, as it invariably is, the percentage of its availability is reduced to 92 per cent., while vegetable foods are proportionately raised to the same figure, we see that the apparent discrepancy practically vanishes to nothing. And when we further take into account the fact that an equal amount of proteid can be obtained from a far *less* quantity of non-flesh food, we see that, from an equal bulk of food material, a far larger *proportionate* percentage would be assimilated from the vegetable foods than from the animal.

Another great argument which has always been advanced in favour of meat-eating, or the ingestion of proteid in the form of animal, as opposed to vegetable food, is that the proteid derived from the animal is far more quickly and readily assimilated by the system than vegetable proteid. The *rapidity* of the digestion of animal food has always been urged as one of the strongest arguments in its favour, and it is largely for this reason that it has been administered to invalids, and to patients in a depressed and weakened state of body. But now we find that physiological research has completely disproved this old dogma! Professor Chittenden, on p. 80 of his " Nutrition and Man," says :

" It is evident from what has been stated that the gastric digestion of proteid foods *is a comparatively slow process*, involving several hours of time ; and further, that food material in general remains in the stomach for varying periods, dependent upon its chemical composition. . . . It is a mistake to assume that the digestion of proteid foods is complete in the stomach. Stomach digestion is to be considered more as a preliminary step, paving the way for further changes to be carried forward by the combined action of intestinal and pancreatic juice in the small intestines. . . . The importance of gastric digestion is frequently overrated."

Dr Sylvester Graham, writing on this subject years ago in his " Science of Human Life," said :

" In vain have they attempted to regulate the diet of

man on the chemical principles, and insisted on the necessity for certain chemical properties in the human element to sustain the vital economy.   That economy has shown them that it can triumph over the chemical affinities and ordinary laws of organic matter, and bend them to its purposes at pleasure ; generating and transmuting from one form to another, with the utmost ease, the substance which human science calls elements ; and while the living organs retain their functional power and integrity, elaborating from every kind of element on which an animal can subsist, a chyle so nearly identical in its physical and chemical character, that the most accurate analytical chemists can scarcely detect the least appreciable difference. . . . Though, while the health and integrity of the assimilating organs are preserved, the physical and *chemical* character of the chyle are nearly identical, whatever may be the elementary substance from which it was elaborated, yet the *vital* constitution of the chyle and blood, and consequently of the solids, is greatly affected by the quality of the food. When chyle is taken from the living vessels, the vital constitution of that which is elaborated from flesh meat is capable of resisting the action of bacterial decomposition only a short time, and will begin to putrefy in three or four days at the longest ; while the vital constitution of that which is elaborated from pure and proper vegetable elements, will resist this decomposing action for a much larger period, yet it will in the end putrefy with all the phenomena of that formed from flesh meat."

The bearing of these facts on physical training, the health of the body, and the decomposition of the body after death, need only be pointed out.

It is really extraordinary how writers on dietetics, seem to take a delight, as a rule, in making as many mis-statements and misrepresentations as possible. Take, for example, the following passage in Dr C. S. Read's Book, " Fads and Feeding " :—

" It is necessary, with the vegetable products, to take the nitrogenous product as Nature gives it to us, which is a drawback ; and secondly, vegetable foods are relatively much poorer in this respect than animal foods. . . . A vegetable diet must needs be bulky, because of its wateriness, especially when cooked, and the large amount of indigestible matter it contains. This tends to abnormally distend the stomach and bowels. The capacity of the stomach becomes greater, more food can be taken, but the distention produces a feeling of satiety before sufficient nourishment has really been ingested. The dealing with such a bulk internally means the expenditure of much nervous energy which might have been better utilised. The wateriness of vegetable foods is extremely disadvantageous, since on absorption it tends to render all the tissues flabby. The individual who leads a sedentary life will feel the disadvantage of vegetarianism more than the active worker."

Now, not a sentence in the above quotation is correct. If Dr Read had studied vegetarians at first hand, he would have found out his mistakes, and would not have written such rubbish. As a matter of fact, vegetable foods *do not* supply less nitrogen than meat, but on the contrary more ; a vegetable diet *need not* be bulky, if properly selected—*less* of it need be eaten than of a mixed diet, because of its greater nutritive value ; while the notion that the absorbtion of water from the foods make the tissues " flabby " is, of course, absurd. Altogether, this is almost the greatest string of inaccuracies regarding diet that I have ever come across.

There is one aspect of this question which it might be well to touch upon in this place. The air that we breathe, as we know, contains a large percentage of nitrogen. Might it not be possible for the system to utilise some of this nitrogen, when the body is in a state of nitrogen starvation ? Dr De Lacy Evans, surgeon to St Saviour's Hospital, in London, contended that this might be the case, and in his " How to Prolong Life," pp. 76-80, wrote :

" It has been argued that fruits will not sustain life, because they do not contain sufficient nitrogen ; this argument is founded upon a *theory* which is demonstrably incorrect, and it is an ascertained *fact* that fruits alone will support life and good bodily health. . . . By experiments on ourselves, on friends, and on natives of tropical regions, we find a comparatively small quantity of nitrogen necessary to sustain life; in fact, fruits, taken as a class, contain sufficient nitrogen to sustain human life. . . . Now fruits will sustain life, and all fruits contain carbon, hydrogen and oxygen, and most of them a small quantity of nitrogen ; and if these fruits which will sustain life do not contain sufficient nitrogen, may not man, who breathes and is in contact with an atmosphere (four-fifths of which is nitrogen), by means of his lungs, the surface of which is supposed to be more than twenty times that of the whole body, *absorb the necessary nitrogen directly from the atmosphere*? From careful observation of the diet of natives in tropical regions, and from direct experiments in England, we may state that this is positively the case.   This is often observed in the herbivora : their natural food contains little nitrogen, still it is found in their flesh in about the same ratio as in the carnivora.   Further, the carnivora live on food rich in nitrogen—yet one is as well nourished as the other. . . . Man may live entirely upon fruits, in better health than the majority of mankind now enjoy. Good, sound, ripe fruits are never a cause of disease ; but the vegetable acids, as we have before stated, lower the temperature of the body, decrease the process of combustion and oxidation—therefore the waste of the system—less sleep is required, activity is increased, fatigue or thirst hardly experienced : still the body is well nourished, and as a comparatively small quantity of earthy salts are taken into the system, the cause of ' old age ' is in some degree removed, the effect is delayed, and life is prolonged to a period far beyond our ' three score years and ten.' " [1]

[1] " On one occasion, when living for five days entirely upon oranges, our temperature was lessened, still we felt a pleasant glow throughout the system ; but to other individuals we felt cold ; animal heat is therefore only *relative*. We further found that only three or four hours sleep was required in the twenty-four hours."

The consensus of modern opinion, however, seems to be against any such supposition. Chittenden, for example, writes : [1]

" Man lives in an atmosphere of oxygen and nitrogen. He can and does absorb and utilise the free oxygen of the air he breathes ; indeed, it is absolutely essential for his existence, but free nitrogen likewise drawn into the lungs at each inspiration is of no avail for the needs of the body."

As, however, all bodies contain more or less nitrogen in excess, there would be no need to call upon the air for its supply. It would be interesting to note the effects in cases of nitrogen starvation ; but the simple fact that animals *do die* when sufficient nitrogen is subtracted from their food, would seem to indicate that but little nitrogen, if any, can be extracted from the air, even under these circumstances.

After the above lengthy argument, which endeavours to show that sufficient proteid can be supplied the body from vegetable foods, it is somewhat amusing to find that, as a matter of fact, *far too much proteid* has invariably been eaten by practically all civilised peoples —and that so far from there being any danger of nitrogen starvation, or lack of sufficient proteid, the danger is all the other way, and four-fifths of all the maladies from which mankind suffers are due to the very fact that an excess of proteid has been eaten ! All physiologists agree that the majority of people eat far more, not only of proteid, but of all kinds of food, than is required, according to their tables ; and Professor Chittenden has recently shown, as the result of an elaborate series of experiments conducted at Yale, that the average proteid standard set by physiologists, as being

[1] " Nutrition of Man," p. 4.

necessary for the maintenance of health, is at least *three times too high*! That is, the majority of persons eat considerably more than three times too much proteid! In view of these facts, it is amusing to find so much fear exhibited on all hands in case the proteid supply should not be sufficient in quantity.

These Yale nutrition investigations are now so widely known that it would be useless to do more than refer to them in this place. As the results of experiments upon University professors, upon athletes, and upon a squad chosen from the United States army, it was definitely proved that the proteid standards were far too high: the men flourishing, improving in every direction, and even doing a *greater* amount of physical work than usual on a diet averaging, in proteid value, about a third said to be necessary by the physiologists. When we take into account the fact that most people eat far more proteid than the physiologists said was necessary, it will be seen at once the tremendous disproportion which exists between the amount actually consumed, and the amount really needed by the body; and how absurd it is, in face of these facts, to persist in demanding an excess of those foods which contain such high proteid percentages! Chittenden says:

" There is no question, in view of our results, that people ordinarily consume much more food than there is any real physiological necessity for, and it is more than probable that this excess of food is in the long run detrimental to health, weakening rather than strengthening the body, and defeating the very objects aimed at. . . . One-half of the 118 grams of proteid food called for daily, is quite sufficient to meet all the physiological needs of the body, certainly under the ordinary conditions of life; and with most individuals, especially persons not living an active outdoor life, even a smaller amount will suffice." [1]

[1] " Physiological Economy in Nutrition," pp. 274-275.

The figures and calculations throughout his works, however, show that the proteid intake may be reduced to fully one-third of that said to be necessary in standard physiologies, with nothing but increased health and strength.

In summing up this question of the necessity of meat-eating, one important fact must not be lost sight of, which, in a sense, may be said to settle the argument in favour of the vegetarian dietary without further additional evidence of any kind. It is this : That the bodies of all animals are built from vegetable foods, and consequently, when we eat those animals, we merely eat the vegetable foods, upon which *they* have subsisted, at second hand ! We appropriate or obtain the *same* chemical elements in organic compound that they originally obtained from their food, *but we obtain nothing else.* Animals have the power to create nothing. The single fact that all nutritive material is formed by vegetables—animals having the power to appropriate but never to form or create food elements—is proof positive, to my mind, that we can derive all the nutriment we need directly from the vegetable world, and that the best food, and that which is most conducive to man's highest development—bodily, mentally and spiritually—is found in the use of these vegetables themselves. Those who eat animal food do not get a single element of nutrition, save that which those animals have obtained from vegetables. Hence man, in taking his nutrition indirectly, by the eating of animals, must of necessity get the original nutriment more or less deteriorated from the unhealthy conditions and accidents of the animal he feeds upon—with the impurities and putrescent matters mingled with the blood and in the viscera of animal substances, which are invariably present. Apart from this aspect of the problem—which is one rather of hygiene than of chemistry, and hence will be discussed in the following chapter—it is evident that man can derive no single element of nutrition from the bodies of animals, which he cannot also obtain from suitable vegetable foods.   He need not eat grass and herbs, as do the cows and sheep, in order to obtain this material—since chemical analysis of the foods will readily show us that these same elements are contained in fruits, nuts and other substances suited to his economy.   This argument alone should, therefore, as a matter of fact, settle the whole case in favour of vegetarianism as against flesh-eating, without any further or additional proof being necessary.

V

THE ARGUMENT FROM HYGIENE

WE have seen in the preceding pages that it is perfectly possible for man to live upon vegetable and kindred foods without necessitating the eating of animal foods of any character—which merely confirms the evidence afforded us by a study of comparative anatomy and physiology. Having thus seen that it is *possible* for man to live and thrive upon these foods, the question at once arises : Can man thrive *best* upon such foods ? Can he maintain a *higher* level of vital and bodily health, and of mental and moral powers, upon these foods than he can upon the usual mixed diet of to-day—including meat and its various products ? If it can be shown that this is the case—that a man cannot only live, but improve in health and bodily strength on the vegetarian régime—then it will be pretty obvious that this is the diet best suited for man, and the diet upon which he can thrive best. It would, in fact, confirm the argument drawn from comparative anatomy, physiology, and chemistry, and would conclusively prove that man can live and thrive best upon a diet devoid of flesh.[1]

[1] " . . . The American must be educated in the principles of the frugivorous diet. ' Its never too late to learn,' and ' now is the appointed time.' Unquestionably man can live on a diet of fresh meats—proof of which is amply afforded by the very fact that the larger part of the people of the North American continent of to-day are living almost wholly or largely on such a diet. When it comes to a discussion of the relative merits of the two diets . . . we need go no further than to chemistry and physiology, which show that the flesh meats do not begin to contain the same amount of nutriment as do the nuts, and some of the other articles of vegetable origin." "The Art of Living in Good Health," p. 197. By Daniel S. Sager, M.D.

In order to understand the evil effects of flesh-eating thoroughly, it will be necessary for us, first of all, to consider the normal body when living, and the process of death. When the body of any animal is living, two processes are simultaneously going on within it—viz. the constructive and the destructive (Anabolism and Catabolism). The former of these processes feeds and bathes the tissues, while the latter is that process whereby the dead matter is thrown off, and conveyed, by means of the venous blood, to the various eliminating organs. The arterial blood conveys the food material to the bodily tissues; the venous blood conveys the dead, worn-out, effete material from the various tissues to the eliminating organs. If either of these two processes ceases, or is in any way interfered with, grave results follow—which, if persisted in long enough, will result in the death of the organism. It must be remembered that all the poisons which are thrown off by the cells, throughout the body, are not really eliminated until they have been conveyed to the depurating organs, and been completely dissipated in that way. If they are still in the venous blood or in the tissues, they are still *in the animal*, and a part of its flesh. These waste substances are poisonous, and are produced very rapidly by an animal in movement, or even by the very process of living, so that every animal, no matter how healthy, must and does contain a vast amount of these poisons, the accumulation of which would soon kill the animal if not removed—as has often been proved by varnishing the surface of the body, *e.g.* When the action of the skin is stopped in this manner the animal soon dies. Again, when a man is strangled, and the blood forced to pass through the lungs several times without being oxidised and purified by contact with the oxygen of the atmosphere, the blood soon becomes almost *black* in appearance

G

(due to retained poisons), and the man dies as the result of the rapid formation of poisons within his system. These facts must be borne in mind, in what follows. This constant formation of deadly poisons, as the mere result of living, is a most important factor in the problem, as we shall soon see ; and is one that cannot be overlooked when considering this question of the propriety and wisdom of flesh-eating.

Having grasped the above facts, let us now proceed to apply them to the problem before us. When an animal is killed in any manner whatever, it does not instantly die. It loses consciousness, its heart ceases to beat, its conscious and somatic life end, but its *tissues* still continue to live—for several hours, in the case of warm-blooded animals, for several days in the case of cold-blooded animals, like the snake and the turtle. During the time which elapses between death, so-called, and the actual death of the cells and tissues of the body, the activity of the animal tissues consumes the soluble food material which is in contact with these cells and tissues—at the same time continuing to produce those waste substances, which, during life, are rapidly removed from the body through the kidneys, lungs, and other excretory organs.

It is by the accumulation of these poisons after death that the tissues are killed. During life, the tissues are washed by a pure stream of blood, which not only bathes but feeds them, and at the same time gathers up the waste substances and carries them to the liver for distribution to the kidneys, lungs and skin, for elimination. When the heart ceases to beat, this cleansing process ceases, and the poisons which are ever forming, accumulate at a rapid rate until the vital fluids are so saturated that every living structure is killed. The arteries continue to contract after death until all the blood which they contain is forced on into the tissues, and still farther on into the veins, so that the flesh of a dead animal contains nothing but venous blood and poisonous juices, in addition to the organised tissues which have not yet been broken down.

From the foregoing, it will be apparent why it is that meat-eating is so destructive. In addition to the useful and necessary nitrogenous products that are contained within the flesh of the animal, there are also, contained within its tissues, these poisons created during life, and retained within the body of the animal after its death. It is almost impossible to extract these poisons by any process which will also leave the tissues of the animal free from them, and wholesome in consequence. By long continued washing, it is possible to extract the greater proportion of them ; but this is never done, as a matter of fact, and even if it were it would leave behind a tough, elastic substance, almost tasteless, which would be quite unappetising to the person attempting to eat the meat. It would no longer have any charms ! This, then, is the greatest objection that can be raised against meat-eating (from this particular aspect)—viz. that, in addition to the nutritious portion of the meat, there are and must always remain, and go along with it, these poisons which are consequently eaten with it. Now, I ask, would it not be better to eat that food which provides us with the useful material (proteid) for the upbuilding of the body ; but food in which these poisons are not present, and which we consequently escape ? Such being the case, why not eat only those foods which supply the nutriment, without the poisons ?

I have observed above that certain poisons are invariably retained in the tissues of an animal which has died ; and that these poisons may be, to a certain extent, washed out by water—they, of course, remaining in the water into which they have been washed. This is the case with " beef tea "—the boiling having the effect of washing out all these poisons, and dissolving them in the water in which the meat has been cooked. Instead of throwing away this water, however, it is carefully preserved, and given to patients, as valuable and precious nutriment! Instead of regarding it as so much poison and filthy excreta in solution, it is given to patients as a restorative tonic! It is really amazing that patients ever get well at all under such treatment. It is certain that none of the real goodness of the meat can be extracted by any process of boiling or washing, for the reason (1) that all the arterial blood has been converted into venous blood soon after the death of the animal; and (2) because animal tissue is *per se* indissoluble in water. Were this not so—if our tissues dissolved in water in this manner—then we should melt and dissolve like a lump of sugar whenever we went out in the rain, or when we happened to fall into the water; but we know that such is not the case. It is obvious, therefore, that only the excrementitious products can be washed away in this manner; and these are the parts of the tissue which are soaked and boiled into the water. In beef tea, therefore, we obtain only the refuse and poisonous excreta of an animal—and very little, if any, of its real nutritive qualities.

But it may be contended that beef tea *does* benefit sick persons: they really do feel better after taking it! Quite possibly; but this feeling of elation is due to *stimulation.* If the public understood what stimulation really is, they would not urge any sick patient to eat or drink anything that in any way stimulated him; but would on the contrary forbid him to eat or drink anything which affected him in this way! If they understood the *rationale* of stimulation, they would never urge or suggest that any stimulating food be administered to the patient again. For how do stimu-

lants stimulate ? What is the *rationale* of their
" action " ?

When we see a horse plodding slowly along the street,
and the driver suddenly cuts it across the back with
his whip, the horse jumps, and reaches the end of the
street more quickly than if he had not been so whipped.
In such a case, does anyone suppose that any strength
has been *imparted* or *given to* the horse ; or is it not
rather that the energy already present in the horse
has been forced, and expended a little more quickly ?
Of course, the latter. In other words, the energy has
been extracted *from* the horse, and not imparted *to* it.
It is the same with all stimulants whatever. In every
case, their action is the same. It is not that energy
has been imparted to the organism, but rather that it
has been abstracted from it—in the process of resisting
and expelling the stimulant. Stimulation does not
impart strength ; it wastes it. Vital power does not
go out of the brandy into the patient, but occasions
vital power to be exhausted from the patient in expelling
the brandy. The system expends its force to get rid
of the alcohol, but never derives any force, great or
small, good, bad or indifferent, *from* the alcohol. Stimulants merely occasion the expenditure of strength and
energy ; they do not impart either *to* the system.[1]

From the above facts, it will readily be seen why it is
that beef tea is a stimulant of the highest order ; and
for that reason an apparent supporter of strength. In
fact, it is now becoming to be realised in many quarters
that beef tea is more of a stimulant than a food ; and,
if you believe in the one, you cannot accept the other.
These facts will also enable us to understand the
stimulating character of meat—a quality which has
gained for it the reputation of being " strengthening,"

---

[1] " See pp. 34-44 of my " Vitality, Fasting and Nutrition," where
this question is discussed at length.

and consequently " good food " for the weak invalid !
But it so happens, unfortunately, that *because* of this
very fact it is really disqualified as a food for the invalid ; and this would be seen clearly enough if the true
rationale of stimulation were properly understood.
The fact of the matter is that the more stimulating
a food, the less nutritious, and *vice versa*. Perhaps I
cannot do better than quote Dr Trall in this connection.
He says :

" Medical men teach us that animal food is more
stimulating. Here, for once, the premise is true. But
stimulation and nutrition happen to be antagonistic
ideas. Just so far as a thing stimulates, it does not
nourish. Just so far as it nourishes, it does not stimulate.

" There is no more widespread delusion on earth than
this, which confounds stimulation and nutrition. This
is the parent source of that awful error—or, rather
multitude of errors—which are leading all the nations of
the earth into all manner of riotous living, and urging
them on in the road to swift destruction. This terrible
mistake is the prime cause of all the gluttony, all the
drunkenness, all the dissipation, all the debauchery in
the world—I had almost said, of all the vice and crime
also.

" But what is this stimulus of animal food ? Let us
see if we cannot understand it. What is a stimulant ? It
is anything which the vital powers resist with violence
and expel with energy. The disturbance of the organism
which denotes this resistance, constituting a kind of
feverishness, is stimulation. It is a morbid process.
It is disease, hence a wasting process. Medical books
have a class of medicines which are called stimulants.
They are all poisons, and not foods. Among them are
alcohol, phosphorus, ammonia, cayenne pepper, etc.
Anything which is foreign to the organism may provoke
vital resistance, and in this sense be called a stimulant.
" But how does animal food stimulate ? It always
contains more or less effete materials—the débris of the

disintegrated tissues, the ashes of the decayed organism —with more or less of other excrementitious matters. These impurities cannot be used in the organism, and therefore must be expelled ; and this expulsive process, amounting to a feverish disturbance, this vital resistance, is precisely the *rationale* of the stimulating effects of animal food. And thus we prove that animal food is impure precisely in the ratio that it is stimulating, and for this reason objectionable.

"All that can be alleged in favour of flesh-eating because of its stimulating properties can be urged, and for precisely the same reasons, in favour of brandy-drinking or arsenic-eating." [1]

There is nothing more certain than that the eating of meat, even if the meat be clean and wholesome, and the eating of it be not excessive, will in time produce grave results and diseases of the foulest and worst type. Not invariably, of course, but almost invariably. The rapid increase in uric acid which results from a flesh diet has previously been pointed out, and is now well known. In addition to this, there are numerous other poisons that are formed, or introduced into the body, as the result of flesh-eating—as Bouchard and others have proved conclusively. These poisons and their effects were carefully studied by Bouchard, and the results of his experiments are very interesting and convincing. He succeeded in isolating a number of poisons from the urea of flesh-eaters, and injecting them into animals, and noted the results. "One of the poisons in most minute doses produces death with violent spasms ; another causes rapid fall of temperature until death occurs ; another influences animal temperature in another direction ; still another produces death with most profound coma."

The basis of the demonstration is this. The urine is really an extract from the tissues ; the kidneys do not

[1] "Scientific Basis of Vegetarianism," pp. 23-24.

manufacture poisons *de novo*, but simply separate from. the blood poisons found in solution therein, which have been washed by the blood-current from the tissues which it bathes in passing through the capillary network of systemic circulation. Bearing these facts in mind, Bouchard and his assistants injected into live rabbits certain known quantities of these poisons, and noted the results. Death invariably resulted—frequently in a very short time, and as the result of taking an extremely small dose of the poison. It was also found that, by increasing the amount of meat in the diet, the amount of these toxins could be increased accordingly, and proportionately ; the greater the amount of meat consumed, the greater the amount of toxin given off by the animal in its urine, and the more deadly its effects. It was even found that a person living almost exclusively upon a flesh diet increased these toxins to fourfold the normal limit !

Again, it is now well known that in all infectious and contagious diseases there are created within the system certain poisons which play a large part in the disease—they are a factor of immense importance. This being the case, it becomes obvious how important it is to keep out of the system all other and unnecessary poisons—such as might be introduced into the system by foul air, bad water, food containing poisons, etc. Since meat and beef tea contain these poisons in excess, it is certain that they should not only form *no* part of the diet of invalids, but should be strictly *forbidden*, just as any other poison is.

Metchnikoff has recently pointed out, with great emphasis, the immense influence upon health of intestinal putrefaction. He insists that it shortens life ; is one of the chief causes of premature old age and death, and is the cause of many diseases and much misery during life—in all of which he is doubtless quite right. The method of checking this intestinal putrefaction, however, does not appeal to me as other than a palliative measure. Lactic acid is, for him, the great preventive of putrefaction of this type ; but is it not obvious that such a treatment is merely one that aims at *results*, rather than at *causes* ? one which attempts to patch up existing conditions, instead of trying to find out what gave rise to those conditions, and checking *them* ? M. Metchnikoff has apparently failed to realise the fact that there is no need whatever for the human intestine being in any such diseased and disgusting condition as it is generally ; that, in certain cases, it may be rendered absolutely sweet and clean—with virtually no putrefaction going on in the bowel at all. In the case of Mr Horace Fletcher, for instance (and in many of his disciples), no such conditions are present or possible. Mr Fletcher, writing in his " New Glutton or Epicure," says (pp. 144-145) :

" One of the most noticeable and significant results of economic nutrition, gained through careful attention to the mouth treatment of food, or buccal-digestion, is not only the small quantity of waste obtained but its inoffensiveness. Under best test conditions the ashes of economic digestion have been reduced to one-tenth of the average given as normal in the best text-books on physiology. The economic digestion ash forms in pillular shape, and, when released, these are massed together, having become so bunched by considerable retention in the rectum. There is no stench, no evidence of putrid bacterial decomposition, only the odour of warmth, like warm earth or ' hot biscuit.' Test samples of excreta, kept for more than five years, remain inoffensive, dry up, gradually disintegrate, and are lost."

To my mind, it has always been so obvious that, if we supplied no food to decompose, there could be no decomposition, that I hardly thought the question was open to debate at all. It would appear to me to be axiomatic that if we only supplied the body with as much food as it really needed, and of the proper quality, there would be virtually no food left to decompose, or to offer pabulum for germs of any character whatever. Certainly this is the case outside the human intestine, and why not in it ? One can quite easily see why it should be—why putrefaction should take place, if the amount of food ingested were excessive in quantity, or poisonous in quality ; *but not otherwise.* The former of these two questions I have discussed at length in my former volume on fasting ; the latter aspect of the problem is the one I propose to discuss in this book.

If we compare the decomposition of various articles of food, we find there is a very great difference (both as to the quality and the quantity) in the various food-stuffs. Under the same conditions, and during the same period of time, the extent of the decomposition, and its character, will be very different, in the two cases. Compare the decomposition of a pear, a peach or a plum, *e.g.*, with that of a piece of beef or mutton ! Animal tissues and products, when undergoing the process of decay or decomposition are particularly offensive ; and this fact is well borne out by a comparative study of the excreta of the various animals. As before pointed out, that of the herbivora and frugivora is comparatively inoffensive, while that of the carnivora is very offensive, and dangerous also. This is particularly the case with man, when he eats meat of any character. His fæces at once assume a characteristic odour and character ; and clearly indicate that he has wandered away from his natural diet, and is living upon food altogether foreign and unnatural to him. His tissues also take on the chemical composition of the resulting mass—being coloured and influenced by it. Meat and all animal products easily decomposing, and being in a moist, warm place, where they might easily decompose at once, they assume a most offensive character ; and it does not require much imagination to see that the results would be disastrous in a very short time, under such circumstances ; and clearly indicate that the individual is living on food unsuited to his needs and his organism.

Even when an animal is perfectly healthy, its tissues begin to decompose as soon as the animal is really dead —as soon as *rigor mortis* has passed away. Even when meat is kept at a very low temperature, it has been found that it decomposes after the first twenty-four hours ; so that the amount of decomposition present in all animals whose carcasses have been hanging up for hours, and even days, in a shop may easily be imagined ! In the case of game, the carcasses are frequently green and blue with decomposition, and the chemicals injected into the animal in order to preserve it from such decomposition. For only in this manner can meats be preserved ; and it has been proved time and time again that meats are treated and " doctored " with drugs and chemicals of all kinds in order to delay their decomposition. . To think that we really eat such stuff, and give it to our children, and even *prescribe* it for invalids, is too revolting for words ! It passes all comprehension. Dr Kellogg, in his excellent little book on this subject, says, when speaking of the deadly effects of the poisons formed within the body :

" Physiologists sometimes, for experimental purposes, separate from its bony attachments one of the muscles of a frog's leg, and arrange it in such a manner, in connection with a battery and a suitable device, that by a repetition of electric shocks the muscle may be made to contract and lift a small weight. After being thus made to work for a longer or shorter period, the muscle becomes fatigued to such a degree that it no longer contracts in response to the electric stimulus. This is shown to be due to the accumulation of the waste matters, of which mention has been made. If at this point the muscle is washed with a weak saline solution, it at once recovers its ability to work. If now a *fresh* muscle is thus prepared, and strong beef tea or solution of beef extract applied to it, the muscle at once becomes expanded or unable to contract, the same as if it had been working for a long time, but without having done any work whatever! The reason for this is that the beef tea or beef extract is simply a solution of the same poisons which are developed in the muscles by work, and to the paralysing effect of which its fatigue and inability to contract are due. . . . By injection of the fluid obtained by compressing a piece of beef steak or so-called beef juice into the veins of a rabbit, it has been proved to be highly deadly in character. The quantity of beef juice required to kill a rabbit of given weight is *less* than the amount of urine required to produce the same effect. . . . The juice obtained from the flesh of a dog was twice as poisonous as that obtained from ox flesh; in other words, it required twice as much beef juice to kill an animal of given weight as the juice obtained from the flesh of a dog. . . ." [1]

Upon this subject of beef tea, Dr Tibbles says:

" Beef tea, mutton broth, chicken broth, and other meat infusions are useful for sick persons, for they are stimulating and restoring, but they are recognised now chiefly as stimulants to tissue change or to metabolism rather than as foods proper. They do not prevent wasting of the body; indeed, when given alone, *they cause more rapid wasting than no food at all. Dogs fed on beef tea die sooner than when they are not fed at all.*" [2]

In the U. S. Dept. of Agr. Bulletin, No. 102, " Experiments on Losses in Cooking Meat," we read :

" Beef which has been used for the preparation of beef tea or broth has lost comparatively little nutritive value, though much of the flavouring material has been removed " (p. 64).

[1] " Shall We Slay to Eat ? " pp. 53-56.
[2] " Food and Hygiene," p. 138.

It will thus be seen that beef tea extracts practically nothing from the meat ; and that the bulk of the nutriment, such as it is, remains in the meat. This, however, is invariably thrown away ! We thus see that neither the beef tea nor the remaining mass of meat is of any use ; while both are certainly harmful. So much for beef tea !

It is now a well-known fact that meat-eating is the more or less direct cause of various diseases. Tapeworm is one of these, most easily and directly traceable to meat ; and a very serious disease it can become. Beef and pork are two great carriers of the cysts, or tapeworm embryos ; and they develop in the intestine, whence it is most difficult to extract them. Fish is another great cause of tapeworm ; and no matter how fresh these meats may be, this same danger is run, and can never be completely guarded against. These facts are now so well known that it is unnecessary to quote authority in support of them. The deadly trichina, found mainly in pork, but also in fish, fowls, and in other meats, is the direct cause of trichinosis—a disease so closely resembling cerebro-spinal meningitis that it is impossible to distinguish between the two at first, and without a detailed diagnosis. The history of the infection is said to be somewhat as follows :—rats visit a cemetery, and become infected with trichinæ. After a time, the rat dies of infection. The hog—the universal scavenger—eats it. Man—the greatest of all scavengers—eats the hog, and thus becomes infected in turn ! It is not a very pleasant thought, or one calculated to elevate man to a position " a little lower than the angels ! "

Tuberculosis is another disease that is very frequently communicated to the human organism from the carcasses of dead cattle. In his " Human and Bovine Tuberculosis," Dr E. F. Brush contends most strenuously that phthisis is very frequently contracted in this manner, and advances strong evidence in support of his claim. He says (pp. 9-10) :

" The total number of cows in the United States for the year 1887 was 14,522.083—that is, one cow to every four and three-fourths (4·7) persons. There exists, according to Lynt. a true parallel between human and bovine phthisis; the curves of double mortality are the same for different districts in the Duchy of Baden. Now this must mean that a larger proportion of the bovine race dies from phthisis than of the human race, because of the difference in the length of life between the races. We have no statistics of this kind in the United States, but Professor R. A. McLean tells me that. where cows are affected by tuberculosis in great numbers, the death rate from phthisis is correspondingly large in the human race in the same districts. This is his observation from his large experience among diseased cattle."

It would be useless for me to enumerate in full all the numerous diseases that are traceable to meat-eating. That alone would occupy an extensive volume. Typhoid fever has frequently been traced to the eating of oysters. A disease closely related to hog-cholera has been known to be contracted by the human being, as the result of eating pork. Meat-eating is known to be one of the chief and most direct causes of the decay of the teeth—the small fibres of the meat becoming wedged in between them, and, decomposing, cause rapid decay of the teeth. It is probable that this is one of the chief causes of the bad teeth we see about us. Gout and rheumatism are now well known to result from the eating of meat. The reasons for this might perhaps be given. As the result of excessive meat-eating, and eating *too much* food, the body becomes choked with an excess of mal-assimilated food material;

and particularly with uric acid—a product of the meat. The blood, being surfeited with this material, deposits some of it in the vicinity of the joints, and this gives rise to the various symptoms of gout. It is beginning to be realised that this disease, formerly thought to be the direct result of the drinking of wine and other alcoholic beverages, is due to " good old English beef." Rheumatism is largely due to the same cause. Meat poisoning shows itself in various forms ; but the cause is the same. It is now known that meat-eating is the chief cause of Brights disease : and to all unprejudiced minds, it will be obvious that this *must* be so. The excess of albumen in the system cannot well be due to any other cause : and the mode of cure thus becomes apparent also.

It is certain, to anyone who has studied the facts carefully, that meat-eating predisposes the body to all forms of disease. In pestilences of any character— statistics, so far as they have been kept, conclusively show that the vegetarians escaped the disease, and that the meat-eaters were the chief sufferers. The excess of poisons introduced into the system predispose it to any form of disease to which it may be exposed at the time ; the general tone of the system being lowered, owing to the lessened resistance, it becomes a ready prey to any contagious disease which might be prevalent at the time. In further support of this, it has long been known that wounds heal far more rapidly in vegetarian soldiers and in all others who live upon foods of this character, than in those who live largely upon meat. Carnivorous animals are far more subject to blood poisoning than are vegetarian animals. These latter may be very badly wounded, and escape with a scar ; but lions and tigers and other carnivorous animals frequently die from blood poisoning, though but slightly wounded. There can be no reason for this, beyond that indicated above.   The tissues of the animal's body are more or less saturated with poison, in the first place ; and it required but a small amount in addition, to turn the scale against the animal, and cause its death.   It is surely the same, to a great extent, in the case of human beings.

Epilepsy is another disease which has been more or less directly traced to meat-eating.   A few years ago, Dr Warner, of the Eastern Illinois Insane Asylum, called attention to the profound influence of flesh dietary upon epileptics.   He found that it had a most pernicious influence.   By experiment he also ascertained that cats fed upon meat, or allowed to eat the mice they caught, frequently become epileptic.

It has been ascertained, further, that a strictly vegetarian diet is the best possible preparation that can be made for a surgical operation of any kind ; and that vegetarians die less frequently, as the result of severe operations, than do meat-eaters.   Paget, in his " Lessons on Clinical Surgery," states that there is a higher death rate from operations in cities than in rural districts ; and he considers that this is largely due to the greater amount of meat consumed in the cities.

Of late years much attention has been devoted to the relations of cancer and meat-eating.   Several authors have called attention to this fact ; Dr Alexander Haig, in his " Uric Acid in the Causation of Disease," strongly contends that the consumption of flesh is one of the chief causes of cancer, and points out that any irritant to the tissues will invariably be one of the chief factors in the causation of this disease.   As he showed that meat-eating created much uric acid in the system, and that this uric acid acts as an irritant upon the tissues, it is obvious that the consumption of flesh-foods is one of the chief causes of this dreaded disease.   Lately, the Hon. Rollo Russell, in his book,

" The Reduction of Cancer," has defended this view very strongly, and has gathered together a great deal of evidence bearing upon this problem—showing that there is a definite connection between the amount of flesh consumed and the number of cases of cancer, in any one locality. He has also advanced strong reasons for supposing that the one is directly *caused* by the other. As a result of comparing the food habits and the mortality tables of a large number of countries and districts, it was found to be the invariable rule that when, in any locality, meat-eating was excessive, the cancer rate was high; and where meat-eating was small, it fell to a comparatively low figure. A number of other authorities could be quoted in this connection. Thus Dr Lambe remarks :

" The effects of animal food, and other noxious matter, in inducing and accelerating fatal disease, are not immediate, but ultimate effects. The immediate effect is to engender a diseased habit or state of constitution; not enough to impede the ordinary occupations of life, but, in many, to render life itself a long-continued sickness; and to make the great mass of society morbidly susceptible to many passing impressions which would have no injurious influence on healthy systems."

Drs Clarke, Buchan, Abernethy, Sir Edward Berry, Drs Sigmond, Copland, Alphonus Lercy, Graham, Wardell, Trall, and many other of the older writers were of the same opinion; and a number of recent authorities have taken the same stand. It is beginning to be realised that meat-eating is one of the most potent of all the causes of deadly and fatal diseases of many kinds—all more or less directly traceable to it. But, in addition to these varied diseases, there are induced states of the body which must rightly be looked upon as diseased—though they are not actual diseases, in

H

the sense generally understood by that term. Meat-eating is, however, one of the most potent of all factors in inducing that state of the body known as " predisposition " to disease—and in deadening and lowering the vitality, and in enfeebling the senses. I shall now proceed to adduce evidence in support of these various statements, and show that the effects of meat-eating are far more insidious and widespread than is generally believed ; and that the effects of this practice, even among the supposedly healthy, are indeed baneful and disease-engendering.

In the first place it must be pointed out and insisted upon that meat is a highly *stimulating* article of food, and for that reason, innutritious. Stimulation and nutrition invariably exist in inverse ratio—the more the one the less the other, and *vice versa*. The very fact, then, that meat is a stimulant, as it is now universally conceded to be, shows us that it is more or less an innutritious article of diet, and that the supposed " strength " we receive from the meat is due entirely to the stimulating effects upon the system of the various poisons, or toxic substances, introduced into the system, together with the meat. It is for this reason that those who leave off meat, and become vegetarians, experience a feeling of lassitude and weakness, for the first few days—they lack the stimulation formerly supplied, and now notice the reaction which invariably follows such stimulation. This feeling of weakness, or " all-goneness," is therefore to be expected, and is in no wise a proof that the diet is weakening the patient. Let him persist in his reformed manner of living for some time, and he will find that this reaction wears off, and that a general and continued feeling of energy and well-being follow.

It is commonly supposed that only by eating large quantities of animal foods can the bodily heat be maintained in cold climates. Such is by no means the case. Although the Esquimaux, and the inhabitants of Greenland and Iceland, do subsist almost entirely upon fats and animal substances, many of the peasants of Northern Russia and other parts of the globe, eat very little meat—for the reason that they cannot secure it. Dr Graham, in his " Lectures," went so far as to say that: " All other things being precisely equal, the man who is fully accustomed to a pure vegetable diet, can endure severer cold, or bear the same degree of cold much longer than the man who is fully accustomed to a flesh diet.". The truth probably is, as Dr Trall pointed out, that, " the ordinary farinaceous foods and fruits contain all the carbon and hydrogen requisite to sustain the animal heat in all climates, and under all circumstances of temperature ; and if ever surplus carbon or hydrogen is taken into the system, it is, of course, thrown off ; and when a large amount of surplus carbon and hydrogen is taken, the labour of expelling it is attended with a feverish excitement—which, instead of warming the body permanently, only wastes its energies, and renders it colder in the end." The body is, in other words, continually in a more or less feverish condition.

In discussing this question in my " Vitality, Fasting and Nutrition " (Book III., ch. 4, " Bodily Heat ") I said :

" There can be no doubt that the oxidation of the tissues throughout the system, and the combination of the oxygen with the carbon are sources of animal heat, in common with all the organic functions and chemical changes which take place in the body. All the conditions requisite for the due regulation of the animal temperature are: good digestion, free respiration, vigorous circulation, proper assimilation, and perfect depuration ; in two words—*good health*." .

It is thought by many that " stamina " can only be maintained upon a diet derived largely from flesh, but this is not at all the case. In the chapter on the experience of nations and individuals, I shall adduce a considerable quantity of evidence tending to show that a *greater* amount of endurance can be secured upon a vegetarian than upon a mixed diet ! But many persons do not mean by the word " stamina," endurance alone. It is often difficult to get a definition of this word, as it varies with individual conceptions. If, however, by " stamina," is meant stoutness of person, and fullness of blood, such " stamina " constitutes the very food of disease, and the person in such a state is not only more liable to febrile and epidemic attacks, but is also in much greater danger while labouring under them, than one whose development is such as to allow all the secretary functions to be performed with ease, and whose blood is not so charged with either natural or extraneous elements. How frequently do we hear of those who are said to be looking well and healthy being suddenly cut off by apoplexy, or some malignant disorder ! The fact is, we are deceived by appearances, by what we erroneously consider the indications of health ; for those whom we are taught to regard as healthy and robust are generally the farthest from safety, and only need a slight exciting cause to bring on a fatal disease. It is not the apparent disease which is the real cause of death, but men die because the body is worn out ; the tone of the fibres is destroyed, and the principle of motion fails. The obvious disease is the mask under which the condition is concealed.

I have referred before to the protection against epidemics afforded by a strictly hygienic life, and particularly by the vegetarian diet. There is an abundance of testimony on this point to which it is impossible to more than refer. Bush, in his "Works," vol. iv., p. 55, observed that the negroes of the West India Islands, were at that time almost wholly exempt from yellow fever, which cut off the resident upper classes in large numbers. Mr Hardy, a noted Scotch philanthropist, escaped the yellow fever in New York, he asserts, by his course of living ; while Mr Whitlaw, of New Orleans, Dr Rush, of Philadelphia, and Dr Copeland, also assert that they escaped yellow fever by abstinence. The poet Shelley, in his "Vindication of Natural Diet," p. 18, says:

"There is no disease, bodily or mental, which adoption of vegetable diet and pure water has not infallibly mitigated, wherever the experiment has been fairly tried. Debility is gradually converted into strength, disease into healthfulness ; madness, in all its hideous variety, from the ravings of the fettered maniac, to the uncontrollable irrationalities of ill-temper, that makes a hell of domestic life, into a calm and considerable evenness of temper—that alone might offer a certain pledge of the future moral reformation of Society. On a natural system of diet, old age would be our last and our only malady : the term of our existence would be protracted ; we should enjoy life, and no longer preclude others from enjoyment of it. All sensational delights would be infinitely exquisite and perfect ; the very sense of being would then be a continued pleassure, such as we now feel in some few and favoured moments of our youth. By all that is sacred in our hopes for the human race I conjure those who love happiness and truth to give a fair trial to the vegetable system. Reasoning is surely superfluous on a subject whose merits and experience of six months would set for ever at rest. But it is only among the enlightened and benevolent that so great a sacrifice of appetite and prejudice can be expected—even though its ultimate excellence would not admit of dispute."

Another argument in favour of the vegetarian dietary, as against meat-eating, is found in the fact that such a diet is conducive to symmetry and normal development of the human frame. We shall see (p. 142) how the abdomens of the pigmies were greatly reduced, as a result of abandoning their exclusive flesh diet. Many men are said to have reduced their weight from ten to one hundred and fifty pounds by an abstemious, non-flesh diet. The body also assumes a more symmetrical form, and the skin and complexion a ruddier and more healthful glow. It must be admitted, however, that the flesh of meat is not, of itself, a fat-forming food; and many persons are put upon a diet of minced beef and hot water, in order to reduce their weight. This they do, generally, however, at the expense of the general bodily health. In the Banting cure, and the various cures which are followed in America and in England, the weight is reduced, but with doubtful benefit to the patient. The large amount of beef creates an excess of acid within the system, which has a tendency to eat away the fatty tissues; and it is in this manner that they are destroyed. The excess of acid which is thus manufactured, however, remains in the system, and is the chief cause of resulting diseases of various kinds.

In addition to all these arguments, it can be shown that a vegetarian diet improves and renders more acute the various senses. Sight and smell, taste and hearing—all are influenced—in some cases more than in others. Frequently patients are enabled to see distances or to smell odours, after living on this diet for some weeks, which they have never been able to do before. The appetite no longer craves the highly-seasoned and stimulating articles of food formerly desired, but is content with the simpler foods. The general acuteness and sense of well-being will more than compensate for any feeling of deprivation that may at first follow the abolition of meat from the diet. There can be no question that the food exerts a tremendous influence over the mental, moral, and emotional life. Says Dr Haig[1]:

" I believe that as the result of a rational, natural and proper diet, producing the best circulation in the great power-house of the human body, we shall get not only freedom from gross disease, but that we shall get, developing gradually, conditions of mind, thought, judgment, and morality, which will, in the future be as different from what they have been in a diseased and degraded past as the light of Heaven is different from the darkness of the dungeon ; and that while there are to-day many things in human nature which all believers in the great, and good, and true, can only most heartily deplore, I believe that in the future there will be more harmony, more strength, more beauty, more unselfishness, more love—in a word, a truer and greater and more complete *sanity*."

It can be shown, further, that the length of individual life as well as its usefulness and freedom from disease, are dependent largely upon the character of the diet. Longevity, properly so-called, is not a prolongation of the period of decrepitude and helplessness, as some imagine ; but an extension of that period of life when men can fully appreciate the blessings of existence. It has been proved that any animal should live, roughly speaking, five times as long as it takes to mature. The dog matures at two, and lives, on an average, until it is ten ; and so on, throughout the animal world. Man, who matures at (say) twenty, should live to be at least one hundred, and probably more, without showing any of the signs of decrepitude and imbecility which at present frequently accompany old age. As a matter of fact, we find that the average length of life is a fraction over forty-two years ; and, in addition to this, these forty-two years are filled with diverse diseases and

[1] " Life and Food," pp. 8-9.

miseries, which should at no time afflict the individual. *Something*, therefore, is wrong, producing this result. In some way we are consciously or unconsciously perverting the laws of Nature. Now, in no way do we so flagrantly and so continually pervert her laws as in this question of food; and we can for this reason account both for the sicknesses which occur—these being engendered by depraved conditions of the body—and for the shortening of life, which we perceive about us on every hand. Philosophically, as well as practically, this should be so. As Dr Graham pointed out years ago: "A life cannot be both *intensive* and *extensive*." And the more it approaches the one, the less can it approach the other. Anything which tends to rapid living —or, what is perhaps the same thing, rapid bodily consumption or combustion—will consequently tend to shorten life. All stimulants would, of course, produce this effect; and, as meat is a highly stimulating article of food, it will be seen that its consumption, if long continued, will ultimately tend to devitalise and wear out the body—for the reason that it hastens the vital wear and tear, and consequently shortens life. This is, further, in agreement with the fact that " the heart of the habitual meat-eater beats from 72 to 80 beats a minute, while that of the person living on a pure diet of fruits, nuts, etc., will beat ten times less per minute. Fifteen hundred extra heart strokes every twenty-four hours makes a very appreciable strain upon the vital forces." [1]

These conclusions are further borne out by the fact that the average standard of longevity is higher among those peoples and nations who subsist largely upon a vegetarian diet, than among the meat-eating races.

There is an additional argument against meat-eating which might be mentioned in this place. It is this:

[1] "Food Value of Meat," p. 45. By W. R. C. Latson, M.D.

That meat, being a highly stimulating article of diet, has a tendency to make us eat *too much*, both of meat, and of other foods, which are before us at the time. When the meal consists largely of simple, non-stimulating food-stuffs, it will be found that this tendency is absent, and there will be no temptation to over-eat, or eat to excess, as is the case when meat is largely indulged in. *Less* food, and not more, will be eaten—which corresponds with the argument drawn from physiology and chemistry—which shows us that we can abstract the same amount of nutriment from less food of another character. Instead of eating more food, when we adopt a vegetarian diet, therefore, we should eat less ! And, as a matter of fact, most vegetarians *do* eat less than meat-eaters. Thus, Mr Henry Salt, in his " Logic of Vegetarianism," p. 68, says :

" If the chemist were a man of action, and not merely a man of study, the practical aspects of this question might, at the outset, give him pause. Had he known vegetarians, lived among vegetarians, and talked with vegetarians, instead of regarding them theoretically, he would have been aware that the average vegetarian eats decidedly *less* in bulk than the average flesh-eater."

This agrees with our argument advanced elsewhere—that meat is not as nutritious as other articles of food ; and, further, when we come to consider the question of a fruitarian diet, we shall find that cooking also destroys a large amount of the vital properties of food, and that less raw food may be eaten than cooked food. For further discussion on this point, I would refer the reader to the chapter on the quantity of food necessary to sustain life.

The question of the influence of the diet upon the mental, emotional and moral life should, perhaps, be insisted upon a little more fully. Many of the older writers have insisted on this fact very strongly, and furnished numerous examples and illustrations of the effects of the diet upon this side of man—either for better or worse. Judge Woodruff, writing on this subject, says :

" On my return to Smyrna, I stopped at Syra. . . . I there became acquainted with Dr Korke, an eminent teacher from Switzerland. He had charge of the principal school at Syra, containing from two hundred to three hundred pupils. . . . I can truly say that these Greek children manifested a capacity for learning which exceeded anything I had ever before or have since witnessed. Dr Korke attributed this extraordinary ability in his pupils, mainly to their habits of living, which were exceedingly simple. Coarse, unbolted wheat-meal bread, with figs, raisins, pomegranates, olives, and other fruit, with water, constituted their diet. Figs and other fruit composed a large portion of their food ; but I am confident they did not consume an ounce of flesh meat in a month."

It is generally conceded that the eating of large quantities of meat tends to make the consumer pugnacious and animal-like in nature. This has been insisted upon over and over again, and innumerable cases could be adduced in support of this contention, if necessary. The Tartars, who live principally on animal food, possess a degree of ferocity of mind and fierceness of character which form the leading feature of all carnivorous animals. On the other hand a vegetable diet gives to the disposition, as in the Brahmin, a mildness of feeling directly the reverse of the former. To many, it would appear that, if a choice had to be made, it would be better to resemble the former class than the latter—since the one conquers and controls and the other is conquered and controlled. This is not invariably the case, however. The pigmies of Africa, and the Esquimaux do not possess this fierce disposition, but are frequently cowardly, and easily over-ruled by other European nations. It would appear, therefore, that dietetic considerations cannot settle this question—which is too largely a matter of philosophy, on the one hand, and of personal idiosyncrasy, on the other, to allow of any definite conclusions being drawn therefrom. If we desire to arrive at definite results, we must experiment upon different individuals of the *same* race ; and then, by observing the *same* individuals, while upon a meat diet, and while upon a vegetarian diet, some definite results might be obtained.

There are two consequences of meat-eating which should be noted, in this place, however—the influence upon the passional nature, and the influence upon the desire for alcohol. Meat, being a stimulant, excites the bodily functions unduly—stimulating and irritating them in an unnatural manner, and exciting the individual to acts which he would not think of performing, were his body less stimulated and more under control. This is not saying that a vegetarian diet destroys or lowers the sexual powers, or the tone of the animal nature—far from it. But it does not keep the sexual organs in a more or less constant state of irritation, as is the case upon a meat diet. The potential energy is there ; but the desire to expend it so frequently is not noted. Here is, at all events, a very important factor in civilisation—how important, few realise (see Sanger's " History of Prostitution "). At all events this is one very strong argument in favour of the vegetarian diet, and should by no means be overlooked.

The relation between meat-eating and the consumption of alcohol is now becoming widely known and recognised. No sooner does the amount of meat consumed, *per capita*, rise, than the quantity of alcohol consumed rises also. The two—meat-eating and alcohol-drinking—invariably go hand in hand; and the reason is obvious. Meat is a highly-stimulating article of food. All stimulants call, after a time, either for an increase in the amount of the stimulus, or for a stimulant of another character—in order to produce the desired result. Now, of all solid foods, there is no stimulant which is more powerful than meat; and for that reason liquid stimulant is sought. One stimulant craves another. And another reason for the invariable accompaniment of the two is this. It would be practically impossible to create a desire for alcoholic beverages while eating fruits, nuts and vegetables. They do not call for alcohol, and there would be no desire for it manifested. In every way we see, therefore, that drunkenness would be largely abolished by the simple introduction of vegetarianism as a diet—and this has been confirmed by the fact that in certain sanatoriums, where the vegetarian diet has been introduced as a cure for inebriety, it has been found to work to perfection; and the patients, while on this diet—and although allowed all the alcohol they craved at first—soon ceased to want it, and the craving left them after a few days—never to return, so long as they maintained their reformed habits of living.[1]

In conclusion, I wish to call special attention to the very great effects of a properly regulated vegetarian dietary upon the body (1) when diseased; and (2) to its power to *prevent* such diseased states. In any form of chronic or acute disease—no matter what its nature may be—only good will follow the adoption of a vegetarian regimen; and the more closely this is followed, and the more sparing and abstemious the diet—the sooner will the patient mend and get well. And if the vegetarian diet be adopted when the patient *is* well, and conscientiously followed, there can be no question

[1] See, in this connection, H. P. Fowler: "Vegetarianism, the Radical Cure for Intemperance"; Dr Jackson's "How to Cure Drunkards," etc.

whatever that he will *stay* well—provided he does not eat *too much*, and that he pays reasonable attention to the general laws of health. The preventive influence of the diet is very profound and far-reaching.

But now, it may be asked, if all this be true; if these diverse and grievous diseases that afflict man result from the eating of meat; how comes it about that it is such a universal article of diet? How is it that everyone believes in its value so thoroughly? The answer to this is simple. The majority simply follow where custom leads, without further thought, and without stopping to inquire into the *reasons* for the course of life they daily pursue. But the scientists, and the physiologists? They surely ought to know better! They ought, indeed; but they do not seem to! It would really appear as though this whole doctrine of meat-eating could be traced back to the old and fallacious dogma that we have canine teeth in our heads! *They* have been the source and the cause of all the trouble! But, as Dr Trall said years ago, in writing of this very question:

" Sometimes, when I think how perfectly ridiculous as well as sad this carnivorous tooth blunder is, on the part of doctors of learning and unlearned people, I am reminded of that very beautiful experiment of a dog running after his own tail. Take a dog, give his head a sudden twist round towards his tail, at the same time holding his tail in the line of his mouth, and say ' catch it,' and the poor, deluded dog will run round and round with all his might, till he falls down dizzy and exhausted, all the while fancying himself going the straightest possible road in pursuit of his tail. And after he has rested a little, and recovered a little breath, he will up and at it again.

" It is very much so with our flesh-eaters. The doctors have given their heads a roundabout twist; told them they had carnivorous teeth; set them agoing; pointed to the beasts of the field, the fowls of the air, and the fishes of the sea, and said ' catch them.' And the whole world has gone to hunting and fishing and fattening and butchering and salting and pickling, and smoking and broiling, and frying and eating, until they have become filled with morbid humours, scrofula, cancer, erysipelas, gout, rheumatism, biliousness and putrid fevers; then they have rested a while, lived on vegetable food until they have measurably recovered, and then resumed their carnivorous raid in the animal kingdom !

" And sickness has not taught them the lesson it ought to have done. Instead of regarding their maladies as the necessary consequences of their eating habits, they have looked upon them as the arbitrary inflictions of chance, or of a mysterious Providence. Even when, in the middle ages, the great pestilences prevailed over Europe, at a period of the world's history when for three hundred years the people literally rioted and revelled . in the abundance of flesh blood and alcoholic beverages; and when, during those three centuries, the terrible plague—the ' Black Death ' and the ' Great Mortality,' as it was then called—desolated London, Paris, and other great cities — sweeping off one hundred millions of the earth's inhabitants—the medical profession, and the people with them, wholly mistook the lesson it taught.

" And so it is now. People eat all manner of animal products, with their morbid humours, foul secretions, diseases, impurities and corruptions; and when their bodies become so obstructed and befouled that they reach, and vomit, and spit, and expectorate, and go into fever and inflammation, and gripes and spasms, they wonder what the matter is ! And then they send for the family physician, and he wonders also. Why, the only wonder is that they are not all matter ! "

Throughout the whole of the above argument, I have assumed that the. meat eaten is from *healthy*

animals, and have assumed that no diseased meat
finds its way upon the table of the average meat-eater—
an assumption which is certainly not warranted by
facts. I wished, however, to give my adversaries
every advantage in this discussion, and for that reason
have assumed throughout that the meat was obtained
from healthy animals, and was not adulterated before
coming to the table. As a matter of fact, however,
neither of these two conditions are invariably fulfilled.
We might say that the second condition is very rarely
fulfilled. It is generally known that meat is inoculated
with chemicals of all kinds before it is placed upon
the market, and for that reason it is enabled to be
shipped from place to place, and to hang in the butcher's
shop by the hour without being kept upon ice—for
how, otherwise, could this be ? We know that meat
decomposes very rapidly—especially in moist or warm
weather—but it is apparently enabled to hang, nevertheless, for hours at a time in the butcher's shop !
If chemicals of various kinds were not injected into the
meat, this would be impossible. Most graphically does
Upton Sinclair describe this process of " pickling "
in his book, " The Jungle," where he says :

" Jonas has told them how the meat that was taken
out of pickle would often be found sour, and how they
would rub it up with soda to take away the smell, and
sell it to be eaten on free lunch counters ; also of all
the miracles of chemistry which they performed, giving
to any sort of meat, fresh or salted, whole or chopped,
any colour and any flavour which they chose. In the
pickling of hams they had an ingenious apparatus, by
which they saved time, and increased the capacity of
the plant—a machine consisting of a hollow needle
attached to a pump ; by plunging this needle into the
meat and working with his foot, a man could fill a ham
with pickle in a few seconds. And yet, in spite of this,
there would be found ham spoiled, some of them with

an odour so bad that a man could hardly bear to be in the room with them. To pump into these the packers had a second and much stronger pickle which destroyed the odour—a process known to the workers as ' giving them thirty per cent.' Also, after the hams had been smoked, there would be found some that had gone to the bad. Formerly these had been sold as ' Number Three Grade,' but later on, some ingenious person had hit upon a new device, and now they would extract the bone, about which the bad part generally lay, and insert in the hole a white-hot iron. After this invention there was no longer Number One, Number Two, and Number Three Grade—there was only Number One Grade ! The packers were always originating such schemes. They had what they called ' boneless hams,' which were all the odds and ends of pork stuffed into casings : and ' California Hams,' which were the shoulders, with great knuckle joints, and nearly all the meat cut out ; and fancy ' skinned hams,' which were made of the oldest hogs, whose skins were so heavy and coarse that no one would buy them—that is, until they had been cooked, and chopped fine and labelled ' head cheese ' ! "

This question of *diseased meat* is, therefore, one which deserves our close attention, largely because it has been treated so ineffectually in the past, in other books dealing with this subject. The defect has been due to the fact that, until recently, no definite *facts* have been available ; and, although everyone knew in a general way that much of the meat said to be " inspected " and found free from disease was, as a matter of fact, unfit for human food, there were no data to which the vegetarian could point, and say : " Here are facts and figures incontrovertible ! What have you to say in defence now ? "

Lately, however, several such exposures have been published. It would be well for us to summarise the facts ; and I cannot do better, in this connection, than to turn to Dr Albert Leffingwell's book, "American Meat." (I would refer all those interested to its fascinating pages.) A very brief summary must suffice. This will be enough, however, for our purpose:

"During the period of 1901-1906 inclusive, over 660,000 *post-mortem* inspections were made of animals, which before slaughter had been rejected in the stock yards as apparently diseased. Of these, only 85,000— *less than one in eight*—were finally condemned as wholly unfit for food purposes. . . . What is it that the United States inspector is required by his regulation to condemn as unfit for human food? The carcasses of animals which he might find affected by cancer or malignant tumours? No. He is directed to condemn *the tumour*, the part of the carcass which was affected, the organ which was infiltrated by disease! The remainder of the carcass—what becomes of that? Is there anything which prevents it from being turned into the food supply of the poorer classes? There is sometimes a silence which accords assent. . . . Suppose the entire liver of a hog to be a mass of cancerous disease; what is there in these regulations of the Department of Agriculture to prevent transmuting the muscular tissues and unaffected organs into various food delicacies or food products, which in due time should find their way to the tables of rich and poor in England and America? Not a word! . . .

"The United States Department of Agriculture advances yet another step, and, under certain circumstances, *requires* the inspector's approval of the flesh of tuberculous animals as fit food for human beings:

"*Rule C.*—The carcass, if tuberculous lesions are limited to a single or several parts or organs of the body (except as noted in Rule A) without evidence of recent invasion of tubercle bacilli into the systemic circulation, SHALL BE PASSED, after the parts containing the localised lesions are removed and condemned."

I

The following table affords matter of interest :—

Number of Carcasses (Approximately) found on inspection to be affected with tuberculosis, of which " parts " were condemned, and the remainder passed as wholesome food.[1]

YEAR			CATTLE			HOGS
1900	.	.	85	.	.	1,061
1901	.	.	256	.	.	44
1902	.	.	152	.	.	4,700
1903	.	.	250	.	.	52,006
1904	.	.	703	.	.	118,820
1905	.	.	647	.	.	142,105
1906	.	.	1,114	.	.	113,491
1907	.	.	10,530	.	.	364,559
1908	.	.	27,467	.	.	628,462
		Total	41,204			1,425,248

The significance of these figures should not escape the reader. Here is the proof, based upon official statistics, of the utilisation for food purposes of animals suffering from tuberculous disease !

But the figures prove far more. They illustrate the terrible indifference to public interests which governed the inspection of meat, especially before the legislation of June, 1906. Note the vast difference which obtains between the number of animals found " partly " diseased in 1907, and the number of preceding years. For instance, the total number of beef carcasses inspected in 1907 showed an increase of precisely 10 per cent. above the figures of 1906. Yet the number of cattle, of which the carcasses were " in part " condemned increased—not 10 per cent.—but *over* 800 *per cent.* above the figures of the years before. Almost as many hogs were condemned in one year (1907) as " in part affected " by this disease, as during the entire seven years that preceded it ! Was there any noteworthy sudden increase in the prevalence of this disease among animals intended for

[1] Abstract from the Annual Report of the Bureau of Animal Industry.

human food ? There is no hint of it in the official report. The only conclusion we can reach is that, following the agitation and legislation of 1906, thousands of hogs and cattle were at least partly condemned, which in preceding years, without even the condemnation of a part, *passed into the food supply of the world.*

During eight years, 1900-1907, there were slaughtered, under Government Inspection, over 208,000,000 hogs. Since there can be no doubt that the trichina was as common among all the animals as among those whose carcasses were examined, it follows that, during this period of eight years, over 5,000,000 carcasses of hogs, or about 1,000,000,000 *pounds of pork*, infested by trichinæ—at least half of which at the time of slaughter were potent for mischief—were turned into the meat supply of an unsuspecting world !

The following " Government Regulations," in this connection, are certainly remarkable and well worth quoting It is hardly likely that the general public suspects what is given to them in the form of meat ; and the following quotations will probably help to open their eyes :

" *Malignant Epizootic Catarrh.*—The carcasses of animals affected with this disease, and showing general inflammation of the mucous membranes with inflammation, shall be condemned. If the lesions are restricted to a single tract, or if the disease shows purely local lesions, the carcass *may be passed.*"

Skin Diseases. Section 16.—" Carcasses of animals affected with mange or scab, in advanced stages, or showing extension of the inflammation of the flesh, shall be condemned. When the disease is slight, the carcass *may be passed.*"

Section 21.—" Hogs affected with urticaria (diamond skin disease) tinea tonsurans, demodex folliculorum, or erythema, *may be passed*, after detaching and condemning the skin, if the carcass is otherwise fit for food ! "

Caseous Lymphadenitis. Section 12.—" When the lesions of caseous lymphadenitis are limited to the superficial lymphatic glands, or to a few nodules in an organ, involving also the adjacent lymphatic glands (N.B.), and the carcass is well nourished, the meat *may be passed*, after the affected parts are removed and condemned."

Tapeworm Cysts.—" Carcasses of animals slightly affected with tapeworm cysts may be rendered into lard or tallow, but extensively affected carcasses shall be condemned " (p. 15).

Section 17.   Par. 3.—" Carcasses or parts of carcasses found infected with hydatid cyst (echinococcus) *may be passed* after condemnation of the infected part or organ."

Similar quotations could be supplied *ad libitum* ; but the above will doubtless. suffice for our purposes. From them we see that—all statements to the contrary notwithstanding—a very great deal of diseased meat *does* get into the market—so much, in fact, ·that it becomes highly probable that a large percentage of it is diseased ; and that we probably run more chance of buying diseased meat than we do of obtaining meat clean and free from infection.

These facts. and figures relate only to the meat slaughtered under Federal Inspection, it must be remembered ; and represent the best possible condition in which our meat is obtained.   This meat is passed by expert Government Inspectors; the packing houses are considered the best and the cleanest in the country, etc.   What, then, of the meat killed by local butchers, on farms, and *without* Federal Inspection altogether ? The reader may think that there are but few cattle and hogs killed in this way ; and that their flesh is not disposed of upon the public market to any extent.   If he is of this opinion, he is sadly mistaken, as the following figures will show.   I take them from Dr A. M. Farrington's Report to the Bureau of Animal Industry, which is published as Circular No. 154, under the supervision of the U. S. Department of Agriculture. As we have seen that the tendency of the Bureau is to under rather than over-estimate the facts in the case, the following statements will appear all the more impressive. The figures given below relate to the year 1907, but much the same conditions prevail to-day, and but little has been done to check the conditions depicted. The following is the result of a careful statistical inquiry, in tabulated form :—

ITEM	CATTLE	SHEEP	SWINE
Slaughtered under Federal Inspection . . .	7,633,365	10,252,070	32,885,377
Estimated Farm Slaughter .	1,500,000	1,000,000	16,500,000
Slaughtered by Butchers without Federal Inspection .	4,972,052	7,793,133	10,316,300

It will be seen from the foregoing that practically 5,000,000 cattle, nearly 8,000,000 sheep, and over 10,000,000 hogs were slaughtered by butchers in 1907 without Federal Inspection, to which may be added about 3,000,000 calves. All these 26,000,000 animals were consumed by the people of the United States, and the responsibility of inspecting them rested wholly upon the State and local authorities, since they are beyond the reach of the Federal Inspectors.

And now, how about the sanitary conditions of the slaughter-houses in which these animals were killed, and how about the state of the animals themselves ? Were they free from disease ? were they sick ? Were the surroundings filthy and poisonous in the extreme ? If I should give an account of the real state of affairs in my own words, I should be accused of exaggeration—to use the very mildest term. I prefer, therefore, to quote entirely from the Report of the Bureau of Animal Industry, before referred to. This Report states in part :

" The slaughter-houses, where animals are killed for local consumption, are usually isolated or scattered about the city or town. . . . Such houses, in addition to being unsightly, malodorous, unclean, and insanitary in the extreme, are actually centres for spreading disease. . . . A recent investigation made by the State Board of Health in Indiana of those slaughter-houses which do not have Federal Inspection . . . states that :

" ' Of the 327 slaughter-houses inspected, only 28, or 7 per cent., were found to fulfil the sanitary standards. . . . At nearly all slaughter-houses inspected, foul, nauseating odours filled the air for yards round. Swarms of flies filled the air and the buildings and covered the carcasses which were hung up to cool. Beneath the houses was to be found a thin mud, or a mixture of blood and earth, churned by hogs, which are kept to feed upon offal. . . . Maggots frequently existed in numbers so great as to cause a visible movement of the mud. Water for washing the meat was frequently drawn from dug wells, which receive steepage from the slaughter-house yards, or the water was taken from the adjoining streams, to which the hogs had access. Dilapidated buildings were the usual thing, and always the most repulsive odours and surroundings existed.' . . .

" One of the butchers was asked what they did with ' sick ' cattle. He laughed and answered ' What do they all do with them ? '

" In another large eastern city there are only four slaughter-houses in the city proper which do not have Federal Inspection. The total kill at these places is about 1,000 cattle and 2,500 hogs per month. The only inspection is furnished by one inspector of the board of health, and this inspector is not a veterinarian. Previous to his employment by the board of health, he was a hotel porter."

It need only be added that such strict economy is practised in all these slaughter-houses that the odds and ends—the " trimmings "—are now valued by the butchers at about 14 per cent. of the whole. The trimmings consist of every part of the animal except the actual refuse it contains, everything else being utilised in one way or another. As one Chicago packer proudly expressed it, when speaking of hogs, " we use everything but the squeal ! "

This, be it observed, is the meat placed upon the market and eaten by the American public, to the extent of millions of carcasses yearly ! Is it any wonder that the people have cancer, and tapeworm, and tuberculosis, and other illnesses, and break down prematurely and become miserable and die ? It would be a wonder indeed if they did anything else !

It is well known that large quantities of diseased meat are constantly being introduced and placed upon the market—far more than the public is aware of. But, for the present argument, it is not necessary that we should force this conclusion, since we can establish the point, even assuming that all the meat eaten is from the carcasses of healthy animals—the actual content of the tissue containing toxic material, no matter how free the animal may be from what is generally known as " disease." This being true, all the arguments advanced above will remain perfectly valid—no matter how " healthy " the animal may be.

VI

THE ARGUMENT FROM EXPERIENCE

(*Nations and Individuals*)

" THERE is a difference," observes Chalmers, " between such truths as are merely of a speculative nature, and such as are allied with practice and moral feeling. With the former, all repetition may be often superfluous; with the latter, it may just be by earnest repetition that their influence comes to be thoroughly established over the mind of the inquirer."

These words are particularly true when applied to the subject matter before us. No matter how perfect, theoretically, an argument may be, it will never appeal to the public mind as do a few concrete facts. The arguments I have presented, drawn from comparative anatomy, from physiology, chemistry, and from hygiene, would weigh but little in many minds against the testimony of human experience. They would contend that, no matter how good the theoretical argument might be, the facts, nevertheless, would seem to prove the contrary; and show that the majority of all the more civilised people of the earth, particularly the ruling and governing nations, *do*, as a matter of fact, eat meat; and hence, practically, meat is a suitable article of diet. I propose to consider these arguments in the following chapter, and see how far they rest upon facts, and how far upon misconception.

Pythagoras, one of the most celebrated philosophers of antiquity, was one of the first to defend the " vegetable diet." He not only totally refrained from animal food himself, but also strictly prohibited the use of it

by his disciples, so that those who abstain from it at
the present time are sometimes known as Pythagorians.
Pythagoras flourished about five hundred years before
the Christian era.   He was a man of immense learning,
and extraordinary powers of intellect.   He was the
first demonstrator of the forty-seventh problem of the
first book of Euclid, and entertained correct views of
the solar system.   Ovid speaks of him with great ad-
miration.

· Zeno, the Stoic, Diogenes, the Cynic, Plato, Plutarch,
Plautus, Proclus, Empedocles, Socrates, Quintus Sextus,
Apollonius of Tyana, Porphyry, and numerous others,
among the ancients, abstained from animal food and,
more recently, Haller, Ritson (celebrated for his numerous works and varied talents) Dr Cheyne, Dr Lambe,
Mr Newton (who wrote a splendid book, " The Return to
Nature "), Shelley, Dr Hufeland, Sir Richard Phillips,
and many others have both advocated and personally
tried for many years a strictly and exclusively
vegetable diet.

Hesoid, the Greek poet, Heroditus, Hippocrates,
Pliny, Galen, and many other writers of antiquity could
be quoted as defending a simple, non-flesh diet.   Of
late years numerous scientific men and physicians have
come forward in support of this claim ; and their testimony will be found in various parts of this work.

If the past has produced individual giants, mental
and physical, who subsisted upon a vegetarian dietary,
the present may also claim its champions ; and there
are doubtless more at the present day than ever before.
Many athletes are now adopting a vegetarian diet,
largely on account of the Fletcher-Chittenden experiments before referred to ; largely because of individual
study and investigation.   The fact that strength and
endurance are greatly increased by a strict vegetarian
or fruitarian dietary cannot be gainsaid.   I have ad-

duced some of this evidence in the chapter on hygiene, and shall adduce further evidence in the present and following chapters. The frequently quoted case of the seventy-mile walking match, that took place in Germany some years ago, should at least be referred to.   Fourteen meat-eaters, and eight vegetarians started on a seventy-mile walking match. All the vegetarians reached the goal, it is said in " splendid condition "—the first covering the distance in fourteen and a quarter hours. An hour after the last vegetarian came in, the first meat-eater appeared, and he was " completely exhausted." He was also the last meat-eater to finish the race, as all the rest had dropped off after thirty-five miles. A further and almost exactly similar illustration is furnished by the Dresden to Berlin walk of 1902. For this, eighteen vegetarians and fourteen meat-eaters started, and ten of the vegetarians, but only three of the meat-eaters came in. The winner (Karl Mann) was upwards of seven hours in front of the first meat-eater. It is to be noted that Mann was a strict fruitarian, and practically never touched the ordinary vegetarian foods. The last meat-eater only just got in within the time limit, and was beaten by more than four hours by a man of fifty-nine, who had been a vegetarian for thirty-eight years.   In this race the championship of Germany was decided, and the winner made two world's records. The proceedings were watched, and the organs and circulation of competitors were measured and recorded by a committee of physiologists, for the benefit of the German government and army.

Dr Alexander Haig, in his " Diet and Food," p. 100, says :

" A week or two after the race I had the pleasure of examining the winner, who had, to a large extent, arranged his diet by the aid of a previous edition of this book. . . . His circulation was far better than that of any

meat-eater, which, to a large extent, explains his victory;
and the records show that his heart was smaller at the
end of the race than at the beginning. I have but
little doubt that the meat-eaters who gave up had
dilated hearts, owing to their obstructed circulation.
. . . In my opinion, a few more hard facts like these
(and plenty more of such records will be forthcoming)
will quite dispel the meat-eating delusion that strength
and endurance can be attained on no food but flesh.
The truth is that 50 per cent. *more* endurance and
strength can be obtained with many other foods;
and the chief reason for this can now be seen and gauged
in a moment by the rate of the capillary circulation of
the individuals concerned; and this capillary circulation is proportioned to the uric acid in the blood, and
is therefore slowed and obstructed by meat, which
introduces uric acid."

Professor Baelz, of Tokio, Japan, made some experiments on vegetarian natives, and, after measuring and
recording some of their feats of endurance, he gave some
of them meat, which they took eagerly, and regarded
as a great luxury, because it was used by the " upper
classes "; but after three days they came and begged
to be let off the meat, as they felt tired on it, and could
not work as well as before. The Professor then made
some similar experiments on himself, and he found that
he also was sooner tired, and more disinclined for exer-
tion when he took meat.

Mr Eustace H. Miles, formerly amateur champion
of the world and holder of the gold prize at tennis,
amateur champion of the world at racquets, and of
American squah tennis, etc., is a strong advocate of
vegetarianism, and has written a number of works on
this subject, defending the non-flesh diet—which books
are too well known to need more than a mere reference.
Mr Miles, though he must be approaching middle age,
is a remarkably young-looking man, with a brilliant

complexion, and thinks that he will be as good ten or
fifteen years from now as he is to-day.   In a conversa-
tion with me, Mr Miles stated that he considered diet the
all-important factor, so far as health is concerned ; and
exercise, and other forms of health-getting " a luxury."
I agree with him absolutely, and defended this very
position in my " Vitality, Fasting and Nutrition," pp.
618-621.   I too think that if the food be regulated in
quality, and sufficiently reduced in quantity, all other
factors might be more or less neglected, and perfect
health maintained.

But it would be useless to refer to a large number of
individual cases of this character.   However many I
might cite, the defenders of meat-eating would be enabled to cite an equal number of cases in favour of
their argument ; and for this reason I do not think that
individual cases are of value in establishing any conclusion beyond this one—viz. such cases show us conclusively that men *can live*, and *can maintain a high
standard of physical health and mental brilliancy upon
a diet derived exclusively from the vegetable world*.   That
is an important point, but would not be conclusive.
In order to arrive at a definite conclusion, far larger
numbers of vegetarians and meat-eaters must be in-
vestigated ; and the question, therefore, becomes one
of statistics and of the diets of nations, rather than of
individuals.   I shall accordingly turn to this aspect
of the problem—after mentioning one additional point
that must not be lost sight of, in this connection.

It must be remembered, throughout, that, for every
vegetarian in England or America, there are doubtless
100 or more meat-eaters, so that the percentage of
success in the athletic field and elsewhere *should be* at
least 100 to 1—and probably a great deal more, if the
balance is to be maintained between the vegetarian and
flesh-eating athletes, and others before the public eye

But, as a matter of fact, we find that the percentage is very much lower than this; and that, within the last few years, at any rate, quite as many vegetarian athletes secured successes and achieved records as did the meat-eating athletes; and in some instances, where the two ran in competition, it was found that a *larger* percentage of vegetarian athletes achieved success than did the meat-eaters. Inasmuch as the number is so disproportioned, in the two cases, it would certainly appear that the vegetarian athletes did, on the whole, achieve a far greater percentage of successes than did the meat-eating athletes.

The diets of the various nations have so frequently been summarised and presented by writers upon this subject that it will not be necessary for me to do more than to mention briefly a few of the most essential points; and to refer the reader to those works in which these facts and arguments are to be found in full. Dr Graham, in his " Science of Human Life "; Dr John Smith, in his " Fruit and Farinacea "; Dr Anna Kingsford, in her " Perfect Way in Diet," and, more recently and fully, the Hon. Rollo Russell, · in his extensive volume, " Strength and Diet: A practical treatise with special regard to the life of nations "—all these writers have discussed this question of national health, as compared with national diet, and found, almost invariably, that in every nation whose diet consisted almost exclusively or even largely of meat, the natives were small in stature, depraved mentally and morally, and afflicted with diverse diseases; whereas those nations which were largely vegetarian did not suffer in the same way from the sicknesses and pestilences that affected their fellow-men; but were, on the contrary, more forceful, superior morally and mentally, and in every way higher in the scale of evolution than those nations which subsisted largely upon meat.

A striking example of this is to be found in the pigmy races of Central Africa. In his work, " The Pigmies," Professor A. de Quatrefages has shown us that this miniature people. stunted as they are, mentally, physically and morally, subsist almost entirely upon meat. He says :

" The Mincopies are exclusively hunters and fishermen, living upon the shore of a sea filled with fishes, close to great forests where boars run at large, and which furnish them, besides, honey and nuts, they have not felt the necessity of wringing by labour from the soil, a supplement to their food supply ; and this very luxuriance of food, perhaps, has been of influence in keeping them at the lowest point in the social scale. Francis Day informs us that a very small tribe of Mincopies camped near the English establishments, and receiving daily rations, took besides, in a single year, five hundred boars, one hundred and fifty turtles, twenty wild cats, fifty guianas and six bugongs. . . . All the descriptions agree in attributing to the Akkas, men and women, an extreme abdominal development, which causes the adults to resemble the children of Arabs and negroes. . . . But it is evident the abnormal development of the abdomen, among the Akkas, is not a true race characteristic, but that it is largely due to their manner of life, the quantity of their food, perhaps also to the general conditions of their habitat. This fact results from some observations of Count Minis Calchi, who has seen, after some weeks of regular and wholesome diet, the extreme development of the abdomen disappear, and the vertebral column resume its normal state."

These people are described as cruel, cowardly and wanting in all the qualities that would raise them in the scale of evolution : yet their diet consists almost entirely of meat—the supposed " strengthening " and courage-breeding food of civilised nations! Emaciation is very common among them, under certain conditions. It cannot be objected to what I have said that this condition is brought about by their cannibalism, for we read ("The Pigmies," p. 155) that: "Far from seeking human flesh, the Andamanese regard it as a deadly poison."

The Esquimaux are another race which is very inferior; and in them nothing is developed, scarcely, save the mere animal nature; hence their stomachs have all the nervous power, almost, of their whole constitutions. They have virtually no mental life beyond that necessary for carrying on the affairs of daily life. One never hears of any mental achievement coming from an Esquimau; more than this, their animal nature is itself actually inferior in muscular power to that of those tribes and races of men whose general régime is comparatively free from fats and animal oils.

Throughout history the general run of the people—the natives—subsisted almost entirely upon a vegetarian diet; and any large quantity of meat was not consumed, for the reason that it could not be procured. The upper classes subsisted more or less upon meat—which might have accounted for their eventual degeneracy!—as the whole nation degenerated when meat-eating became general, as in Greece and Rome. But in the early stages of the history of these nations, and of others, meat was a luxury, to be eaten on holidays and fête days, rather than a steady article of diet; it could by no means be procured every day or every meal, as is now the case. The principal food of the natives of Egypt, India, Mexico, Chili, Brazil, Cyprus, Arabia, Bolivia, the Canary Islands, Italy, Ceylon, Japan, Sierre Leone, Greece, Malta, Turkey, China, Palestine, Algiers, the African Coast, Poland, Russia,

Norway, Spain, France, Switzerland, Belgium, Prussia, Saxony, Bavaria, Sweden, Switzerland, Scotland, Ireland, and, until recently, England—is some form of vegetarian food—bread, rice, fruits, cheese, and various grains. The details of these dietaries are to be found in Russell's " Strength and Diet," where a very full summary of all these dietaries are to be found. I refer my reader to that work for further information upon these lines. But one or two examples are needed to illustrate this. Thus we read :

" It is indeed surprising to see how simple and poor is the diet of the Egyptian peasantry, and how robust and healthy most of them are, and how severe is the labour they undergo. The boatmen of the Nile are mostly strong muscular men, rowing, poling and towing continually ; but very cheerful and often the most so when most occupied, for they amuse themselves by singing."

The staple food of India is, of course, rice, to which is added a poor grain called râgi, pulse, roots, fruits, and one or two other articles of diet. The men from the hilly district are described as tall—being from five feet ten inches, to six feet high. They used to carry the mail from Calcutta to Bombay by foot—but twenty-five days being allowed for this journey, an average of sixty-two miles a day.

Few people surpass the Arabs for longevity, agility, and power of endurance ; yet they subsist largely upon dates, milk, and honey. The peasants of Italy are a splendid, hardy set, living almost entirely upon cakes and porridge of chestnut, bread, garlic, and a little wine. The Greek boatmen are exceedingly abstemious, their food consisting of a small quantity of black bread, made of unbolted rye or wheat meal, a bunch of grapes or raisins, figs, etc. They are extremely vigorous and active, as well as blithesome, jovial and full of hilarity. Sir William Fairbairn, in his "Report on Sanitary Conditions," says :

"The boatmen and water carriers of Constantinople are decidedly, in my opinion, the finest men in Europe, as regards their physical development, and they are all water drinkers ; they take a little sherbet at times. Their diet is chiefly bread, now and then a cucumber, with cherries, figs, dates, mulberries, or other fruits which are abundant there ; now and then a little fish."

In Dr Mackenzie Wallace's "Russia," we read :

"Eggs, black bread, milk and tea—these form my ordinary articles of diet during all my wanderings in northern Russia. Occasionally a potato could be had, and afforded the possibility of varying the bill of fare. . . . The people of Russia generally subsist on coarse black rye bread, and garlics. I have often hired men to labour for me in Russia, which they would do from sixteen to eighteen hours, for eight cents a day. They would come on board in the morning with a piece of their black bread weighing about a pound, and a bunch of garlics as big as one's fist. This was all their nourishment for the day of sixteen or eighteen hours labour."

The fare of the Swiss workmen is very frugal.

"They rarely taste flesh, their food being principally, bread, cheese, potatoes, vegetables and fruit, though in the towns the consumption of meat is somewhat greater. The middle classes fare pretty much as the working classes, all consuming large quantities of milk."

Mr H. Irving Hancock, in his "Japanese Physical Training," says of their diet :

"When making their phenomenal marches, Japanese troops often carry no food except a small bag of rice.

K

When practicable, barley and beans are issued in small quantities, though this is only done for the sake of adding variety to the diet. . . . A bowl of this grain (rice) and a handful of fish is considered an ample meal for the coolie who is called upon to perform ten or twelve hours of hard manual work in a day."

It would be possible to add quotations and references such as the above *ad lib.* ; but it is hardly essential for our argument, since this has been done so frequently by able writers on the vegetarian diet, that it hardly needs recapitulation in this place. Anyone may test the value of the diet for himself, and thus verify from that most satisfactory of all sources—personal experience—what has been outlined here, as a theoretical possibility. Before closing, however, I desire to call attention to one or two aspects of this question which have been more or less overlooked, or wrong inferences drawn from the facts—apparently vitiating the argument, and showing that meat-eating has a substantial basis, and that there are valid objections to the vegetarian dietary that have hitherto been lost sight of. Let us consider these briefly.

One great argument will always be raised against this theory of vegetarianism, or non-flesh-eating—at first sight a very rational objection. It will be said that all the nations who are flesh-eating are the most progressive and dominating races or nations ; and that those who are largely vegetarian on principle are invariably overruled by the nations who eat meat. The old case of the Hindu and the Englishman may be cited here : it being contended that the meat-eating. Englishman dominates and holds in check the vast hordes of India, and this largely or exclusively on account of his meat diet ! Many other examples of this character might be referred to, and in fact a strong case apparently made out from these arguments alone.

I do not think that the argument is in any way valid, however; for the following reasons, among others :—

In the first place, the Hindu is the man he is—peaceful, docile, kind—more on account of his philosophy than on account of his diet. He is opposed to killing and bloodshed in any form whatever, and will not kill any animal (except, very occasionally, a snake) because of his belief in reincarnation and the trans-migration of souls. It can readily be seen, therefore, that, holding such beliefs as these, and being naturally of a philosophic and introspective turn of mind, and being, moreover, a rural, rather than a warlike people, killing their fellow-men would not appeal to them as it does to us. With them, the aim and object of life is, not to acquire material possessions, but true spiritual progress. They look upon material possessions as so much ephemeral matter, which shall count for very little, when compared with the ultimate destiny of the human soul. European nations, on the other hand, who consider the material nature only, cannot under-stand that attitude of mind; they are so saturated with materialism and the materialistic thoughts of the age that they cannot even conceive the viewpoint of one such as the Hindu, who considers and values only the immaterial. Both consider the other as dreamers, and as victims of illusion—people carried away by vain baubles—in the quest of mere delusions! Holding such views, therefore, it can hardly be wondered at that Hindus should view with more or less indifference the conquests and despotism of foreign nations : to them these are mere incidents in the passing of one life. This argument can, therefore, hardly be pressed against the Hindus and similar nations; it is invalid, for these reasons alone.

Again, it must be admitted that the highest evidence of civilisation—the most advanced evidences of evolution—are hardly those of war and bloodshed, but rather peace and tolerance ! As a friend of mine expressed it : " If you mean that those nations are the most advanced and progressive which shoulder a gun and go out and kill their fellow-man, then I must admit that European nations are the most advanced ; but if you mean anything else, this cannot be said."

As Dr Trall, when discussing this question, remarked :

" If it be alleged, as an argument against the position I am endeavouring to occupy, that the milder and more civilised and peaceful nations are degraded and enslaved by their more ferocious and warlike neighbours, I can merely reply that human beings may, and in fact do, like predacious animals, riot upon and tyrannise over the more amiable and more lovely, as the wolf preys upon the lamb, and the vulture upon the dove. And I can see no end or remedy for this seeming cruelty—save in that law of benevolence and progress which permits suffering for a season, and as a means of development, and overrules all for good, by that law which, in due process of time, will not only exterminate from the face of the earth the beasts of prey, but also all the appetences of human beings for preying upon other animals."

Lastly, I must contend that it is by no means invariably the case that vegetarian nations are subservient to the meat-eating; but they are, on the contrary, almost invariably superior to them physically, as well as mentally and spiritually. The Japanese have only lately given us an excellent example of this fact ; and it is illustrated in the histories of all nations. It might almost be said that meat-eating nations have never stood at the head of the military world until recently. The Greeks and Romans were not meat-eating, but were strictly vegetarian, for the most part ; when meat-eating and wine-drinking and debauchery generally were introduced, the Government speedily disintegrated and went to pieces. The same is true of every nation of which we have any authentic account. The great mass of the people were always vegetarian, and must have been. Even a hundred or so years ago meat was considered a luxury, and was served only on special occasions; bread and vegetables were eaten the rest of the year. Even in our own day, the majority of the peasantry in all countries are almost entirely vegetarian, and only in the large cities can the very poor buy meat. A brief glance at the " diets " of various nations will confirm this statement.

There is slightly more excuse for natives of frigid or temperate zones eating meat than there is for any inhabitant of the tropics; but, as a matter of fact, when an inhabitant of the temperate zone *does* visit the tropics, he still clings to his meat diet—his rich, greasy dishes, his wines, and his roast beef! Even upon his own showing these should be largely sacrificed, when visiting the hot countries; and yet, as a matter of fact, they are not given up—showing the illogical stand taken by those who defend the flesh diet, and conclusively proving that it is merely a matter of habit and prejudice rather than bodily requirements. Mr Salt, in his " Logic of Vegetarianism," has indeed tersely and wittily summed up this argument as follows :—

" *British Islander*.—Vegetarianism ? No thank you ; not here ! All very nice in Africa and India, I dare say, where you can sit all day under a palm tree and eat dates.

" *Vegetarian*.—But I have not observed that when you visit Africa or India you practise vegetarianism. On the contrary, you take your flesh-pots with you everywhere—even to the very places where you admit you don't need them, and where, as in India, they give the greatest offence to the inhabitants.

" *British Islander*.—Oh, well, it's no affair of theirs, is it, if I take my roast beef ?

" *Vegetarian*.—Yet you think it your affair to interfere with the cannibals when they take their roast man. And have you observed that it is in the tropical zone, not the temperate zone, that cannibalism is most rife ?

" *British Islander*.—Why do you remind me of that ?

" *Vegetarian*.—To show you that all this talk about vegetarianism being ' a matter of climate ' is pure humbug. The use of flesh is a vicious habit everywhere, and nowhere a necessity, except where other food is not procurable.

" *British Islander*.—But do we not need more oil and fat in northern climates ?

" *Vegetarian*.—Undoubtedly ; but these can be obtained without recourse to flesh.

" *British Islander*.—Then how do you account for the fact that northern races have been, to so great an extent, carnivorous ?

" *Vegetarian*.—Perhaps because in primitive times hunting and pasturage were less toilsome than agriculture. But I am not called on to ' account ' for such a fact. Their past addictedness to flesh food no more proves the present utility of flesh-eating, than their gross drinking habits prove the utility of alcohol.

" *British Islander*.—Can you quote any scientific authority for your contention ?

" *Vegetarian*.—There is one which is all the more valuable because it is an admission made by an opponent. Sir William Lawrence wrote : ' That men can be perfectly nourished, and that their physical and intellectual capabilities can be fully developed in any climate by a diet purely vegetable, has been proved by such abundant experience that it will not be necessary to adduce any formal argument on the subject.' ' In any climate,' mark ! And a diet ' purely vegetable '; whereas all *you* are asked to do is to forego the actual flesh foods, and not the animal products. But come now, let me ask the great question !

" *British Islander*.—What is that ? There is only

one other I have in mind.   What would become of the Esquimaux ?

"*Vegetarian.*—Of course ! I have always been profoundly touched by the disinterested concern of the Englishman (when vegetarianism looms ahead) for the future of that arctic people.   Well, perhaps the question of what ice-bound savages might do or might not do, need scarcely delay the decision of civilised mankind. For that matter, what would become of the polar bears ? If you cannot dissociate your habits from those of the Esquimaux, why don't you eat blubber ? At least they have a better reason for eating blubber than some people have for eating beef—they can get nothing else." [1]

This whole question of diet, so far as it is decided by experience at all, can in reality be summed up in a very few words.   In the first place, all that it is necessary for anyone to do is to experiment upon himself.   Let him study the subject sufficiently, first of all—so that he may be sure he is balancing his diet properly, when the meat is discarded ; and then give up meat, and continue the new dietary for a year or so—or even a few weeks, for that matter.   The result will soon be apparent.   In the next place, it is ridiculous to raise the question at all, as a matter of fact—as to its " possibility "—when we consider that seven-tenths of the inhabitants of the whole globe are vegetarians ! They are not the scattered few, here and there, as the majority suppose ; but the great bulk of the people in every country. The peasantry in every land have always subsisted almost exclusively upon fruits, grains and vegetables ; and it is only recently, when the price of meat has been so greatly reduced, and the average wages of the people increased, that they have been enabled to buy meat at all, with any regularity.   Meat-eaters have always been in the minority—and have, as a rule, shown signs of

[1] " Logic of Vegetarianism," pp. 67-68.

degeneracy before many centuries or even generations have passed. To anyone knowing these facts, it is little less than absurd to speak of the " impossibility " of subsisting without flesh-foods! It displays the greatest short-sightedness.

Dr Trall, in writing upon this question some years ago, said :

" They say that vegetable food is not sufficiently nutritious. But chemistry proves the contrary. So does physiology. So does experience. Indeed, it can be demonstrated that many kinds of fruit are nearly as nutritious as flesh. Many kinds of vegetables are quite as much so, and the grains and nuts several times as nutritious. They allege that human beings cannot have permanent strength without the use of animal food, right in face of the fact that the hardest work is now being done, and has always been done, by those who use the least animal food ; and right in the face of the fact, too, that no flesh eating animals can endure prolonged and severe labour. I should like to see them try the experiment of working a lion or a tiger, or a hyena against an ox, a camel, or a mule. Examples exist here and there, all over the world, of men of extraordinary powers of endurance who do not use animal food at all ; and history is full of such examples in all ages of the world. And again : the largest and strongest animals in the world are those which eat no flesh-food of any kind—the elephant and rhinocerous." [1]

I cannot refrain here from alluding to the most common objection to vegetarianism we meet with in this country ; and I do so for the purpose of explaining it away. The objection is, that vegetarians are themselves poor specimens of health. And the answer is that the great majority of those who are the subjects of notice and comment are invalids who are restricted to a

[1] " Scientific Basis of Vegetarianism," p. 20. As a matter of fact, all the work in the world is done by vegetarian animals—the horse, ox, camel, elephant, etc.

vegetable diet, because they can recover health in no other way ; and many of them are living on a strict vegetable regimen because it is the only way they can live at all. At the various hydropathic establishments in this country the most desperate cases are put on a vegetable diet, simply because it affords them the best chance of getting well. The casual observer, who judges by appearances, will always find an argument in favour of flesh-eating in the fact that the best-looking persons, physiologically, are those who eat meat.

There are, however, scattered, in America, in England and elsewhere, many persons who will not suffer by comparison, either physical or mental, with the flesh-eaters of any country that can be found. In bodily vigour and in mental capacity they are equal to any meat-eaters. Let us consider this a little more fully.

It is usually thought that athletes cannot be developed upon a non-meat diet (though the fallacy of this argument has long since been disproved, in reality). It will be well to give a few instances, from among many, of the success of vegetarians over their opponents. It is true that these have not been numerous, but then, there are but few vegetarian athletes ; and *proportionately* their triumphs have been singularly frequent. A useful summary of some of these successes is given in Mr Charles Forward's book, "The Food of the Future." He says :

"In the latter part of the year 1880 Gaston de Bennet, a young Austrian, 17 years of age, and a vegetarian of the strictest sect, using neither eggs nor milk, won the first prize in a grand swimming contest in Lord Harlick's Park . . . against 11 flesh-eaters, most of them full-grown men. He also won the first prize in the 'Cooler' race, and, though well drenched, kept his wet clothes on for hours, and took no harm. As a flesh eater, he had been extremely delicate, very subject to cold, and constantly taking physic.

" In the year 1884, the Brothers Whatton and Mr A. W. Rumnay, as representatives of Cambridge. in the inter-university races, carried all before them—a fact which directed considerable public attention to their vegetarian dietary.

" The first path race of the vegetarian cycling club took place in 1891, but it was not until 1893 that the performances of Messrs S. H. Potter, H. Sharp, and W. Kilby, turned out so far in advance of previous work that the Committee decided upon issuing a Club Challenge Shield. During 1895, two of its members . . . gained first and second prizes, in the North London Club's Road Race ; and, in the same year, Mr H. E. Brinning wrested the Club Challenge Shield from Mr Warlow, who had won it a year previously.

" Since then, Mr Brinning had been to Calcutta, and soon after his arrival, won from scratch nearly every race he competed in, besides becoming possessor of three challenge shields put up for competition in Calcutta, and securing the cycling championship of India.

" The achievements of the members of the Vegetarian Cycling Club were much discussed in vegetarian circles all over the world ; and particularly among German vegetarians ; and when, in 1898, a walking competition took place from Berlin to Vienna, several vegetarians were amongst the competitors, who numbered 16 in all. The winner was Otto Peitz, who reached the judge's box at 4.40 P.M., on the 4th of June.   About an hour later, another vegetarian, Elsässer, arrived. No other competitors arrived until about 22 hours later, when, at about 8 o'clock on the following day, Carl Nauhaus passed the post. He was not a vegetarian, but he expressed the opinion that it was a mistake to eat much flesh on a long walk. The fourth arrival was a Berlin university law student, arriving on the sixth of June, at 6.52, whilst a few minutes later Fritz Goldbach reached the Committee Box. Dr Heller, a Vienna physician, and an opponent of vegetarianism, partook of raw flesh on the journey ; but on the second day he began to reconsider the task before him, and he subsequently posted a dispatch to the Committee, announcing his withdrawal from the contest, and went on to Vienna by train. Owing to a technical breach of the rules, Elsässer put in a claim for the gold medal. He had been a strict vegetarian for over four years, not even using eggs, milk, butter or cheese. All that he took during his walk was bread, fruit and water, and, on one or two occasions, a glass of seltzer. He had undergone no regular training at all. Otta Peitz, who secured the second prize, consumed bread and butter, and occasionally eggs and milk. He was a compositor by trade, and being poor, had to ' rough it,' not being able to pay for a bed during the walk. . . .

" On the 21st of January, 1894, the ' Winter Walk ' of the German Long Distance Walk Society took place, the route being from Berlin to Fredericksburg, a distance of about 80 miles. The roads were soft and muddy, and the weather rainy and windy. Of the first four competitors who arrived at the winning post, two were vegetarians—namely, Frederick Bruhn and Carl Harmann. That the result of these walking matches was no mere ' fluke ' is clear from the fact that the vegetarian competitors have repeated their successes on subsequent occasions ; and impartial students of dietetics were ready to admit the soundness of the vegetarian position."

VII

IN the five preceding chapters I have advanced a number of reasons for thinking that the natural diet of man is vegetarian or fruitarian, and have endeavoured to show why flesh-eating is injurious. We saw that, from anatomical structure, from physiological function, from chemical - analysis, for hygienic reasons, and because of the past experience of nations and individuals —for all these reasons man should abstain from meat. In the present chapter I shall adduce a number of miscellaneous arguments, tending to show that flesh is not man's natural food; and that he cannot make it an article of his diet without violating many of the laws of his organisation—mental and moral, as well as physiological. These laws are important, also, and have their rightful place, just as mental and moral considerations have their place in any other question; and I shall accordingly consider them here.

There is first of all the humanitarian argument. This argument is perfectly legitimate, so far as it goes, and a most forceful one. The idea of taking life unnecessarily is very repellant to some—those who have not become hardened, and who have thought of this matter at all. To see a cartload of young animals going to the slaughter-house is a sad if not a disgusting sight—especially when we consider that these animals are soon to be cut up, and made into human food! The ill-treatment which the animals receive, during shipment, is certainly not in favour of their flesh being in any too good condition when it is received at the slaughter-house; and, if mental conditions count for anything, in their effect upon the composition of the blood and tissue juices, there is very good reason for thinking that their bodies are pretty well poisoned before they are killed— even if they were healthy when they left the stock-farm. But, apart from such considerations, every animal has its right to live ; the ox and the calf, and the sheep, and even the swine, has its mental life, just as man ; and there is a universal life running throughout the animal kingdom, which it is no part of man's duty to take needlessly. This brings me to a very important factor in the argument. It is the taking of life *needlessly* which the vegetarian protests against so strongly. If it were necessary to kill these animals ; if man could not live without flesh, then killing and eating would be perfectly justifiable. It would simply be a case of the survival of the fittest, and man would be entitled to kill and eat other animals, just as the carnivora do. But it is not necessary in any degree. Man can live perfectly well without meat of any kind ; and not only live as well, but far better ! My arguments in the chapter devoted to the hygiene of this subject should prove that to the satisfaction of the reader. Man can live without animal flesh ; consequently the eating of this flesh is purely to gratify an appetite—and a perverted appetite at that. No normal appetite could possibly crave flesh of any kind. So that there is no possible excuse for the killing and eating of animals, than this—except, of course, ignorance. After all, that is the greatest factor !

It is against this taking of life unnecessarily that the vegetarian protests ;—not the taking of life at all. Besides, there is a difference between killing a highly organised and sensitive animal, and one far lower in the scale of Evolution. Shedding the blood of such animals is against all normal instincts. Said a lady once, to a gentleman who was eating beef: " How can you eat a thing that looks out of the eyes ? " The very plaintiveness, coupled with the helplessness of such animals, should inspire a certain pity in the breasts of all who have any humanitarian instincts.

This aspect of the controversy throws a different and a more rational light upon this question. It has frequently been contended, *e.g.*, that, if this humanitarian argument were carried far enough, it would become absurd, for the reason that every drop of water we drink, and every breath of air we breathe contains living animals, which we kill within our bodies ! Moreover, every vegetable we cut or pick, takes life (such as it is) and consequently this argument cannot be carried to its logical conclusion, and is consequently worthless !

The position I have indicated above answers this objection. If we cannot live without taking the lives of certain animalculæ, or that of certain plants, then we must take their lives (for the most part, be it noted, unconsciously). But there is a great difference between this and taking the lives of highly organised animals intentionally and voluntarily. Besides, the one is necessary, the other not. As I said before, if meat were a necessary article of diet, there could be no possible objection to making it an article of food ; but it is *not* necessary. That is the *crux*.

Further, it can be shown that, on a fruitarian diet, it is not necessary to take the life even of the fruit eaten ! If a cabbage be cut, *e.g.*, we thereby kill the cabbage— its psychic life, that is. The same is true of all other vegetables. But it will be observed that, when fruits are eaten, nothing is destroyed ; no life taken unnecessarily. Fruits, when they are ripe, fall from the tree, and rot upon the ground—thus exposing the seed, and allowing it to become buried in the soil. It will be seen that the pulp of the fruit is of no further use to the seed ; it has nourished it up to the time of its falling to the ground, but thenceforward, it is virtually useless to the seed. So that we might with justice feel that we were taking no life at all in eating this pulp of the fruit —which, again, would seem to indicate that fruit is man's natural diet.[1] However, as I said before, I do not think it is necessary to split hairs so finely on this question. The valid ground to take is that it is wrong and cruel to take highly organised life uselessly ; and I do not think that such an attitude is in any way open to criticism.

I may as well answer, in this place, one objection that has been frequently raised against vegetarians by the meat-eaters, which is that, if we did not eat meat, we should soon be overrun by the various animals, and there would be no room for man upon the earth ! They would eventually crowd man out ! This supposed argument is really absurd. In the first place, hardly one-tenth of the animals now brought into the world would be raised. They are now especially bred for eating purposes, and if the demand decreased, the supply would decrease also. Further, how is it that we are not overrun by wild animals of all sorts ? We have never been in any danger from *them*, somehow ; but it has invariably been found that they tend to recede before the advance of civilisation. Many survive, to be sure, but Nature seems to take care that their numbers are not unduly increased, so as to be a menace to the human race. If this be true of wild animals—which might really be a menace to the human race, if their numbers were sufficiently increased—it is certainly all the more true of the harmless domestic animals. Nature would

---

[1] *Cf.* Genesis i. 29, where man is distinctly told that he is a fruitarian ; and not only that, he is told the character of fruit he must eat. "And God said, Behold, I have given you every herb bearing seed, which is upon the face of all the earth, and every tree, *in the which is the fruit of a tree yielding seed* ; *to you it shall be for meat.*" The seed-fruits are here clearly indicated, as well as man's originally frugivorous diet.

see to it that man was not overrun by animals of any sort, as she always has in the past. People need not worry about the future welfare of the bovine race, if they would only be a little more humane in their treatment of its present representatives !

There is an ethical and an æsthetic aspect of diet, just as there is a hygienic and chemical aspect. There is a wider view of this question of diet than merely that of supplying the body with pabulum for the tissues ; the body itself cannot be built equally well from all food-stuffs, but the body is cleaner and internally purer on some foods than upon others. The keeping of the body in a clean, pure state—a fit tenant for the soul—is in itself an aspect of the diet problem that should affect us most keenly. It is not as though food had no effect upon mental life and morals. Far from it. There is the closest inter-relation. The whole process of in-gesting food is disgusting, in one sense, but that is no excuse for choosing, in consequence, carrion and offal to feed upon ! Think of the condition of a man's stomach who has eaten a regular *table-d'hôte* dinner, and compare it, in the mind's eye, with the stomach of a man who has dined on peaches and Brazil nuts ! Were one to stop and think of what meat *is*, and what it *was*, it is doubtful if one could eat it. It is merely dead and decaying flesh—flesh from the body of an animal. There is nothing more repellent to think about than the " scorched corpses," as Bernard Shaw calls them, which grace the tables of so-called civilised people. The sight, the smell, the taste, all are repellent. Only by the fact that they are covered up, and their true nature con-cealed by cooking, and basting, and pickling, and pepper-ing and salting can we eat them at all. If we were naturally carnivorous animals, we should delight in bloodshed and gore of all kind ! We should go out and kill our dinner, just as we now eat it ; and the one would seem no more repulsive to us than the other. Carnivorous animals secure their food in this way, and so should we, if we were naturally carnivorous. We should eat our flesh warm and quivering—just as it comes from the cow ! But instead of this, what do we find ? That the majority of people in civilised nations will not even consent to go near a slaughter-house ! And when they *do* go, they come away sickened at the sights and the odours which they encounter. Take for example the following extracts from a diary—the notes being descriptive of a Chicago meat market :—

" Slithered over bloody floor. Nearly broke neck in gore of old porker. Saw few hundred men slicing pigs, making hams, sausages, and pork chops. Whole sight not edifying ; indeed, rather beastly. Next went to the cattle killing house. Cattle driven along gangway and banged over head with iron hammer. Fell stunned : then swung up by legs, and man cuts throats. Small army of men with buckets catching blood ; it gushed over them in torrents—a bit sickening. Next went to sheep slaughter-house. More throat-cutting—ten thousand sheep killed a day—more blood. Place reeks with blood ; walls and floor splashed with it, air thick, warm, offensive. Went and drank brandy. . . :" [1]

And so would anyone else who had witnessed like scenes ! I say *witnessed* them merely : how would it be if each one had to perform the actual process of killing, before he could have a piece of his " delicious beef-steak " ? How would our society women like to spend the morning in a slaughter-house, before they could procure their meat for the evening dinner ? And yet *someone* has to do this work—work disgusting and degrading enough to be below the lowest of men, and fit only for the lowest of animals. The butcher does this, you say ; he is paid for it ? Very true, but he

[1] " Logic of Vegetarianism," p. 55.

L

only learns to do this work after many days and even weeks of revulsion : and it is invariably against his nature to do it. And this brings me to one very important factor—the degradation of the butcher. Of all recognised occupations by which in civilised countries a livelihood is sought and obtained, the work which is looked upon with the greatest loathing (next to the hangman's) is that of the butcher. He becomes depraved mentally, morally and physically. His is a dangerous business, and it is well known that slight cuts and scratches, which, in the average man, would amount to very little, frequently cause blood-poisoning and death to the butcher. Their work brutalises them, too—as it necessarily must. This is well known ; and butchers are forbidden to sit in a jury, in certain countries, as we know, because of the perversion of their moral natures. And all this because certain persons, under the delusion that they " must have meat " demand this from these men ! The crime, and the ugly, dirty work in connection with meat-eating, does not rest upon the butchers—who are paid for their work, and would doubtless starve, lacking it—it rests upon the eaters of meat throughout the country ! As the Whitechapel butcher remarked to the flesh-eating gentlemen : " It's such as *you* makes such as *us* ! " Yes; the stain rests upon the flesh-eaters, not upon the flesh providers !

But there is another argument in favour of the vegetarian diet, and more especially in favour of the fruitarian diet, as against meat-eating. It is that any given area of land will supply far more food per acre in the one case than in the other. When the soil is given up to the feeding of cattle, upon which man is to feed, the given area of land would supply far less nutriment, so to speak, than would the same soil, if grains were raised upon it ; and that would give less, in turn, than if fruit-trees were grown upon it.

Dr Smith pointed out this fact in his " Fruits and Farinacea " years ago ; and stated that twenty times the
population could be supported upon a diet of grains,
coming from a given limited area, than could be supplied, if that area were devoted to the raising of cattle.
And far more would this be the case if fruits were grown
upon this same area. It is safe to say that, if one
person could be fed from a certain area of land, provided he ate the meat it produced, ten could be fed
from the same area, upon grains and cereals, and twenty
upon the fruits and nuts such an area could provide.
This fact is in itself of great importance and significance.
Although the time is doubtless far distant when man
will have to figure so closely on his land space for feeding the people, that time must come some day ; and it
would be well to know that many more persons can be
fed from the same area of ground upon one diet than
upon another.

These and many other arguments could be urged
against the practice of meat-eating. They are all
valid arguments, though all of them, in my estimation,
subordinate to the hygienic argument. If it were
necessary to kill animals, in order to live, I should have
no compunction in doing so ; but as it is not necessary,
I must protest against this useless waste of life ; and
more especially so since this meat is positively pernicious
and harmful to the system. There is a sort of half-
formulated idea in men's minds that they must have
meat, because the blood is *red*, and because the blood
of their own bodies is red ; and they think that, by
eating large quantities of meat, they can increase the
quantity and improve the quality of their own blood—
thereby curing anæmia, etc. ! Of course there is no
foundation at all for this superstition. In the first
place, the tables of the chemical values of the various
foods show us conclusively that meat is far *less* nutri-

tious than many other articles of diet; while it contains, in addition, certain poisons which are extremely harmful to the system. Further, all food, no matter what its nature, is converted into a creamy substance known as chyle before it is appropriated by the system; and, no matter what the food may be, it is resolved into this cream-coloured chyle before it is digested. Where, then, is the " good, red blood " of the meat ? And I have previously shown that, although there are practically no chemical differences between the chyme formed from vegetable and that formed from animal substances, nevertheless, the vital properties of the chyme vary greatly—and are in favour of the vegetable foods. Finally, I would point out that, if this argument were sound, we should not eat the flesh of animals, for the reason that " it most nearly resembles our own," but would become cannibals and eat *human* flesh—since *that* most nearly resembles our tissues ! And yet it has been found by actual experiment, that, so far from being wholesome food, human flesh is exceedingly indigestible and unwholesome !

If flesh-eating is as harmful as I have been endeavouring to show, however, how comes it about that the practice is so universal ? And how did the practice of flesh-eating originate, in the first place ? These are questions often asked of vegetarians, and there is a simple answer to both of them. Flesh-eating is all but universal, simply because people follow habit and custom blindly, without thinking of their actions in the least—and, strangely enough, on this most vital of all questions —food and diet. On most other topics, people are quite capable of thinking for themselves; but in this question, they take not the slightest interest ! So long as the food *tastes* nice, that is all they care to think about it; and the actual preparation of the food, and all questions concerning its composition and combination with other foods, they are content to leave to an ignorant Chinaman or Irish cook, who knows as much about the physiology and hygiene of dietetics as a cow of the constitution of the moon. It is really amazing that this should be so. It shows, of course, that people have not really thought about their food in this light, and realised the tremendous consequences of a false and perverted diet, or the benefits of a simple and nutritious one. Flesh-eating doubtless sprang into existence ages ago, at a time when little or no other food was to be obtained, and they had to live upon it or starve. But we are not called upon to explain the origin of meat-eating, as a matter of fact, any more than we are the origin of alcohol-drinking. We must take conditions as we find them, and endeavour to better them, as best we can. It is certain that animals can be taught to eat meat, quite contrary to their natural dietetic habits—as indicated by their structure, and by the unperverted dietetic habits of the rest of their species. Thus, horses have been taught to eat meat and drink beer; and, at certain seasons, the horses on the coast of Norway are said to dash into the sea, and endeavour to catch fishes in their mouths. Dogs and cats can be taught to like alcoholic beverages of all kinds; and similar perversions of taste in the animal world might be cited by the score. If animals can thus be trained to like foods and drinks of this character, certainly man can be taught to like and to eat and drink them also; and it is doubtless due to this fact that the habit of meat-eating originated. Once perverted, the appetite would have a tendency to stay perverted, by reason of heredity; and in any case the environment and education of the growing child would be quite sufficient to engender the desire for meat—especially if the individual were brought up under the notion that he " cannot live " without meat, and that it is a most essential article of his diet ! The medical profession is to blame for much of this perverted reasoning, and the public for blindly following it, without investigating its doctrines for themselves. Only when this is done can we hope for a widespread and radical reform—one which will revolutionise diet and cookery and spread health and harmony among the human race and the animal kingdom—as well as restore man to a position of elevated spiritual insight.

VIII

DAIRY PRODUCTS

COMING, as these do, from the animal world—more or less directly—they are eschewed by many strict vegetarians and hygienists, as being open to all those objections which might be urged against the use of flesh-meat, only in a lesser degree. There is no doubt that this is the only logical ground to assume, in this question, and the one which many of us occupy from choice. There can be no question, moreover, that man *can* persist, and maintain all his faculties—physical and mental—on a diet devoid of all these articles of food. They are not open to any such serious objections as are the flesh-meats, however; and are certainly to be preferred to them. As found upon the market, they are all more or less adulterated, unfortunately; and preservatives, in the shape of salt, etc., introduced, to prevent rapid decomposition. Eggs are also objectionable, on the ground that they have been kept on ice, as a rule, for long periods of time, before they are offered for sale. But, even granting that these articles of diet are fresh, and the best that can be procured, there are still weighty objections to their use, as I can readily show. Let us consider them a little more fully, in turn.

Milk.—Milk is, of course, the natural food of man for the first year or so of his life. This is no reason, however, for supposing that man can continue to eat, or rather drink, milk, for the rest of his life with impunity—especially when this milk comes from the cow. Milk as an article of diet has been highly praised by many authorities. For example, in the pamphlet issued by the U.S. Department of Agriculture, we read :

" Milk is peculiarly adapted for use as a food by man for several reasons. It contains all the four classes of nutriments—protein, fats, carbohydrates and mineral matter—in more nearly the proper proportion to serve as a complete food than any other food material, although no one substance can furnish a complete food for an adult."

While this may be true, the differences that are noted between human milk and cow's milk are highly important ones. It is to be remembered, in this connection, that the blood and chemical composition of the calf's body are different from those of man ; and its natural food—milk—must consequently be different, for that reason. The chemical composition of cow's milk is therefore not suited exactly for the human being, and, in order to render it more nearly ideal in composition, various other ingredients have to be mixed with it, in order to make it more nearly resemble the milk of the human species.

Mr Otto Carqué, writing in his " Folly of Meat Eating," said :

" Milk is a nutritious food which is best suited for the newborn mammal. Only the infant's digestive apparatus is adapted for the proper digestion of milk ; his salivary glands are not yet developed and his alimentary canal is almost a straight tube, quite different from that of the adult. There is a little bulge in the tube, from which the stomach gradually develops, and during this time very little gastric juice is formed. When milk enters the stomach of an infant it goes easily through and down into the intestines where it can be digested. In the stomach of the adult, which is of different shape and secretes more acid gastric juice, milk forms large, tough curds which are not easily digested.

" *Cow's milk is a splendid food for calves, but it cannot be recommended very well for human beings.* The natural food-supply of the infant—mother's milk—forms very small, soft curds which are easily broken up and digested. They are entirely different from the curds formed by cow's milk which are tough and only adapted to the four-stomach digestive apparatus of the calf. An exclusive diet of milk may often increase the weight of a person, but this is due to its large percentage of water, while it does not contain enough organic salt for the adult who needs a larger percentage of iron, sulphur and silicon in his food.

" Cow's milk is sometimes diluted with water and sweetened with refined sugar to serve as food for children. Warning cannot be sounded often enough against this injurious practice of diminishing the percentage of organic salts in the milk, a circumstance which at once interferes with the proper oxidation and circulation of the blood, giving rise to a larger number of infantile diseases. *Refined sugar* is entirely deficient in mineral matter and therefore always injurious to health."

But there is a far greater danger in milk than any we have so far considered. I refer to the unhealthy condition of cows. Bovine tuberculosis and other diseases are very prevalent among cows of all sorts— far more so than is usually believed. E. F. Brush, M.D., in his book, " Human and Bovine Tuberculosis," says:

" My occupation brings me into close contact with dairy cattle, and I have therefore been compelled to devote my attention to the diseases afflicting dairy stock, and that there is a large number of dairy cows afflicted with tuberculosis I can affirm ; that there has never been any attempt to exterminate the disease is a fact of which I am also cognisant. . . I have been told by inspectors of the Bureau of Animal Industry that a much larger percentage of our cows are affected than is the case in England. Indeed, among the thoroughbred Jerseys in the Northern states, twenty per cent. are affected, as I have been told by Professor R. A. McLean, chief of this district from the bureau."

And in his work on " Milk," this author says :

" Diseases may be conveyed by milk taken from an animal suffering from disease, or by milk contaminated in a dairy, or by contact with diseased or affected persons."

These words were written some years ago, and it is probably true that conditions have somewhat improved since that time ; but there can be no question that a large number of diseased cattle still exist and supply milk to the various cities—their standard being kept somewhat low by continued in-and-in breeding.   And it must not be overlooked, in this connection, that no matter if the animal be perfectly healthy, the milk partakes of the nature and general character and composition of the animal's body ; and while this may not be actually diseased, it is doubtless in a more or less depraved condition—as are practically all domesticated animals, particularly the cow—during the confined period of winter.   And the milk, being a secretion, naturally takes on the conditions of the body of the animal—as would any other secretion.

Indeed, Professor L. B. Arnold, an excellent authority on all dairy matters, says :

" Milk is the scavenger of the cow's body."

But now suppose we have the best of milk, from perfectly healthy cows, there would still remain several objections to its use.   In all conditions of torpor of the liver, or in all dyspeptic conditions, or whenever there is a tendency towards biliousness, milk is sure to cause distress, being unsuited to the organism.   Milk contains a large percentage of liquid (upwards of 90 per cent.) to a very small percentage of solid ; and while this proportionate percentage is right for the body of the babe, it is not suited for that of the adult. He should eat more solid food, and, if necessary, drink water separately.

Milk contains a large percentage of fat, and but a small percentage of proteid and mineral salts, and the adult can usually balance his diet better by leaving out milk and by ingesting a smaller bulk of more nutritious food material, which he is able to assimilate, but which the babe cannot.

Cream, if used to the same extent as n ..., would doubtless be far more injurious. Those who partake of large quantities of cream usually become bilious, as is evidenced by the colour of the complexion, the whites of the eyes, blotches and eruptions which appear upon the skin, etc. But, taken in the very limited quantity that it usually is, it is probably less harmful than milk, on that account. Both milk and cream, if taken at all, should be considered a food rather than a drink, and should be thoroughly masticated before being swallowed—since important chemical changes take place in the mouth, and the milk is also prevented from curdling in the excessively large clots that would form, were milk drunk in quantity, without being separated in the mouth.

Butter.—If we dispense with milk—that is, leave it to the calf, for whom nature intended it—there will, of necessity, be no butter; and, from a sanitary point of view, the absence of it would perhaps be no great loss, it being by no means as wholesome an article of diet as either milk or cream. Like other oils, it is, to a degree, indigestible; not that it gives " a pain in the stomach," as a general thing, but it does not enter into those vital changes which are necessary to convert food into chyle proper. It mixes with the pancreatic juice in the form of an emulsion, simply, and goes into the blood in that crude condition ; and being carried through the system by the capillaries, it is deposited *as fat* in the various tissues, and largely in the skin. From the very nature of its constituents, butter has but little nutritive value It usually contains 3 to 5 per cent. of casein (due to the presence of the milk) and about twice that amount of water ; the other substances are oils, fixed and volatile. These readily decompose upon exposure to the atmosphere, and butyric and other fat acids are set free.

Persons who live largely upon butter emit a strong odour from the skin, very perceptible to those who do not use animal foods. The salt which has to be mixed with it to make it " keep " is not, to the hygienist, a desirable addition, for reasons which will be hereafter stated. Pereira says : " Fixed oil or fat is more difficult of digestion and more obnoxious to the stomach than any other alimentary principle." Indeed, in some more or less obvious or concealed form, I believe it will be found the offending ingredient in nine-tenths of the dishes which disturb weak stomachs. Many dyspeptics, who have religiously avoided the use of fat in its obvious or ordinary state (as fat meat, marrow, butter, and oil) unwittingly employ it in some more concealed form, and, as I have frequently witnessed, have suffered therefrom. Such individuals should eschew the yolks of eggs, livers (of quadrupeds, poultry and fish) and brains, all of which abound in oily matter. Milk, and especially cream, disagree with many persons, or, as they term it, " lies heavy on the stomach," in consequence of the butter it contains. Rich cheese, likewise, contains butter, and on that account is apt to disturb the stomach.

Schlickeysen, in speaking of the use of butter, eggs, and cheese, remarks :

" These cause an excess of fat in the system, and an offensive, slimy, condition of the mucous secretions of the mouth and nose, quite apparent to those who, contrary to their usual habit, eat them. Their effects are apparent also in eruptions upon the skin, especially upon the face."

Eggs.—Eggs are pretty generally conceded to be a "bilious diet"; and if eaten freely at each meal for a few weeks, the whites of the eyes usually show the presence of bile. They contain an excess of sulphur. The albumen (whites of the eggs) cooked soft, would be less objectionable than the yolks, which contain about 30 per cent. of oil. If eggs are eaten they should be fresh, their use not too frequent, and confined to cool weather. The fowls should be allowed plenty of clean territory to run over, and an abundance of fresh pure water, pure air, and good grains. Unfortunately, the habits of the bird are not the cleanest; it will pick up and eat almost anything that comes in its way. This is why country eggs and country fowl (provided there are good and healthful surroundings) are always to be preferred. In towns or cities the chickens are necessarily confined to the house and yard; whereas in the country they have access to the open fields, and feed largely on grains.

Persons who are subject to torpor of the liver would do well to refrain from the use of either eggs or butter; and those who have sound livers—and desire to keep them so—can take a hint !

A great many vegetarians are strong advocates of dairy products, and particularly eggs. They claim, rightly enough, that they contain a large amount of proteid, and hence are valuable meat substitutes. But this same proteid can be obtained from nuts and vegetables, as we have seen—without the necessity of resorting to eggs in order to secure it. From the ethical point of view, there is no excuse whatever for the eating of eggs ; and there are many objections to their use on purely hygienic grounds. It is remarkable, in this connection, to find so strong a belief in egg-eating, when we take into account the fact that these eggs are all intended to be chickens by nature, and we are really eating chickens *in embryo*—a very disagreeable thought, when we come to consider it. All other eggs—swallow's eggs, ostrich's eggs, robin's eggs, etc.—we think of as existing only for the purpose of bringing into the world little swallows or ostriches or robins : but the hen's egg we consider, for some mysterious reason or other, laid for our especial benefit—as a suitable and even necessary food ! It is really remarkable that such curious ideas should have originated in the human mind. Doubtless they originated in the days of savagery, when but little else could be obtained for food, but which culture and modern ideals should have outgrown long ago.

Cheese.—" The fresh curd of milk is perfectly wholesome, and pot cheese is also a practically harmless article of diet. Green cheese is not very objectionable, but old, strong cheese, is one of the most injurious and indigestible things in existence. It is also one of the most constipating articles of food that can be found. It is a common fancy among medical men, and a common whim among the people, that old, strong, rank cheese, though itself very indigestible, stimulates the stomach to digest other things. Hence almost all the medico-dietetic works quote the old adage :

> " ' Cheese is a mity elf,
> Digesting all things but itself.'

" There is more poetry than truth in the doggerel quoted. Old cheese occasionally undergoes spontaneous decomposition, during which process acrid and poisonous elements are developed, as is frequently the case with bacon and sausages." [1]

[1] " Hydropathic Cook Book," p. 107.

Although cheese is, in one sense, a valuable article of diet, in that it contains a large percentage of fat and proteid, it is nevertheless objectionable in many ways The fact that it is derived from milk, and hence indirectly from the animal world, necessitates the same objections to its use as have been raised against all the other animal products. The same proteid may be obtained from nuts and purely vegetable substances, without the injurious admixture of possible toxic materials, impurities, and adulterants. In this connection it may be added that the common salt which is generally introduced into cheese in order to preserve it, renders it an unhygienic article of diet; and hence it is to be debarred, since other substances (containing the same amount of proteid, etc.) can be obtained, in which these mineral ingredients are lacking.

IX

Peas, Beans, Lentils, etc.—It can be seen by referring to the tables of foods that these articles of diet contain a large amount of proteid, and are consequently good substitutes for meat; and, if the ordinary vegetarian diet be adhered to, they should form the staple foods in place of the meat that has been omitted. They are very hearty articles of diet, however, and contain a large amount of proteid in a concentrated form, and for that reason should be eaten in the winter months, if at all. These articles of food, moreover, all contain a certain percentage of uric acid-forming materials, and for this reason should be avoided whenever possible. Dr Haig, throughout his writings, has argued very strongly against the legumes as food for man, and has shown that an excessive consumption of such foods tends to create uric acid—and results in the evil consequences which follow from its presence, whenever eaten in large quantities. He recommends in their place nuts, cheese, and milk. Cheese and milk we have already considered, and the value of nuts we shall ascertain when we come to the chapter on the fruitarian diet. On the whole, then, it cannot be said that peas, beans, and lentils are desirable articles of food, whenever they can be avoided. Their chief value consists in the amount of proteid they contain, and this can be supplied by nuts, as we have seen, and shall see further. In addition to this, we now know that large amounts of proteid are not required by the system, and are detrimental rather than beneficial to it.

" In the early spring," says Dr Dodds, in her " Health ·

in the Household," p. 40, " when we have grown tired
of ' last year's leavings,' the tender vegetables fill our
markets, and delight our eyes in glad anticipation of a
change in the repast. The young beets, the spinach,
and asparagus, the early cauliflower, and even the
lettuce and onions have charms for us then. As summer
draws nigh, the varieties of choice vegetables multiply,
giving us green peas, tomatoes, string beans, summer
squashes, and an almost endless variety of products.
Then come the autumn days, and with them the great
lima beans, the hubbard squashes, and the sweet
potatoes. Nor does the supply fail us when winter
approaches ; there are still turnips, potatoes, cabbage,
winter squashes, and other good things. Really it is
little less than wonderful what varieties of vegetable
products there are even in a single latitude of climate."

Although vegetables are capable of supporting life,
and contain many of the nutritious properties most
necessary for bodily sustenance, there are, nevertheless,
objections to be raised against almost every one of
these foods. Personally, I do not believe that they are
suitable articles of diet for the human race. When we
come to the chapter on the fruitarian diet, I shall endeavour to show that fruits and nuts in their uncooked,
primitive form, are the suitable and proper diet for
mankind ; and I believe that, although he can subsist
upon vegetables, and even maintain a certain degree of
health upon the ordinary vegetarian diet, I do not think
that it begins to compare in excellence with the fruitarian or raw-food diet. Throughout this book, I have
been used to speaking of " vegetarian " as opposed to
a " mixed " diet—including meat—and I certainly think
it preferable to that generally followed ; but the diet
I would advocate is as far superior to the ordinary vegetarian diet as *that* is superior to the mixed diet. It
consists almost exclusively of fruits and nuts. The
fruitarian diet, then, is, in my estimation, the ideal diet,

and the reasons for this I shall endeavour to give in full in Chapter XII.

All vegetables, to be rendered fit articles for human food, must be *cooked*, in the first place, and this fact alone renders the ordinary vegetarian diet less nutritious and less wholesome than the fruitarian or raw-food diet. With few exceptions, moreover, the vegetables contain but little nutritive matter. Those which *do* contain a high percentage of proteid are open to the same objections as were raised against meat—namely, that they create urid acid. But the majority of vegetables supply nothing that cannot be derived in simpler and in better form from the fruit and nut dietary ; and they contain, moreover, a large percentage of indigestible and fibrous material — refuse — from which the other foods are free. A brief glance at each of the vegetables individually will confirm this. *Potatoes* are nearly all starch ; they contain practically no proteid, fats, or mineral substances of value, and are, generally speaking, constipating articles of food. The objections to *peas, beans* and *lentils* we have discussed. *Asparagus, spinach,* and similar vegetables contain but little nutriment, and much waste, and on the whole can be considered little better than weeds. *Cabbages* of various sorts, *brussels sprouts, cauliflower, broccoli,* etc., are also open to these objections. They contain a large amount of fibrous, indigestible matter, with but a small amount of nutriment. Cabbage, eaten raw, is not such a bad article of diet, but cooked in the way in which it usually is, the iron, and its valuable salts, pass into the water in which it is cooked—so that there is, in one sense, more nutriment in the water than there is in the mere " skeleton " that is left, and which we eat ! *Onions, leeks,* and *garlics* may have their uses in certain diseases, when eaten raw, but they would doubtless lose these properties when cooked, and many persons cannot eat them. They are very strong articles of food, and it is doubtful if they are intended for human aliment at all. *Turnips* and *parsnips* consist almost entirely of water, and are practically valueless as food. They contain a very small percentage of carbohydrates, but they are spongy and fibrous, and frequently hard to digest. The same objections would apply more or less to *carrots*, *beetroots*, and *artichokes*. *Mushrooms* should by all means be avoided. They are exceedingly indigestible, in a large number of cases, and there is, in addition, a great danger of becoming poisoned by toadstools, or other fungi. *Corn* is an exceedingly indigestible food— especially if insufficiently masticated, as it invariably is. The proteid it contains can be supplied in many other more wholesome foods. *Celery* consists almost entirely of fibre, and cannot rightly be considered as suitable for human food. *Endives, cresses, capers, dandelions, radishes*, etc., are all weeds, and, if uncultivated, would be totally unfit for the human stomach. *Lettuce* contains a certain amount of opium ; and *cucumber* is widely known for its great indigestibility.

Summing up the nutritive values of these various vegetables, then, we can fairly say that none of them contain the essential properties suitable for human food. The majority of them are indigestible and are, by their innate composition, improper foods for the human race. All the nutritive materials which they contain can be supplied in a purer and better form by the various fruits and nuts, while the tough, fibrous nature of most of the vegetables necessitates an enormous outlay of the energy of digestion, which should be conserved and utilised for other and better purposes. The fact, further, that these various food-stuffs have to be cooked in order to render them palatable and edible, is another objection to their use. Even Dr Tibbles, who strongly insists on the value of vegetables as human food, is forced to write in his "Food and Hygiene," p. 198 :

"Persons in robust health with healthy stomachs, and leading active lives may eat all kinds of vegetables, however cooked, without injury, except when they are taken in excess. . . . Those who are only able to digest vegetables, especially green vegetables, with difficulty should have them in the form of consommé or purée. In their preparation, the cooked vegetable is minced and pounded in a mortar until it is reduced to a pulp, and then rubbed through a hair sieve to remove skin and rough fibres."

In other words, it is practically admitted that vegetables are hard to digest at all times, and that as soon as the energy of digestion is lowered, this fact is immediately apparent! This is evident from the directions that are given to remove the skin and tough fibres. On the fruitarian diet none of these objections would be encountered—the bland, soothing, cooling, antiseptic properties of the fruit juices being readily seen, and practically never cause indigestion, no matter how enfeebled it may be, or how sick the patient —provided eating be possible at all—and provided that they do not contain an excess of acids and other substances injurious to the body in its then state of health. Vegetables are, further, a very *bulky* food, and for this reason, also, I consider them objectionable.

X

CEREALS

THERE is much dispute, as to the relative value of wheat, and other cereal foods, as articles of diet. Numbers of authors contend that they are in very truth the "staff of life"; others, on the contrary, maintain that they are totally unsuited for human food, and that it would be far better for the human race if cereals of all kinds were replaced by other articles of food, containing somewhat similar constituents. We shall examine these opposite opinions a little later on. Let us first of all consider these foods, their functions, and how far they may be supported to nourish the body and maintain the health. Let us take first of all *wheat*. The five outer layers of the bran contain very little except cellulose—a woody, fibrous substance, forming the cell walls. When burned, the ash of bran is found to contain a large proportion of phosphoric acid, potash, and a small amount of other mineral matters. The cereal layer is, of all parts of the grain, the richest in nitrogenous substances—the chief of which is the creatine, from which it takes its name. Gluten is one of the most important constituents of the wheat.

Unfortunately, this is separated from the grain, as is well known, and adheres to the husk, when this is removed; and for this reason " superfine " white flour contains but very little nutriment, and a large quantity of starch—a very constipating food and one which necessitates a large amount of vital expenditure when converting it into bodily tissue. As is well known, all starch must go through several processes or stages of digestion before it can be used by the system. The body can never use starch *as starch*. It must be converted into glucose sugar before the body can make use of or appropriate it.   It must first of all be converted into various substances—dextrose, maltose, etc.—before it is finally transformed into glucose—in which form the body can utilise it. *Starch, then, must be converted into sugar (glucose) before the body can use it* ; and must be transformed into this substance at the expense of the bodily energy, of which a great amount has to be expended in these varied processes of conversion.   Now, this being the case, *why would it not be easier and better for us to eat those foods that supply this glucose or grape-sugar direct*—without necessitating any of these energy-wasting transformations ?   Were we to take this grape-sugar directly into the system (stomach) as an article of food, we should thereby save all the energy of digestion, which would otherwise be wasted in useless processes of conversion. There can be no valid reason why this should not be the case.[1]   And, since fruits contain this very grape-sugar in a free and natural state, it becomes obvious that we can obtain from fruits all that we derive from grains and cereals (with the exception of proteid matter, which we can get from nuts) and in a far better state—because more appropriable by the system.   I am strongly convinced that nothing is to be derived from wheat or similar grains and cereals that cannot be derived equally well or better from fruits and nuts of

[1] It is important to note, in this connection, that but a small percentage of the starch is ever converted into sugar, even by the most thorough mastication.   I say this on the authority of Dr John Goodfellow, F.R.C.S., author of " The Dietetic Value of Bread," etc., who conducted a number of careful experiments on this very point. (See his letter to Dr Densmore, in " How Nature Cures," pp. 237-239.) In raw cereals, only about one per cent. was converted | As this process of conversion cannot go forward in an acid medium—*i.e.* in the stomach—it is evident that the bowels must be called upon to effect this conversion—a useless tax upon them, and a cause of constipation as well.

various kinds. And this applies to all other grains—rye, barley, oats, etc.—as well as to wheat. They are all objectionable for the same reason; and a properly balanced diet of fruits and nuts is superior to any diet of grains and cereals.

It is well known that toast is more wholesome than ordinary bread: it is given to invalids, when bread is debarred. The reason for this—which comparatively few persons know—is that a portion of the starch contained in the flour is converted into dextrine, by this process of toasting. In this manner, a portion of the original starch contained in the bread is " predigested," and hence saves the vital energies so much tax—when it comes to the digestion of this starch. But would it not be better to give the patient fruits, in which *all* these processes of conversion have already been performed by nature—and hence save far more of the bodily energies than even the giving of toast? It must be remembered that starch contains nothing that is useful to the system except this grape-sugar, which can also be obtained from fruits of all kinds, in a natural and appropriable form. This being so, why not give fruits in the first place—thus saving all this useless expenditure of energy? There is also the additional argument that fruits of all kinds are cleansing and slightly laxative—instead of being constipating—and have also powerful germicidal properties. However, I shall consider this question more at length in the chapter devoted to the fruitarian diet.

Many writers upon the subject of dietetics are very laudatory of wheat and other cereal foods. Dr Tibbles, indeed, in his " Food and Hygiene," p. 229, says that " so large a part do they fulfil in domestic preparations that it is almost safe to say that if the entire crop of cereals failed for one year nearly 90 per cent. of the inhabitants of the earth would die " ! This might be true in a certain sense, for there would be no article of food to take the place of the cereals destroyed; but if nuts and fruits had been cultivated instead, it would be found that all the cereals could be dispensed with easily enough, and that none of the inhabitants would die; but, on the contrary, that they would retain a high degree of health—far higher than they now possess.

If the whole wheat, containing all the grain—the nutritious gluten as well as the (comparatively speaking) innutritious starch—were supplied to the body, there would be far less objection to the use of grains and cereals; but as a matter of fact, this is rarely the case, and only health-reformers insist upon having bread made of whole wheat flour or gluten bread. The majority eat bread made of white, " superfine " flour—flour totally divested of its nutritious elements. Such flour contains none of the valuable salts which the whole grain contains; it is devoid of the proteid matter; it is constipating, and in other ways objectionable. And a practical proof of the correctness of this position is afforded by the fact that dogs, fed by Magendie upon superfine white flour, *all died*; while those dogs which were fed upon whole-wheat flour lived and retained their health. Such an experiment is worth any amount of theorising, for or against.

Dr S. Rowbatham, writing some years ago on this subject, said :

" Bread [from wheaten flour], when considered in reference to the amount of nutritious matter it contains, may with justice be called the staff of life; but in regard to the amount of earthy matter, we may with equal justice pronounce it the staff of death. . . . It is quite right to suppose that nutritious food is necessary to support and strengthen the fœtus; but the nutritious and the solid earthy matter in food are very different substances. Wheaten flour, on account of its containing so much earthy matter, is the most dangerous article a female can live upon, when pregnant. The other grains are bad enough, but better than wheat. . . . Persons of a dull, cadaverous appearance, with harsh rough skins, who are thin and bony and continually troubled with some complaint or other, I have always found to be greatly attached to a food of a solid, earthy nature, such as bread, puddings, pies, tarts, cakes, and flour preparations in general. . . . Heavy, clumsy persons, whose movements—when they do move—are stiff and awkward are always great consumers of solid food, especially of bread and pastry of all kinds. . . . Among children and young persons too, it may be seen that the dull, heavy, ill-tempered ones are mostly great consumers of solid grain foods ; while the more active and lively are less anxious for food of a solid character, but mostly fond of light, fluid, saccharine substances. . . . These facts and many others which could be advanced, all tend to support and prove the position that food and drink alone are the source of the calcareous earthy matter which is generally deposited in the body, and which by degrees brings on a state of induration, rigidity and consequent decreptitude— which ends in a total cessation of consciousness, or death. We have seen that different kinds of food and drink contain these earthy elements in different proportions ; and we cannot avoid the conclusion that the more we subsist upon such articles as contain the greatest amount, the sooner shall we choke up and die ; and the more we live upon such substances as are comparatively free, the longer will health, activity and life continue."

In the twenty-second and twenty-third chapters of the third book of Herodotus, describing a visit of some Persian ambassadors to the long-lived Ethiopians (Macrobii), the Ethiopians asked what the Persian king was wont to eat, and to what age the longest-lived Persians had been known to attain. They told him that the king ate bread, and described the nature of wheat—adding that eighty years was the longest term of man's life among the Persians. Hereat, he remarked : " It did not surprise him, if they fed on *dirt* [bread] that they died so soon ! Indeed he was sure that they never would have lived so long as eighty years, except for the refreshment that they got from that drink [meaning the wine], wherein he confessed that Persians surpassed the Ethiopians."

From what has been said, it will be apparent why I do not consider grains and cereals valuable articles of food—far less the indispensable articles they are usually supposed to be. As generally purchased, these flours and grains are innutritious, clogging, and particularly unwholesome articles of food; but even at their best, and taking the whole grain, they contain nothing that cannot be supplied in a better state by an exclusive fruit and nut diet. We must remember Magendie's experiments on dogs. One died in forty days, while fed upon fine wheat and flour, while another dog, fed upon brown bread, lived without any disturbance, and in good health. This should show us conclusively that the fine flour upon the market—the flour invariably consumed—is practically useless as food; but since all the nutritive properties of grains may be derived in a better form from fruits, nuts, etc., the only remaining reason for eating grains and cereals vanishes.

XI

CONDIMENTS, SPICES, ETC.

WE now come to consider the various "food accessories," as they are called—meaning the various condiments, etc., which go to make unappetising food palatable! If the food were natural to the organism, it should need no such appetisers : but I let that pass. Let us consider the relative values of these articles of diet, and see how far each of them may be considered as necessary and beneficial to the human organism. I shall begin with the one in most common use, and one that the majority think they cannot live without—salt !

Salt.—The arguments in favour of salt-eating, as found in the books, may be summarised thus :

1. It is natural to man, the habit being universal.

2. It is necessary to life. Human beings deprived of it die.

8. Wild and domestic animals crave and seek it.

4. It is an invariable constituent of the solids and fluids of the body ; hence it must be supplied.

5. Cattle, when given it, increase greatly in weight, so that if not itself food, it may take the place of food by making it " go further."

6. It retards the waste of the system, and in this way may prolong life.

7. It is essential to promote the secretion and flow of saliva and bile.

8. It promotes appetite by rendering the food more palatable.

The first three of the above propositions constitute what may be styled the prescriptive or old-fashioned argument. The next four, grouped together, are the chemical theory of the value of salt, and are of more recent origin. The last, though seldom advanced as a scientific reason, partakes of the character of science as well as of tradition.

In regard to No. 1, let us see how far it is borne out. To destroy logically the value of the proposition it would only be necessary to establish the case of a single individual who does not and has not used salt—raw salt—in his food. The universality, that which it rests upon, would then be broken. We ought not to be content with that, however. I think it would not be difficult to show that there are whole nations and tribes of people who do not eat salt. I am told by an Italian, who has lived among them, that the Algerians do not. I was myself informed, while in that region, that the Indian tribes inhabiting the banks of the Columbia River and Puget Sound do not. It is noteworthy also that those tribes are among the most peaceful, intelligent and industrious tribes in North America, and are of fine personal appearance. I think there is little doubt that the inhabitants of the islands of the Pacific Ocean lived from a period of vast antiquity, until their discovery by Europeans, without putting salt crystals on their food. It has continually happened that hunters, tourists, soldiers and explorers have been left for weeks, months and years without a supply of salt, by accident or otherwise, and have survived without apparent injury. Finally, there are many persons in the United States who have voluntarily abandoned the use of salt for periods ranging from one to twenty years (and for aught I know longer), not only without injury but with increased health, strength and activity. So far from being natural to man, the instincts of children, especially when born free from an inherited bias in its favour, go to show by their rejection of it that it is *un*natural. Like the taste for coffee, tea and various seasonings, it is an acquired one. Few if any children do not prefer unsalted food.

It should not be overlooked that the manufacture and distribution of salt as an article of commerce is a thing of history, and has attained its enormous dimensions within the past century and a half. It is inconceivable that in past times the population of the world, made up as it was largely of pastoral and nomadic people inhabiting the interior of the great continents, should have supplied themselves with salt as an ingredient of food, as we do. The omission of any mention of it in the older chronicles and even among the more perfect records of the classics, except at the luxurious tables of the rich, goes to confirm this supposition.

Propositions Nos. 2 and 3 are of the same character, and have a like origin. It is discouraging to discover how little thorough sifting of beliefs there is among mankind —especially concerning matters of such primary importance as their daily diet—a neglect for which their hairsplitting casuistry on topics of faith and morals in no way atones. The foundation of the notion that men die when deprived of salt (and the inference therefrom that it is because of it), so far as I have been able to trace it, rests on an experience related in the older works on physiology, and copied with childlike confidence into the later ones, to the effect that, more than one hundred years ago, during the wars waged by England on the Continent, several thousand British soldiers, being shut up as prisoners of war in the low countries—at the Hague, I believe—and after an incarceration of many months, all died of disease, induced, it is stated, by being deprived of salt ! The same cry, it will be remembered, has been charged to modern nations in more recent wars, and notably during the American Civil War, when the mortality was so great in the southern prisons. It needs no great natural acumen nor book learning to discover that there are other and far more potent disease-inducing causes at work to account for the dreadful mortality—even in these days of superior civilisation and greater humanity. Observation satisfies me that inattention to ordinary sanitary precautions—partly incident to confinement and partly to the rooted superstition in the minds of those who had charge of them, that disease is a something to be fought out with specific medicines after it has appeared, rather than prevented from making its appearance—will abundantly reconcile the facts, if they be facts ; and in this I am confirmed by a comparison of the appalling ratio of mortality recorded in some of the most famed of London and Paris hospitals, where gangrene and fevers alone did their deadly work, in spite of the attentions of doctors, without appreciable aid from those inevitable attendants of war-prisons—homesickness, filth and bad diet. Such evidence as this would hardly be received in a trial for larceny ; and yet it is solemnly repeated generation after generation by those who should be teachers of teachers.

The third proposition, in regard to the wild and domestic animals, is, like the preceding, not formidable when examined. I have diligently inquired of old hunters and pioneers for confirmation of the story that deer and buffalo are in the habit of visiting regularly the salt springs or " licks," in order to eat the salt. I have not been able to find one who has ever seen the licking process himself. There is reason to believe that hunters do take their positions at certain brine-springs to find their game, and that the deer at certain seasons of the year resort to them—precisely why is not determined. Nothing of the kind is now claimed of the buffalo ; that is a tradition. But suppose it were all true, as claimed, does that justify man in sprinkling the solid residue of the brine on his food ? Is there not here too lofty a structure upon too slight a foundation ? It is notorious that all the salt springs hold in solution (sometimes found encrusted on their sides) large amounts of lime, sulphur, iron, and commonly other ingredients.

The very purest of our table salts of commerce contain from 2 to 4 per cent. of the sulphate of lime, after they are supposed to have been purified and larger amounts of it removed. May it not be that at certain seasons, as in the winter when the herbage is covered by snow, or during pregnancy, when the foetus requires it, the deer (or buffalo, if you will) repair to these spots instinctively for that which nature denies them at the time ? We know that cows on a scant pasture, at such times, will chew and partly dissolve an old bone ; yet it would be equally reasonable to put ground bones on our food as an inference from this trait ; indeed, more so, as the latter is an admitted fact of everyday occurrence, while the other is somewhat in doubt ; and besides the economy of lime in the system is patent.

In regard to domestic animals we are on more solid ground ; only it is constantly necessary to remember that we are dealing with creatures domesticated and subdued in some degree to the will of man. It is a common notion that salt is necessary to the well-being, if not the preservation, of horses and horned cattle. It is, I am persuaded, a great mistake. In the first place, although it is undoubtedly true that some domestic cattle will eat salt, and follow impatiently to get it, it is not true of wild cattle. I am assured by many of the great herders in Texas, Colorado and California, that the native cattle are not fed salt, never see it, and will not eat it if offered. Of course it is a transparent absurdity that salt could be hauled hundreds of miles to feed these great inland herds ; and it is not done, as is supposed. They derive salt enough from the grass of the plains to supply nature's demand, if any there be. This, if it

furnishes any analogy at all, points to the food itself
as the true source of supply for the human species.

But in regard to the craving of horses and cows kept
within fences, enclosures and buildings, it is susceptible
of proof, and has been proved many times, that it is an
artificial and not a natural appetite. I have seen both
horses and cows which will not eat salt if offered to
them. The parents, when the supply was cut off, did
not suffer perceptibly, and in a short time unlearned
the habit. Neither the old ones nor their progeny will
touch it now. I have not space here to enter into the
question of the great injury done to the health, and
consequently to the wholesomeness of the flesh of both
improved and native or Texas varieties of cattle, by
the pernicious practice of thrusting salt into their
food, while preparing for, or on the way to, market, in
order that the weight may be increased. It is worth
the while of the State to institute an inquiry to see if this
be not one of the provoking causes of the cattle diseases.
and rinderpests of America and Europe.

The tendency in the human mind—the more so with
the untrained intellect—to find the class of facts it is
seeking for, and to overlook or ignore the class which
makes against its preconceived notion or desire, is
always to be guarded against. It is a little singular
that the advocates of the salt habit should have selected
the one or two species of wild animals, and the two or
three allied species or varieties under domestication
which do or can be made to eat salt, while the vastly
greater number of both classes of animals which do
not and cannot be made to, are overlooked. True
enough, a hungry cow will eat what is called " salt hay,"
whereon the brine from the sea has crystallised, but invariably the same cow will turn from it to good well-
cured meadow hay. Hunger is a terrible temptation,
hence many of our animals (and the same is true of

children) acquire their taste for salt by its mixture with their food; and a reprehensible practice has begun of mixing salt, or lime, with the new hay in the stack in order to "cure" it—that is, to prevent its decay by excess of moisture—on the theory that the hay is improved thereby. Surely no argument can properly be drawn from appetites so engendered. On the same principle might we sprinkle sawdust with a horse's oats, because, if kept up, he will gnaw away the boards within reach. For this, by the way, there are good physiological reasons.

Look, however, at the other side of the argument as drawn from the lower animals. How numerous are they by whom salt is rejected or to whom it is hurtful? The whole of the birds avoid salt. It is fatal to chickens and tame birds, as every housewife knows. Indeed, there is strong ground for supposing that much of what is called " chicken cholera," " gapes," and the like, is in part due to the presence of salt—not always in minute quantities—in the food taken from the table. Wild birds have no such epidemic diseases affecting the mucous linings of their organs. It is also fatal to the hog, that foulest and hardiest of omnivora, which, out of some stress of famine, or from its peculiar prolificacy, men have been led to dwell with and propagate as a food supply. I believe it is well ascertained that when hogs get a moderate amount of brine, or pickled salt meat, it is impossible to save them. To vary the phrase a little: that which will make a hog sick cannot, *prima facie*, be good food for his owner. Of all the range of wild animals, clean or unclean, it is yet to be shown that a single one eats salt voluntarily as food. Why should man be the exception?

It is further claimed that salt is a necessary constituent of the diet, for the reason that, when the body is examined, *post-mortem*, a certain amount of salt is found

N

therein. From this it is argued that salt is therefore necessary to the human body ! It is queer logic. Were opium or nicotine found in the body of the dead man, would it be argued that *therefore* opium or nicotine were necessary to the body in health ? Yet the argument is just as logical, and the conclusion just as warranted.

All that can be urged, logically, is that salt is a necessary article of diet ; and that, no one would deny. Certainly I would not. But I must insist that this salt can be supplied to the body in its *organic* form—just as any other salt can. It is contained in fruits and vegetables, together with other salts : why not eat it in that way, just as we eat those other salts ? To be sure, we need common salt, just as we need iron, and potash, and sulphur, and lime, and other mineral salts ; but no one thinks of sprinkling lime and potash and iron filings over his food, just the same ! There is no more reason why we should sprinkle sodium chloride, or common salt, over our food, than there is why we should sprinkle any of these other salts. Both are equally mineral elements : both are inorganic substances ; and hence both are equally unusable by the system. Salt can have no more effect upon the economy than iron filings can ; and there is no more reason for taking the one into the system in this crude form than there is for taking the other. Only habit and prejudice sustain the custom.

It is urged, again, that salt preserves the waste of the tissues, and that animals, fed upon salt, become fat. There is but little evidence for this ; but I shall grant its truth, for the sake of argument. Granting it to be true, what then ?

We know that the antiseptic property of salt, its affinity for moisture, makes it valuable in the arts for some purposes, among which, of course, are conspicuous the preservation of dead animal meats. We see its

effect in the beef or pork barrel, or on dried fish.
It hardens and keeps dry the fibrous tissue so that
oxygen enough cannot be reached to oxidate and break
down the tissue by what is known as decomposition. If
the salt were all withdrawn by solutions of water (whatever might be the effect on the meat itself) there would
ensue no harm in its use in preserving food. Notoriously
it is not done, and even greater is the necessity for re-
moving the nitrate of potash with which the curing is
assisted.

Is not the action of the salt in the system on the effete
or dying tissues the same, in kind, as upon those in the
brine barrel ? I see nothing in the vital economy to
negative the presumption. The particles of dead and
oxidised tissue on their way out of the body, so far as
they are brought within the influence of the salt—and
this, as it floats in solution all over the body with the
blood, must be general—are robbed of their moisture,
dried, hardened, pickled, and their passage along the
finer canals made more difficult. They lodge and remain, and hence account, in part, for the increased weight
of the body. The added weight represents in part filth
which ought to be outside of the body, not inside.

Many other objections might be urged to the use of
salt, in this place ; but space forbids. When anyone
examines the evidence carefully and impartially, he
will find that there is not one solitary argument in
favour of the habit that will stand the test of criticism ;
while there are many arguments, on the contrary, which
conclusively prove it to be injurious and unphysiological.
The single argument, based upon the undoubted *fact*
that many hundreds of people in the United States,
and elsewhere, have totally abandoned salt, and have not
depreciated themselves in consequence, but have, on
the contrary, improved their health and general physical
condition, is proof in itself that salt-eating is a habit—

is not necessary, but is, on the other hand, positively injurious. When we take these facts into consideration, we can come to no other conclusion but that salt-eating is a *habit*, pure and simple, which is not only unnecessary, but is exceedingly detrimental to the physical health of the individual who continually eats it.

Pepper is not, like salt, a mineral substance ; it is a vegetable poison. Flies will not touch it, neither will they eat salt. Black pepper, if taken upon an empty stomach in the moderate quantity of a teaspoonful, will either be promptly ejected, or it will cause great disturbance in the stomach and bowels, and also in the heart's action, after it enters the circulation. It is in no sense a food, but in every sense a stimulant, which is but another name for a substance non-usable by the vital organs, and therefore to be thrown out of the vital domain. Red or black pepper is a prolific cause, as are all stimulants, of enlargement of the blood vessels, and ultimately of disease of the heart. Its immediate effect upon the tongue, throat, stomach and bowels is to cause an increased action, not only of the capillaries, causing temporary congestion and even inflammation of the mucous surfaces, but also of the organs which secrete the digestive fluids. Its ultimate effect is to weaken and deaden these organs, by repeated stimulation, to abnormal action ; it also impairs or destroys the organs of taste within the mouth, together with the gastric or other nerves which aid in the process of digestion. When these are weakened by stimulants, the functions themselves are necessarily impaired, and confirmed dyspepsia, with its attendant train of bad symptoms, brings up the rear.

It is needless to say that *ginger, spices, nutmeg, cinnamon,* and all that class of condiments, however much they may vary in quality, are stimulating to a greater or a less degree, and must be put in the list of " things forbidden " in the hygienic dietary. The habit, every year increasing, of using spices and condiments in almost every article of food, and in such large quantities, cannot be too severely condemned. The end must be hopeless indigestion, with prostration of the nerves which supply the digestive organs, and detriment or ruin to the entire system.

In the language of Sylvester Graham :

" The stern truth is, that no purely stimulating substance of any kind can be habitually used by man, without injury to the whole nature."

Nor does Dr Graham stand alone in his views upon this subject. Pereira says :

" The relish for flavouring or seasoning ingredients manifested by every person, would lead us to suppose that these substances serve some useful purpose beyond that of merely gratifying the palate. At present, however, we have no evidence that they do. They stimulate, but do not seem to nourish. The volatile oil they contain is absorbed, and then thrown out of the system, still possessing its characteristic odour."

Dr Beaumont is essentially of the same opinion. He remarks :

" Condiments, particularly those of a spicy kind, are non-essential to the process of digestion in a healthy state of the system. They afford no nutrition. Though they may assist the action of a debilitated stomach for a time, their continued use never fails to produce an indirect debility of that organ. They affect it as alcohol and other stimulants do—the present relief afforded is at the expense of future suffering."

In doing away with spices and condiments we must also dispense with *pickles* ; 'there is nothing in a pickle to redeem it from hopeless condemnation. The spices in it are bad, and the vinegar is a seething mass of rottenness, full of animalculæ, and the poor little innocent cucumber, or other vegetable, if it had a little " character " in the beginning, must now fall into the ranks of the " totally depraved."

Mustard.—Dr William Tibbles, in his " Food and Hygiene," p. 218, says :

" Mustard is a greenish yellow powder, without smell, when it is dry, but when moist, having a pungent taste and penetrating odour, which is irritating to the nose and eyes. Mustard is the most familiar of all condiments. It produces a sensation of warmth in the mouth and stomach and augments the digestive secretions, by increasing the circulation in the blood-vessels in the alimentary canal. It increases the appetite and the desire for food, and assists in its digestion."

In other words, what really happens is this : Mustard is an irritant and a stimulant to the mucous membranes at all times, and for that reason, harmful. Delicate membranes, such as those of the nose and eyes, detect and resent this irritation at once ; but the throat and stomach, being rendered more or less inert and unresponsive, because of years of perverse living on cooked foods, spices, stimulants, and irritants, do not resent and react against this particular irritant as forcibly as do the other membranes. The fact, however, that the secretion is increased, and that the circulation in the blood vessels of the stomach is augmented, clearly indicates that nature is endeavouring to offset and rid the system as speedily as possible of this irritant poison. When any poison is introduced into the alimentary canal, the system immediately pours out its secretions, in an attempt to liquefy, antidote, and wash through the invading poison as rapidly as possible. That is the *rationale* of the action of all purgatives, and is the reason why increased secretion and circulation is noted whenever stimulants or irritants are introduced into the alimentary canal. The very fact that these physiological disturbances take place indicates clearly that the substance that has been ingested is poisonous, and detrimental to the vital economy. For that reason, and because of these symptoms, mustard must be debarred from any hygienic diet ; and for the same reason, white, black, and cayenne pepper, paprika, cloves, nutmeg, curry powder, garlic, salt, and similar substances must be eliminated from any diet that is to be considered wholesome, and in accordance with the laws of nature.

Indeed, in writing of all condiments, Dr Tibbles himself was forced to admit that :

" Healthy individuals with normal digestion do not need them, and they should most certainly be withheld from children."

I would add to this that if they are to be withheld from healthy individuals and children, they should most certainly and more particularly be withheld from invalids, and from the debilitated and enfeebled. Were the true *rationale* of the action of stimulants understood, this would be so apparent as to render further comment unnecessary. If it were once fully understood that stimulants, instead of adding energy *to* the system, merely called it forth *from* the system, there could no longer be any excuse for their use, upon the ground that they are necessary and suitable articles of food. Condiments and spices of all kinds might easily be eliminated from a hygienic diet, and nothing but increased health and energy would follow the results of this process of elimination.

Vinegar.—So far from being a true article of food, or an alimentary substance, vinegar, like alcohol, is a product of vegetable decay, and is always injurious to the human stomach. In addition to this, it contains a large number of germs which, introduced into the system, are liable to cause great havoc. If acid is required, it may be obtained in a variety of forms, and is readily supplied by all acid fruits, and particularly by lemons. The citric acid of the lemon is appropriable by the system, and is one of the most wholesome acids known to us. It will readily take the place of vinegar—on occasions where we have been in the habit of using the latter substance. It should be noted in this connection that lemon juice, when ingested into the human system, is invariably split up, in the course of a few hours, and the all-day effects of the acid is to *decrease* the acidity of the system, and to increase the alkalinity of the blood. This was conclusively proved by Dr Haig, in England, and now forms a large part of his treatment for all uric acid diatheses. The immediate effect of the acid is to increase the acidity ; but, owing to the fact that it is split up, as stated, the all-day effects are invariably to decrease the acidity, and rid the system of its uric acid. No such beneficial results are observable from the practice of drinking vinegar.

Oils—Olive Oil.—Under " oils " may be classed, roughly speaking, all fats, animal and vegetable, such as suet, lard, tallow, marrow, grease, butter, blubber, and the oils of various nuts. Animal oils are amongst the least nutritious, and most injurious kinds of alimentary substances. The oils from the vegetable kingdom are far more wholesome, and, to a normal stomach, almost innocuous. If oils or fatty matter of any kind are desired in the diet, these might just as well be supplied from the vegetable world as from the animal ; and the oils are obtained free from the impure materials, which invariably accompany animal fats. In other words, the same amount of fatty materials may be obtained, without ingesting at the same time the toxic substances which invariably accompany the fats derived from the animal kingdom. Of those fats which are derived from the animal world, more or less directly, butter and cream are doubtless the most wholesome ; but there are many objections to both of these, as I have pointed out elsewhere.

Olive oil, when obtained pure, is doubtless the best form of oil that we know. The chief difficulty is in obtaining it in a pure state. Cotton seed oil is generally sold on the market in place of olive oil, and is in many ways detrimental to the organism. " Sylmar " olive oil is a pure oil of the first quality, made from ripe olives, and can heartily be recommended. A few of the best French and Italian oils are also excellent, if they are obtained direct and unadulterated.

The ripe olive contains just what an ordinary vegetarian—especially fruit—diet lacks. In being a wholesome source of fat they materially add to the value of other vegetarian dishes. Nuts also supply oils in a healthful form. Those oils are serviceable in nervous disorders, rheumatism, diabetes, and other diseases.

XII

THE FRUITARIAN DIET

ANYONE who has followed me through the preceding chapters will probably have come to the conclusion that there is no article of diet left which he can live upon and eat without detriment! Apparently everything has been condemned in turn. Meat, game, fish, shellfish, soups of all kinds, vegetables, grains, flours, cereals, milk, cheese, butter, eggs and dairy products of all kinds, stimulants, spices, jellies—all have been examined in turn, and found unsuitable for human food. But man must live, and the question remains: Are there *any* foods which he can eat freely and live—not only without detriment to himself, but with positive benefit—feeling assured that they are upbuilding his body, his mind, and his energies, and sustaining his physiological integrity, throughout, in a wholesome and natural manner? It will be seen in going over the list that two important articles of diet have been omitted—viz. fruits and nuts. These, and these alone, supplemented, perhaps, by one or two other articles of diet, can, I contend, sustain man in a perfect state of health; can supply all the needs of his body, and preserve the highest standard of health and energy; while the diet is in accord with his physiological mechanism, and his anatomical structure. The one or two articles of diet that might be added (though I do not consider it necessary that they should be added) are honey, olive oil, and, occasionally, perhaps, whole-wheat bread. It is an interesting fact that there are only two articles of diet in the world, apparently, made exclusively for food—milk and honey. The milk is to nourish the young of the animal which secretes it, and normally the supply would be terminated when the animal was weaned—if nature were not perverted, and the process of milking instituted. But we have considered milk as an article of diet in the former pages. Honey is manufactured by the bees for the express purpose of supplying them with food during the winter months, and man only obtains his supply by robbing the bees of their hard-earned food, and substituting other food in its place. Honey contains a large amount of valuable saccharine material, and I have endeavoured to show on a previous page that a certain amount of saccharine matter, or sweet-stuff, is necessary for the maintenance of health —probably a larger quantity than we are in the habit of supposing. This, honey will supply. It may be noted, however, that certain sweet fruits, notably dates, also contain large amounts of sugar, and if a quantity of dates were eaten, they would doubtless supply all the demands of the system for sugar, without recourse to honey at all. Olive oil is a suitable and nutritive food, when pure. Its chief value, of course, consists in the large amount of oil or fatty matter it contains, but this is also contained in nuts of various kinds in a pure form, and hence is not a necessary article of diet. As found on the market, moreover, it is generally impure and adulterated. Whole-wheat bread has certain advantages, but is also open to numerous objections, as before pointed out ; and, if made from the whole grain, including the husk, it acts as an irritant on the mucous membrane of the bowel, and hence exercises a slightly purgative action ; the same action, however, may be induced by a plentiful supply of non-irritating fruit juices, and for that reason they are consequently to be preferred. We thus come to the conclusion that, although these few remaining articles of diet are not positively pernicious, as are the general run of foods, they are, nevertheless, of secondary importance, and can readily be dispensed with, and their place taken by simple fruits and nuts.

If any lingering doubt exists in the minds of those upholding a strict fruitarian dietary, as to its sufficiently nutritive value, these doubts have been cleared away by the investigations of Professor M. E. Jaffa, of the University of California. His researches, published by the U.S. Department of Agriculture, make an epoch in the history of dietetics, and his researches are most conclusive. In his " Nutrition Investigations Among the Fruitarians and Chinese," he says, in part :

" It would appear upon examining the recorded data and comparing the results with commonly accepted standards, that all the subjects were (*i.e.* should have been) decidedly under-nourished, even making allowances for their little weight. But when we consider that the two adults have lived upon this diet for 7 years, and think they are in better health and capable of more work than they ever were before, we hesitate to pronounce judgment. The three children, though below the average in height and weight, had the appearance of health and strength. They ran and jumped and played all day like ordinary healthy children, and were said to be unusually free from colds and other complaints incident to childhood." [1]

Professor Jaffa then showed that N. was actually *stored* on this diet, although these fruitarians were eating but two meals a day, in place of the usual three of civilised people. He stated (what I have invariably found to be the case) that *less food* was required and

[1] It is an error—though a common one—to suppose that the fruitarian diet causes a loss of weight. My own weight has remained about the same for ten years, no matter what I eat, or how much. On this diet the weight will go *to normal*—and, generally speaking, it is necessary that some weight should be lost, in order to effect this.

was eaten, than is the case with ordinary cooked foods. Further, many of his subjects were found actually to *gain* weight—one patient seven pounds in less than three months! Professor Jaffa was forced to the conclusion that fruits must be considered as *true foods*, and not mere food accessories; and was bound to admit that they alone (with nuts) can sustain a healthy and vigorous life.

" While it is true that 10 cents will buy more animal protein than fruit protein, it will on the average purchase fully as much energy, when spent for fresh fruits, and more in the case of dried fruits than when expended for lean meats. When considering nuts, it is readily observed that 10 cents will buy about the same amount of nut protein as of animal protein, except in the case of cheese and skim milk. If spent on peanuts, it will furnish more than twice the protein and six times the energy that could be bought for the same expenditure for porter-house steak." [1]

I would also refer the reader to Professor C. F. Longworthy's " Fruit and its Uses as Food " (Year-book, U.S. Dept. of Agr.).

Speaking of the value of fruit, Dr Tibbles, in his " Food and Hygiene," p. 174, says :

" The value and importance of fresh fruit, especially to dwellers in towns, cannot be too freely written about. . . . The organic salts in fruit arouse the appetite, and aid digestion, by increasing the flow of saliva, and, indirectly, of the gastric juice; they are stimulants and sialagogues. As the fruit reaches the intestines, the acids increase the activity of the chyme, and stimulate the secretions of the liver and the pancreas, the intestinal glands and muscles; their influence upon the blood is marked: they render it less alkaline, but *never acid*. By combining with a portion of the alkaline salts of the serum, the phosphoric acid increases the phosphates in

[1] " Further Investigations Among Fruitarians," etc., p. 79.

the red blood cells ; they are anti-scorbutic and of value in anæmia, general debility, and convalescence from acute illness. Fruits containing oxalates, as tomatoes, gooseberries and strawberries, are useful in amenorrhœa and for persons subject to bronchitis and asthma ; such as contain salicylic acid—as strawberries, raspberries, currants, blackberries, and oranges—are a valuable addition to the dietary of rheumatic persons. The final stage in the digestion of fruit is the conversion of fruit acids and salts into alkaline salts, chiefly carbonates ; they are therefore useful in scurvy, rheumatism, gout, and other diseases of the uric acid diathesis ; they increase the secretion of the urine and its alkalinity—indeed they are one of the most certain agents to render it alkaline, to stimulate the kidneys, and indirectly the skin, and thereby increase the total excretion of salts and other materials. Briefly, fresh fruit is cooling, refreshing, and tends to correct constipation."

Only recently, at the Congress of Surgery, Paris, 1909, Dr Victor Pauchet, surgeon of the American Hospital, stated—when indicating what in his opinion were the ideal bodily conditions for the successful performance of an operation—that it was necessary for the subject to have the colon and rectum empty ; the bowels free from gas ; the liver and kidneys washed with pure water in proper quantities, etc., and then went on to say :

" . . . It is necessary to give foods, which, besides being devoid of toxins, should at the same time be a bad culture-medium for intestinal germs. These conditions are fulfilled by a vegetable or especially a fruit régime. Fruit juice is a purer water than that of the best spring. Glucose is the best assimilated food. It is the sustaining, diuretic and nontoxic food. Fruits should be taken fresh, ripe and of good quality. If unavailable, cooked dry fruits with a little sugar." [1]

[1] "La réforme alimentaire," vol. xiii., No. 2. For much valuable information on this subject consult Dr J. L. Buttner's book, "A Fleshless Diet" (1910).

The general advantages of fruit as food—instead of the usual cooked diet—have been so far enumerated, and are so numerous, that it would seem almost unnecessary to dwell upon the advantages of each fruit in turn. The whole system being so much superior, this detailed defence would seem unnecessary. Nevertheless, in order to show the great superiority of this diet, it may be well to enumerate some of the beneficial effects of each fruit in turn, and point out, briefly, some of their many excellent qualities. Let us see what these are.

Apples have been called the "king of fruits." They contain an abundance of potash, soda and magnesia, also phosphorus, and for this reason have been considered especially valuable for nerve and brain food. The natural acid of the apple is excellent for the teeth and gums; also for the stomach and intestines. It seems to possess a great antiseptic and germicidal quality. They do not increase the acidity in the stomach, but, on the contrary, decrease it. They possess fine tonic properties, and are a valuable food, at the same time. Apples are naturally laxative, and the proportions of their composition are more clearly adjusted to the human constitution than any other single fruit. It is almost possible to live upon apples alone, and an exclusive apple dietary might be tried for some time during every summer, at least. In the form of cider they supply us with almost the only wholesome article of drink, besides water, that can be found.

The *banana* is a very heavy food, and must be eaten with discretion. It has been called the "bread of the tropics," and this fact must be borne in mind when they are being consumed in large quantities. One must be sure that the banana is sound and thoroughly ripe when eaten—so soft, almost, as to be taken with a spoon. The skin should be almost black, and this should be peeled back, and the outside of the fruit scraped with a knife, cleaning it of the soft, pulpy covering about a sixteenth of an inch thick all round the fruit, which is highly indigestible. Bananas do not agree with many persons, and when this is found to be the case they should be avoided; but when they have been treated in the manner indicated, it will be found that many persons can eat them, when formerly this was impossible. Bananas should be very thoroughly masticated, and possibly mashed up with a fork before they are eaten. They combine well with but few foods, and generally should be eaten alone. Under such conditions, bananas will be found a highly nourishing and valuable food.

Pears, quinces, plums, damsons, peaches, apricots, cherries and *grapes,* all contain a fairly high percentage of carbohydrates, and a high percentage of valuable food-salts. As is well known, it is possible to live upon grapes alone for several weeks at a time, as has been abundantly proved at the various resorts where the " grape cure " is taken. At such places, several pounds of grapes are eaten daily, and in phthisis and other wasting diseases this cure has been attended with some remarkable results. Sweet grapes are exceedingly valuable as a food: they contain a large percentage of water in the purest form; they also contain glucose, or grape-sugar, in a condition in which it is readily assimilated into the circulation. Instead of eating great quantities of starch, therefore, which requires much effort for proper conversion into this same grape juice within the body, why not eat the grapes themselves—thereby obtaining this material in its original and purest form ? In chronic bronchitis, heart disease, gastric and intestinal atony, and frequently in Bright's disease, grapes are very beneficial.

Raspberries and *strawberries* contain a large amount of acid, and for that reason must be eaten with discrimination, especially at first. Yet they are as a rule an exceptionally wholesome fruit, their natural acidity clearing the blood of uric acid and kindred poisons, and acting as a natural tonic and stimulant. The strawberry also contains a large quantity of iron, and for that reason is very valuable for anæmic patients. There are a few individuals who cannot eat strawberries without unpleasant consequences. Needless to say, such persons should refrain from eating them, though the fault in such cases is probably more in the patient than in the fruit.

The *pineapple* is a spurious fruit, or rather a collection of berries, each corresponding to a flower which, under cultivation, is seedless. The juice is highly antiseptic, and of great benefit in certain affections of the throat. In diphtheria it appears to be especially valuable, the juice possessing a cleansing quality of remarkable power. Its effect upon diseased mucous is very noticeable, yet, strange to say, its action upon healthy mucous, in limited quantities, is quite harmless and rather invigorating. This is proved by the fact that pineapple juice has often been given to babies less than a year old, with nothing but beneficial results.

The great value of *oranges* and *lemons* is now beginning to be appreciated. In all uric acid diatheses, the juice of either one of these fruits—particulary lemons—is exceedingly beneficial, and Dr Haig, of London, strongly recommends lemonade and lemon juice for gout, rheumatism, etc., throughout his writings. Lemon juice has also been advocated as a curative agency in malaria—this having the support of so orthodox an organ as *The Lancet*. It is now frequently administered in cases of diphtheria, since it has been found to afford great relief to the sore and

o

inflamed throat and gullet. Lemons are strongly germicidal and antiseptic, and, although their immediate effect is to increase the acidity of the blood, curiously enough, their all-day effect is to increase its alkalinity. The juice of oranges is antiscorbutic, and is said to be valuable in influenza. A patient can live on oranges alone for several weeks together, while the juice is free from the excessive acidity noticed in the lemon.

Bilberries, whortleberries, cranberries, mulberries, gooseberries, etc., are all more or less laxative and soothing, and some of them especially valuable in affections of the throat.

Raisins and *currants,* properly speaking, belong to the class of dried fruits, and possess all the advantages and disadvantages they possess.

Rhubarb, strictly speaking, is not a fruit, but might be classed with fruit. It is slightly tonic and aperient.

Melons contain but little nutriment, but, on the contrary, nothing deleterious.

Citrons and *limes* possess very much the same properties as oranges and lemons, and are now considered of undoubted value in scurvy and rheumatism, and for checking nausea and vomiting.

The *tomato,* which might be classed as a fruit, contains a large amount of saccharine matter, and salts, and is stated to have beneficial effects upon the secretions of the liver.

Figs contain from 60 to 70 per cent. of sugar, and are very nutritive. They also contain some valuable food-salts. *Dates* are the great sources of sugar in the fruit kingdom. They are very nutritious and also contain valuable food-salts.

Coming now to *nuts,* they are, as before pointed out, the great source of proteid—outside meat and certain legumes. When thoroughly masticated, they are a wholesome and very nutritious article of diet. They are less liable to cause indigestion when they form the sole element of the meal, or when mixed only with fruit, than when eaten in combination with any other food. They contain practically the elements of a perfect food in due proportion—supplying the system with proteids, fats, carbohydrates and salts in a concentrated form, with but little waste. In addition to the nitrogenous matter which they contain, they are also a valuable, and in fact the chief, source of fats. Brazil nuts, almonds, filberts, pecans, walnuts, etc., all contain about the same proportions of carbohydrates, fats and proteids, and all contain valuable food-salts. On the whole, it may be said that they are the most valuable articles of food that we know, and when supplemented by a few fruits, form a perfect and nutritious diet. Occasionally, it may be found that nuts disagree or cause gastric disturbance. In such cases, various nut-butters may be substituted, or the nut-food omitted altogether for a few weeks, as it is more than probable, in such cases, that the system is already overstocked with nitrogenous matter. But I believe that, if properly masticated, eaten in limited quantities, and judiciously combined with a small number of other foods—especially fruits—it will be found that they do not disagree, but, on the contrary, are a sustaining and nourishing food—in fact *the most* sustaining and nourishing food that can be found.

Fruit juices are especially cooling and refreshing in the heat of summer. They supply organic fluids to the system, in the form of water, combined with organic salts, and this water is the purest that we know. Sour fruits of all kinds are especially valuable in cases of biliousness, inactive liver, thickening of the blood, and general clogging-up of the system. They are especially valuable in cases of disordered digestion.

Fruits should not be cooked, but eaten raw, and upon an empty stomach, or combined with nuts. When combined with cooked foods, and especially with vegetables, they tend to create, as we have seen, gastric disturbances. The cooking of fruits ruins many of their most valuable properties. Ordinary sugar should never be added to fruits, since it excites fermentation ; and, for cooking purposes, if fruits are cooked and it is desired to sweeten them, dates may be added for this purpose. By all means fruit should be avoided at the end of a meal consisting of a combination of foods, and particularly of cooked foods ; they are sure to disagree, and the fruits will then get blamed for the whole disturbance !

Sylvester Graham, in writing of fruits as food, says :

" It should always be remembered that fruit of every description, if eaten at all, should be eaten as food, and not as mere pastime, or merely for the sake of gustatory enjoyment ; and therefore it should, as a general rule, be eaten at the table, or constitute a portion of the regular meal. . . . All cooked food, even under the best regulations, impairs in some degree the power of the stomach to digest uncooked substances ; and therefore, so long as we are accustomed to cooked food of any kind, we must be somewhat more careful in regard to the times when we eat fruit and other substances in their natural state."

Now, if we compare the fruitarian dietary—meaning by this a diet composed of fruit and nuts, in their natural and uncooked state—with other diets, we shall ascertain the following facts :—

First, that such a diet is suited to man because of his anatomical and physiological structure. We have seen in Chapters II. and III. that, were we to judge from his anatomy and physiology, man must be classed as a frugivorous animal—with the higher apes—and that he is totally dissimilar in construction to any of the other animals.

Second. By comparing these foods with other food-stuffs, we found, in the chapter on the chemistry of foods, that all the elements essential for sustaining the physiological integrity were supplied by a judicious fruitarian diet—the proteids, carbohydrates and fats all being supplied by such foods.

Third. While all these elements are supplied, we do not ingest into the system at the same time injurious toxic substances as we do in the case of meats; or enormous quantities of fibrous, indigestible elements, as we do in the case of vegetables; or innutritious and constipating substances, as we do in all starchy foods. In addition to this, condiments and spices are not called for, and in fact cannot well be eaten with such foods. The oils and fats furnished by this diet are also pure, and are free from all the objections that can be raised to these same substances when derived from the animal kingdom.

As a further argument, it will be found that *less food* in quantity is eaten and called for upon this diet, and that the system is in less danger of becoming surfeited, blocked and choked with an excess of food-matter. Fruits are also easily digestible, and act as a stimulant upon the various internal organs, and as a mild aperient. They also contain the minimum amount of earthy matter, which various authors have contended is the chief cause of obstruction, induration, ossification, premature old age and natural death.

It will thus be seen that there are many advantages, and no disadvantages, to this diet. Since it contains all the elements which the system requires in a purer and better form, and can be assimilated with less energy; and since, moreover, it does not engender any of the diseased states or conditions which result from an ordinary diet, it will be seen that this system presents many advantages over any other so far presented—or, in fact, any other that can be formulated.   In addition to this, and one very strong argument in favour of the fruitarian diet, is the fact that a certain *vital energy*—too subtle to be analysed by the chemist, and which will only be recognised by science when it becomes less materialistic —is imparted, upon a raw fruitarian diet, which is invariably lost whenever food of any kind is cooked. Dr Graham, in his " Science of Human Life," was probably the first to call attention to this fact.   He said :

" It may be laid down as a general law that all processes of cooking, or artificial preparation of foods by fire, are, in themselves, considered with reference to the very highest and best condition of human nature, in some degree detrimental to the physiological and psychological interests of man."

He insists, further, that if man lived upon uncooked foods, he would have to use his teeth, and would therefore preserve them ; he would masticate his food more thoroughly, and by thorough insalivation fit it for the stomach ; he would swallow it slowly, instead of bolting it down in a crude condition ; he would take it at a proper temperature, and not weaken the stomach with hot food ; he would eat the food as nature prepares it, not served in the form of a highly concentrated aliment ; he would partake of the simple, individual food substances, and would not suffer from all manner of injurious combinations ; and finally, he would be less likely to suffer from over-eating than he would if he lived upon soft, cooked foods.   There can be no question that the thorough mastication of nuts, which is rendered necessary by their nature, is one of the best means possible of preserving and strengthening both the teeth and the gums.

Dr Gustave Schlickeysen, in his " Fruit and Bread," has adduced very strong arguments in favour of an uncooked fruitarian diet. Writing of the advantages of such a diet, he says :

" Of all the artificial forms of treatment to which foods are subjected, that of cooking is the most universal and therefore demands our special attention. If we rightly consider the influence of this process upon all the natural properties of a plant, we must perceive that it is, in almost every case, injurious, and that it must be dispensed with, so far as our present habits of life will admit of, with a view of its final and complete disuse. The natural fluids of the plant are in great part lost in cooking, and with them the natural aroma so agreeable to the senses and so stimulating to the appetite. The water supplied artificially does not possess the same properties as that which has been lost, and all the less so since it has been boiled. The cellular tissue of the plant loses also its vitality, and ripe, uncooked fruits and grains with their unbroken cellular tissue, their stimulating properties, their great content of water, sugar and acids, and their electrical vitality are calculated to supply to the human body a rosy freshness ; to the skin a beautiful transparence, and to the whole muscular system the highest vigour and elasticity. Uncooked fruits especially excite the mind to its highest activity. After eating them we experience an inclination to vigorous exercise, and also an increase of capacity for study and all mental work—while cooked food causes a feeling of satiety and sluggishness. Not only do plants lose their vital, but to some extent also their nutritive properties when cooked. The vegetable acids and oils, the latter being of especial value in the development of the bony structure of the body, are, by cooking, dissipated ; while the albuminoids are coagulated, and thereby less easily digested, so that the nutritive value of the food is reduced to a minimum. Another injury that results from cooked food is that caused by artificial heat. All heat excites, through expansion, an increased activity, but this activity is not normal in the case of food eaten hot.

" Again, the sensory nerves of the lips and the nerves of taste are weakened by hot food to such an extent that they no longer serve as an infallible test of its quality, and hence articles that seem in the mouth to be palatable and good may be very injurious to the system, both on account of their natural properties and their artificial heat.   In a similar manner the sense of smell is blunted ; and not less injuriously does hot food act upon the teeth, the enamel of which is destroyed, rendering them unfit for their work of mastication, in consequence of which the food passes unprepared into the stomach.   The eyes are also injured by the action of hot food upon the nerves connected with them.   That condition of weak and watery eyes, so apparent in the habitual drunkard, exist in a certain degree in all whose systems are enervated by hot and stimulating food..   But the greatest harm from hot food is caused in the stomach itself, the coats of which are irritated, reddened, and unnaturally contracted by the heat, so that they lose their vigorous activity and capacity for the complete performance of their natural functions.   The blood, excited by the heat, flows in excess to the stomach, and thence feverishly through the body.   One result of this is the flushed condition of the head after eating. Hot food also causes an excess in eating, so that it is rather by a sense of fullness and oppression than by a natural satisfaction of the appetite that one is prompted to cease eating.   An evidence of the weakening of the stomach by hot food is seen when one eats an apple after the usual hot meal.   Fruit thus taken lies like a stone upon the stomach, the enfeebled nerves being injuriously affected by its presence ; whereas in their normal condition, they are stimulated to a most agreeable activity by it.

" From the abuse of the organs of digestion result a number of diseases.   A life-long weakness of the gastric nerves, with cramps and inflammation of the stomach, are its common fruits.   To this cause also is attributable the almost universal prevalence of colds, which are the direct result of unnatural temperatures of the body. The blood, artificially heated, causes an excessive perspiration, since it produces increased but injurious activity of the skin; and upon the least change of temperature the perspiration is condensed upon the body, and causes colds and stiffness, and this is all the more certainly so when the blood is impure and the tissues overloaded. From the same prolific cause results the uneasiness and languor experienced after eating hot food. The evil effect cannot be overcome by the usual after-dinner nap. This cannot replace the elements lost from our food, nor give the enlivening impulse experienced after partaking of ripe fruits in their natural state.

" It is indeed argued that our northern climate requires that food should be eaten hot as one means of maintaining the bodily temperature; but if this be true of man, it must apply with equal force to all animals; and since man alone seems to require hot food, the argument loses its force. In the polar regions the conditions of animal life show plainly that the natural process of generating heat is not by putting heated substances into the stomach, but by the normal action of the vital forces upon food taken in its natural state. Greater thirst is experienced after eating cooked than uncooked food, and this results both from the change that the food has undergone, and from the perspiration caused by the increased heat of the body. The artificial solution of the food impairs its nutritive properties, and weakens the natural functions of the body by depriving them of their natural employment; and this has been so long continued that we are now almost incapable of digesting uncooked grains, so that their enlivening and invigorating action is almost unknown."

Dr Schlickeysen argues very strongly for what he terms the " electrical vitality " of food, which he contends—I think rightly—is ruined by cooking. He says:

" Finally—and this is a point which physiologists have hitherto quite overlooked—the food must contain

a certain *electrical vitality*. Although the real origin
and nature of the vital force is not yet known, we believe that it is closely related to electricity; not less
so, indeed, than to light and heat. Electricity is
abundant in all purely natural products, and indeed,
everywhere where a free and uninterrupted exchange of
the influences of light, heat, and air, exist. It is less
abundant in closed dwelling and sleeping rooms than
in the open air. An outdoor walk refreshes us, not only
by the increased consumption of oxygen, but by the
increased action of the electrical forces. The same
vitality is stored up in uncooked plants and fruits, but
it is greatly impaired by all our culinary processes.
Fruits act also through their natural acids, their refreshing coolness, and the easy assimilation of their
albuminous products, and other nourishing materials.

" By the ' electrical vitality ' of food we do not mean
its nutritive worth, nor indeed any material element of
it, but rather an imponderable fluid, which is related
to the vital and electrical forces of the human system.
The organic vital force has not incorrectly been called
the interrogation point of physiology, and the physiologists and chemists of the old school thought to maintain
this force by supplying albuminoids to the system.
The fact, however, is the reverse. The albuminoids
demand rather a great expense of vitality for their
solution and digestion. We know now, with great
certainly, and by practical experience, that the human
system is maintained and strengthened by the consumption of fresh air, fresh water, and ripe fruits, and
grains; but these essential means of sustenance are
reduced from the rank of vital to merely nutritive substances by any treatment that, through heat or otherwise, destroys their natural vitality. Our physiologists
have not hitherto understood this difference between the
vital and the merely nutritive properties of food, and
hence, as we have already pointed out, have regarded
foods as merely chemical substances. They have dis-
covered and laid down with wonderful exactness, the
chemical elements of the living body, and hence of the
food requisite, according to their views, to its mainten-

ance ; but we hope to show that their methods and consequently their dietetic conclusions, have been one-sided,
and therefore essentially erroneous. So long as the
electrical vitality of food is overlooked, and the bearings
of anthropology upon the question is ignored, a scientific
system of diet must remain impossible." [1]

This whole question of the injurious effect in cooking
food may be summed up in a very few words. Heat
destroys the life and vitality of the food, and practically nothing is left but the " ashes," as it were, which
are dead, inert, and comparatively of far less food value
than the raw foods. It can readily be seen why this
must be so. At a temperature of 150° F., certain
properties of all organic substances are destroyed, or
even at a temperature below this. This can readily be
proved in the case of all living organisms, and it is also
true, to a large extent, in the case of all vegetables,
fruits, and other organic compounds, whose life is also
destroyed at these high temperatures. A leaf of cabbage
immersed in water not too hot to be borne by the hand
will wilt. The effects of heat upon all flowers can very
readily be seen. Their life becomes extinct, and the
vital properties of all organic substances must be ruined
by subjecting them to the tremendous heat necessary
for cooking them. A large part of the nutritive value of
the substance cooked is thus ruined, while, in many
cases, valuable nutritive material passes out of the
substance into the water in which it is cooked, or escapes
altogether. It will thus be seen that, from the physiological and chemical sides of this question alone, there
are many strong reasons for believing that the cooking
of food is injurious, lowering its nutritive value, and

[1] If this theory were true, it would agree very well with Professor
Loeb's recent physiological researches. He has come to the conclusion that the energy of food-stuffs is not due to the production of
heat, or to chemical energy, but to electrically charged molecules.
This would seem to agree very well with the theory outlined above.

ruining many of its most valuable properties. But since fruits are almost the only.form of food that can be eaten in a raw state—or rather as cooked by nature— this would indirectly prove that fruit is man's natural diet, thus agreeing with his anatomical structure ; and the fruitarian diet would, on the other hand, indicate that a raw-food diet is the best that man can adopt. When we come to consider the fact that no other animal cooks his food, and that the higher apes—man's dietetic counterpart—eats his fruits and nuts in a raw state, we can readily see that there is no valid reason, apart from custom, for man cooking his food—so long as the natural or fruitarian dietary be adopted at all. It is curious to note the attitude various authorities have taken upon this subject, when writing of foods in relation to man's relative place in nature. Thus, Dr Mattieu Williams, in his " Chemistry of Cookery," p. 295, says :

" At the outset it is necessary to brush aside certain false issues that are commonly raised in discussing this subject. The question is not whether we are herbivorous or carnivorous animals. It is perfectly certain that we are neither. The carnivora feed on flesh alone, and eat that flesh raw. Nobody proposes that we should do this. The herbivora eat raw grass. Nobody suggests that we should follow their example.

" It is perfectly clear that man cannot be classed with the carnivorous animals, nor the herbivorous animals, nor with the gramnivorous animals. His teeth are not constructed for munching and grinding raw grain, nor his digestive organs for assimilating such grain in this condition.

" He is not even to be classed with the omnivorous animals. He stands apart from all as *The Cooking Animal.*"

Here it will be seen that Dr Williams classes man as a " cooking animal " merely because he has no other class (according to his own classification) in which to place him ! But it will be observed that no mention whatever is made of fruitarian diet, or the possibility of man living upon fruits and nuts alone. He does not even mention the fact that there are fruitarian animals ! Naturally, if one eliminates a whole class in this way—that class being the one to which man belongs—it is impossible to find a rightful place for him ; but once recognise the fruitarian class of animals, and it will be found that man, structurally, and in every other way, belongs to it ; and for that reason he does not stand apart by himself as a " cooking animal," but is simply one member of the fruitarian family.

There are many other reasons for thinking that the fruitarian diet is the best, and that uncooked foods should form man's staple diet. One of these is that they are more economical in the long run. While certain other foods may be purchased at a less cost, particularly in the winter-time, they are not nearly so nourishing to the system ; and it can be shown that the nutritive value, per pound, is far greater in the case of fruits and nuts than is the case with any other articles of food. For this reason, although fruits and nuts may cost more, they will ultimately be found to cost *less*—because they contain a higher percentage of nutriment ; and indirectly because they avoid doctor's bills, and maintain the body in a higher state of health and energy. They thus enable it to accomplish more work ; and, since work represents, as a rule, financial return, it will be seen that these foods are in the end most economic. As before pointed out, moreover, they do not induce over-eating, as do cooked and stimulating articles of food.

Fruits also exert a very cleansing and purifying effect upon the system. Their medicinal value is therefore not to be omitted from our consideration ; and further, were the fruitarian diet followed, humanity would escape nine-tenths of the ills from which it now suffers, because of its over-eating, and its living upon gross and highly stimulating articles of food, and bad food-combinations. The choking and blocking effects of the more solid and earthy food would be avoided—while indigestion, fermentation, constipation and all the ills which accompany them would also be entirely done away with.

This question of the prevention of disease by diet is a very important one, both from the economic and from the physiological point of view, and if any diet can be found which will prevent a large percentage of the diseases from which mankind suffers, that diet should surely be adopted. Inasmuch as fruits and nuts are man's natural diet, it should be obvious that they are the ones best suited to his organism, and consequently those which will maintain it in the highest state of health. Let us consider this question a little more fully.

In my previous work, I argued that every article of diet must be more or less healthful or more or less injurious, and this being so, only those foods should be eaten which had been proved by philosophy and experience to be the most wholesome. The fact that the system *can live* upon other foods, and maintain a certain degree of health, argues merely that it can *withstand* the bad effects of these other foods, and by no means shows us that they are the best! I further contended that the same foods are alike detrimental or beneficial to all, and that the old doctrine which Dr Page called "the most foolish of all aphorisms "—namely, "one man's meat, another's poison "—is totally false. I contended that, while there might be certain deviations and variations in the details of the diet, still all men are *rudimentally* alike, and that the body of each human being is made after a certain pattern, which pattern is in accordance with the general principles which apply to all individuals. Man, that is, belongs to a certain *genus*, and consequently his food must be, within certain limits, the same as that of the rest of the family to which he belongs. That is, as we have seen, the frugivora, and his diet must accordingly consist of fruits and nuts in their uncooked, primitive form. There may be certain individual differences, and there doubtless are. Thus, some individuals are unable to eat strawberries, others bananas, others onions, others mushrooms, but this would show, merely, that these particular individuals, *while in the peculiar state of body in which they then are*, are unable to appropriate and utilise, with benefit, these particular food-stuffs. The chemical composition of their bodies has become altered in some way unknown to us, and, as the result of this altered chemical composition, they are unable to appropriate, with profit, food containing certain elements with which they may already be overstocked. In other words, this would prove, merely, that, in their present physical condition, they are unable properly to assimilate and digest those particular food-stuffs. It does not show that, if they were normal, these foods could not be appropriated and used with benefit. In other words, the fault is rather with the individual than with the food. Still, I admit that these differences have to be taken into account; and that no two individuals can be treated exactly alike—especially at first. To use a simile, no two spokes of a wheel are identical—that is, each spoke is individual, and different from all other spokes—but they all lead, nevertheless, to the hub, the central point which unifies and combines them all. In a similar manner, I can see that there is an ideal diet for the human race, which should be followed by all who are in health, and could be eaten by all with equal profit and benefit, if the chemical composition of their bodies were altered.   But, as each spoke must be treated individually at first, so must each individual be treated individually, and, by gradual changes in the diet, be brought more nearly to a normal standard, when it will be far easier for it to adopt a simple fruitarian diet, without any of the disturbance or unpleasantness that might otherwise follow.   As Dr Jackson expressed it :

" If I had his ultimate good in view, I should seek to change the state of his stomach that he might eat what was in itself better for him, rather than to have his morbid necessity say what he should be compelled to eat."

Some readers may contend that I have gone too far in thus insisting upon an ultimate unification of diet, and that such a state can not only *not* be hoped for practically. but is false theoretically.   I myself do not think so.   When discussing this question in my former book, I said :

" It must be noticed that, with the single exception of man, every class of animal feeds upon its own particular and especial kind of food.   All dogs, for example, eat practically the same food, and about the same amount of it. . . . When a dog is fed upon milk, meat, and biscuit, in certain amounts, when living in England, we do not think of modifying his diet to any appreciable degree should we take him with us to America or to the Tropics.   The diet might, in the latter case, be somewhat *lessened*, but that would effect its bulk only, not materially effecting the quality of the food-supply.   Again, we should be surprised to find dogs fed upon altogether different substances in any portion of the globe to which we might travel ; if, *e.g.*, they were fed upon turnips, oysters, mince pie, hay and saurkraut—yet I must earnestly insist that this unholy combination is no more bad and unnatural than some that supposedly ' civilised ' men and women take into their stomachs in the course of twenty-four hours ! To be sure, there might be modifications or alterations in the diet, but the changes would not be of *kind*, merely of *degree*, and we should feel, doubtless, that these dogs, having their diet altered to an altogether different kind, live under such abnormal and altered conditions rather *in spite of* than on *account of* their newly acquired régime, and would be inclined to feel that the same dogs might be infinitely more healthy and live longer lives on their normal diet. Similarly with every other species of animal ; each *genus* has its proper and natural food, allotted by nature, and any attempt to depart from this diet, and to live upon other and altogether unnatural food, must of necessity weaken, devitalise and eventually destroy the organism of the animal so attempting to live contrary to nature's unchanging dietetic laws."

Now, since we have seen that man is anatomically and structurally a member of that family whose normal food is fruits and nuts, he too should live upon that diet if he wishes to maintain the highest degree of health. There is only one valid objection to this theory, which is that man, having lived so many ages upon the cooked diet, is now more adapted to that diet than to his original uncooked foods, and that an attempt to return to such a diet would be attended with grave and possibly disastrous consequences. As Professor Goodfellow put it : " The conditions of life have so altered that the natural food of our ancestors would be unnatural now, living as we do under such different conditions." [1]

This objection, however, is completely refuted by the fact that *no anatomical change whatever* has taken place in man's digestive apparatus since the most primeval times. If the body had gradually grown accustomed to the cooked and unnatural foods, this should not be the case—certain modifications in the digestive apparatus

[1] " The Dietetic Value of Bread," p. 166.

P

and perhaps throughout the body should be noted, corresponding to this altered adaptability. But no such changes have been observed. As we have seen, man corresponds structurally throughout with the higher apes, and he has altered not one whit since the days when he more closely resembled them than he does now !

The second point to be noted is that such an objection is not in accord with facts. It is a comparatively simple thing for the majority of persons to adopt a fruitarian dietary. They can do so almost at once, having made up their minds to do so, and thereafter live upon it exclusively, without harm to themselves, but, on the contrary, with added health and strength. There is no real reason to think that, because a thing has been done for many generations, it is the best thing which *can* be done. Experience merely shows us what *has* taken place, not what *might* take place ; and, so far as that goes, experience has shown us in the past that, living upon the diet they have been accustomed to, human beings have been constantly suffering from one form of disease or another, and that they almost invariably become aged prematurely, lose their faculties before their allotted time, and die a premature death. So far as experience can teach us anything, therefore, it shows most conclusively that such a state of affairs as has existed in the past is by no means the most ideal, but, on the contrary, one which should be avoided and changed, if possible, and rendered more in accordance with nature's laws—thus ensuring a greater degree of health, and a more prolonged and happy existence.

There is another strong argument in favour of the fruitarian dietary, and an adoption of the simpler foods, which is that the adoption of this way of living would ensure a practical emancipation of women. Under the present conditions, a wife—if she has a husband and

family, and if she is forced to do her own work, as a
large number are (in America, at least)—spends four or
five hours a day in the kitchen preparing and clearing
up after the three daily meals supplied to the
family. The anxiety and mental tension that she
undergoes in ensuring the correctness of her dishes ;
the bending over the hot stove—especially in summer-
time—the constant inhaling of smells and odours,
arising from the cooking food, the fumes from the oils
and fats, the constant tasting of dishes which is necessitated, all these tell against her health, and age her
prematurely. In addition to this, there is the time
wasted in the preparation of all these foods, and in the
clearing up of the remnants ; and when we stop to consider that all this cooking is not only useless, but positively detrimental ; not only a waste of time, but an
actual injury to the body ; and when we know that far
greater health and strength may be preserved upon a
diet consisting wholly of uncooked foods—which require
no preparation and practically no clearing up—we
can see how false is the doctrine at present enunciated,
and slavishly followed by the majority, which tends to
keep woman in a state of bondage, and her time filled
up with petty details of a wholly useless nature—
which time might be better occupied in mental pursuits.
And when we remember, in addition to all this, that
such foods, even when they are prepared, are by no
means so wholesome as a simple fruitarian diet, but are,
on the contrary, positively harmful, we can see that
no time should be lost before we adopt this simplified
diet, and insist upon its acceptance by all persons
calling themselves civilised. From all these points of
view, therefore, we see that there are very strong
grounds for believing that the fruitarian diet is the one
most suited to the body's needs, and is in every way
the most wholesome and hygienic. I shall now proceed

to adduce another whole set of facts showing that fruitarianism is the natural diet of mankind, and that fruits and nuts, eaten in their uncooked form, are those most suitable to man, and those best calculated to preserve him in a high state of mental and physical health.

Not only do fruits and nuts contain a higher percentage of nutriment than ordinary foods, and particularly cooked foods ; not only do they maintain the system in a better state of physical, mental and moral health ; not only do they simplify the wants of the household, and the toil of the woman ; not only are they more economical in the long run ; not only would the adoption of this diet prevent nine-tenths of the misery and physical suffering in this world ; not only would it prevent a large part of the crime, debauchery and drunkenness, but, in addition to all this, the adoption of such a dietary would be the chief factor in all social, ethical and agricultural reform. This should be apparent to anyone who has read through the above list of reforms made possible by this simple change of diet. The practical abolition of the traffic in alcohol, which would certainly result from an adoption of this diet, would be in itself a tremendous revolution. In addition to all this, there would be the increased ease and comfort afforded by the simpler diet. The economic aspect of this question is one very important factor. It is possible to live far more cheaply upon fruits and nuts, when they are in season, than upon any other foods—quite apart from the general question of health. The freeing of the body from diseases and the prolonging of useful life would also be strong arguments in favour of the simpler diet—since there can be no question that both these results are effected by its means.

There are also other arguments in favour of this diet—

arguments that should appeal to many of my readers. It will be found, *e.g.*, that the texture and the general colouring of the skin will improve, upon this diet ; the complexion will become clear, and the eyes will become bright. This is very noticeable, in many cases. The brain is also rendered clearer, and more fitted for continued mental work. Far more work can be performed, without the exhaustion formerly noted, upon such a diet. There can be no question whatever that the temper will invariably improve upon the fruitarian diet. I have seen many cases of this character. It is only natural that such should be so. On the ordinary " mixed " diet, the system is surcharged with toxic substances, which mix with the blood and irritate the brain cells. When these irritating substances are removed, the mind will become clear, and a more even and just view of the world will be obtained. There can be no question that there is a close, even intimate, relation between the mental life and the state of the body ; and nothing demonstrates this more certainly than the adoption of a fruitarian dietary. I have already referred to the brutalising effects of meat and the slaughter-house upon the butcher. It is true, in a lesser degree, with everybody. The natives of India and elsewhere look with horror at the practice of meat-eating, and cannot understand how anyone can be spiritual, or even decently humane, who kills and eats animals. And yet missionaries, knowing this, continue to eat their roast beef, in spite of the fact that natives of the more intelligent order must despise them in consequence. No wonder they can accomplish very little, so long as they are so totally incapable of appreciating the viewpoint of others, and are unwilling to reform their diet, and adopt a more simple and humane one—for the sake of their religion, if not for hygienic reasons !

There can be no doubt that the adoption of fruit as

a food would relieve many cases of hitherto incurable diseases. In cancer, gout, eczema, tumour, etc., the exclusive fruit diet has been found to bring rapid and remarkable cures. Moreover, the salts found in fruits of various kinds are a very important factor—and this, not only in the sick but in the well.

Dr H. Benjafield, writing in the *Herald of Health* says :

"Garrod, the great London authority on gout, advises his patients to take oranges, lemons, strawberries, grapes, apples, pears, etc. Jardien, the great French authority, maintains that the salts of potash found so plentifully in fruits are the chief agents in purifying the blood from these rheumatic and gouty poisons. . . . Dr Buzzard advises the scorbutic to take fruit, morning, noon and night. Fresh lemon juice in the form of lemonade is to be his ordinary drink ; the existence of diarrhœa should be no reason for withholding it."

Florence Daniel, in her excellent little book " Food Remedies," says of fruits :

" Salts and acids as found in organised forms are quite different in their effects to the products of the laboratory, notwithstanding that the chemical composition may be shown to be the same. The chemist may be able to manufacture a ' fruit juice,' but he cannot, as yet, manufacture the actual fruit. The mysterious life force always evades him. Fruit is a *vital* food, it supplies the body with something over and above the mere elements that the chemist succeeds in isolating by analysis. The vegetable kingdom possesses the power of directly utilising minerals, and it is only in this ' live ' form that they are fit for the consumption of man. In the consumption of sodium chloride (common table salt), baking powders, and the whole army of mineral drugs and essences, we violate that decree of nature which ordains that the animal kingdom shall feed upon the vegetable and the vegetable upon the mineral."

So far back as the beginning of last century, the famous Dr Lambe, of London, wrote in favour of the fruit diet, and several vigorous reformers soon followed his example. The system was bitterly attacked, but these attacks served only to strengthen the defence, and show the inconsistency of its opponents. Objections to the fruit diet are constantly being urged, but not one of them has been shown to rest on a solid foundation.

Take, for example, the notion that the acids of fruit injure the teeth. Dentists will frequently tell you that acids are injurious to the enamel of the teeth, and for that reason acid fruits most certainly should not be eaten! The position sounds perfectly logical, and, if the acids of fruits had the same effect upon the enamel of the teeth as mineral acid, it would be true. The fact is, however, that this is not the case, but one does not really find this out until he becomes a fruitarian. He then finds that he has no further " use " for the dentist, and that his fine theoretical knowledge is overthrown by the actual facts.

Persons often notice that they become—especially at first—much more acutely sensitive and almost nervous upon a fruitarian diet. Of course the diet is blamed; but as a matter of fact it is but indirectly responsible. The sensibility and nervousness is the result of previous habits of life—and this transitory condition is but the manifestation of certain nervous, vital energies which had, till then, remained "smothered," as it were, by the excess of food eaten. Now they rise to the surface and tend to become noticeable to us (v. my " Vitality, Fasting and Nutrition," pp. 520-523).

Further, sensibility, it must be remembered, is merely another word for extreme sensitiveness or a degree of reaction of the nervous system—which is its normal function. A nervous system is made for the express purpose of reacting immediately, to the most delicate stimulus—and if it does not do so, it shows that the nervous mechanism is in some way out of order. It is only because we constantly keep the nervous system poisoned, by our perverted food habits, that it does not react as it should. It merely regains some degree of its normal powers when the fruit diet is adopted.

But I shall probably be told that there are cases in which a hyper-sensitiveness has become apparent—the sensitiveness, not of health, but of disease. That I admit : but I must contend that this extreme sensitiveness would not have resulted had it not been for the previous habits of life, which resulted in an accumulation of irritating poisons within the body; so that, when these habits are discontinued and the nervous system invigorated by the improved dietetic habits, the nerves begin to react vigorously against these irritating poisons. The result is that a great irritability and hyper-sensitiveness is noted, *pro tem.*—which, however, will be found to disappear (if the diet be persisted in) when the nervous system again approaches a more normal standard.

There remains one very strong argument in favour of a fruitarian diet, to which I have not so far referred. Able authorities affirm that many of the waste places and deserts of the earth once teemed with fertility and foliage, and that the existing sterility of these deserts has been brought about by the destruction of their forests. The influence of trees upon the rainfall, and consequent support of vegetation, is so well known that some of the foremost nations are fostering tree-culture and taking means to preserve existing forests by Government enactment. There can be no doubt but that trees improve the climate, in any neighbourhood ; they improve the soil, reduce the severity of storms and the cold of winter, and prevent undue evaporation of moisture from the surface of the ground. But it is unnecessary to enlarge upon the great value of trees, which is well known. Now, the point I make is this :

if the fruitarian dietary were adopted, more fruits and nuts would be eaten, and hence a large number of trees would be planted—huge orchards would exist throughout the land. Whereas under cereal culture there is a constant temptation to the farmer to cut down his trees to make his lands available for grain-growing; as soon as a market for fruits and nuts is established, the same law of pecuniary gain will induce him to transform his pastures and his grain fields into orchards and nut groves. This would be highly advantageous in every respect.

I think it probable that fruits alone contain about all the nutriment that an average man wants, who is not working out of doors, and who does not take much exercise. Oxen will get fat on apples and pears; but when we set them to work, we have to supply an extra amount of grains, and foods containing proteid, to offset the greater destruction of muscular tissue. It is probably the same with man. In the majority of cases, fruits alone would probably supply all that the body needs; but when it was called upon to perform an extra amount of work, nuts and other proteid-forming foods will be craved and called for. This, I think, indicates the true place of nuts and of all foods rich in proteid in the diet.

M. Metchnikoff has argued strongly against the use of fruits and all raw foods, as liable to introduce bacteria into the intestines! He believes that old age and natural death are largely brought about by bacteriological decomposition in the intestines (in which he is doubtless right) and believes that raw foods are one of the chief causes of this intestinal putrefaction. I would point out, in reply, that bacteria can only exist in a locality in which there is a suitable soil; and if this soil is lacking, they cannot exist, no matter how many of them may be introduced. Now, when the bowel is kept sweet and clean, as it invariably is by a fruit diet, it will be apparent that there is no soil in which such bacteria could multiply, hence their continued presence would be quite impossible.   M. Metchnikoff has only studied cases in which the patient had been nourished by the ordinary cooked foods, and his conclusions were drawn from the facts presented to him ; but when the diet is entirely fruitarian, there can be no doubt that such a state of the bowels would be quite impossible, and there would consequently be no bacteria present ; and if they *were* introduced, they could not live in such a medium.   The bowel, in the case of those living upon a fruitarian diet, is almost entirely free from all bacteria ; and their infection and action upon the system would consequently be rendered practically impossible.   There would be no danger of infection if the body were maintained in a high state of health—as it would be upon a fruitarian diet.

Frequently, throughout this book, I have referred to man's " natural diet," and, it may be asked, what is his natural diet, in what does it consist ?   I answer : fruit and nuts—or a combination of these—is man's natural diet, and this is proved by all the arguments of comparative anatomy, of physiology, and all the other evidences I have adduced.   I think there can be no mistake and no hesitation about this, once we have mastered and appreciated the force of these arguments. They alone would determine the issue.   But, further, I think there is one simple test that will settle this question—an instinctive test.   After eating a full meal of any article of food, let a man look back, and contemplate having to eat it all over again, and he can soon tell whether what he has eaten is " natural " for him or not !   If the meal has consisted of fish and meat, and all the other " luxuries " of modern civilisation, there can be no doubt that such a thought would repulse and sicken him ; the very idea of it would nauseate him.

But if the meal had consisted of peaches and dates, let us say, the idea of going back and eating as much again of the same food would not prove in the slightest degree repellent to him. This instinctive testimony is very suggestive and valuable, it appears to me, and clearly indicates man's natural diet.

Let us consider this question of instinct further.

If we take a little child into a room in which there are two tables, one covered with meats of all kinds (choicely cooked, if you will) and the other groaning under a multitude of fruit, which one would the child turn to, without any hesitation ? Most certainly he would turn to the table spread with fruit—in every single instance where the appetite has not been perverted so early as to render all natural taste and instinct impossible. The child would turn to its natural food—fruit, and would in that manner demonstrate his natural cravings and instinct, and clearly indicate that his natural food is fruit, and that consequently he is frugivorous by nature. But now let us take a dog or a cat, or a lion or a tiger into the room, and leave him there. To which table would *he* turn, and that without a moment's hesitation ? We can have no doubt on that point. He would instantaneously show his carnivorous nature and appetite, and would not, in all probability, even touch the fruits, even if he were hungry and there was no meat in the room at all. Our primary instincts, therefore, clearly indicate that man is frugivorous, and not carnivorous in his nature.

Again, if man were naturally carnivorous, he should eat his meat as do the carnivora—and he should be provided by nature with the bodily structure, teeth, claws, etc., for doing so. Were man naturally carnivorous, he should prey upon his food by night ; he should lurk in the dark places, and pounce upon his rightful prey, rending it with his teeth, tearing it with his claws, lapping the warm blood as it oozes from the life-less body before him ! He should catch and eat his prey as do all the other (naturally) carnivorous animals. If Nature pointed us to such a diet, we should feel the same instinctive appetite for raw flesh as we now feel for ripe fruit ; and a slaughter-house would be more delightful to us than an orchard. Yet we know that such is not the case, and that even the mere thought of such a thing is sickening to any sensitive person. Why is this ? Does it not clearly indicate that man is not naturally carnivorous by nature, but that he can only tolerate the idea of flesh-eating because of long deadening of the higher moral centres, in this direction ; and because the food is so pickled, and spiced, and peppered, and salted, and roasted, and fried, and smothered in onions, and in other ways covered up and *concealed*, and its taste and nature so *disguised*, that we can eat it at all?

As Mr Salt so well remarked [1] :

" Our innate horror of bloodshed—a horror which only long custom can deaden, and which, in spite of past centuries of violence, is so powerful at the present time —is proof that we are not naturally adapted for a sanguinary diet ; and, as has often been pointed out, it is only by delegating to others the detested work of slaughter, and by employing cookery to conceal the uncongenial truth, that thoughtful persons can tolerate the practice of meat-eating."

If all persons who enjoy " a good, juicy beef-steak," or a rasher of bacon, first had to go out and kill the cow or the hog, how do you think they would like it ? And how many of us would or could do such a thing ? Aside from the fact, before pointed out, that, were we naturally carnivorous by nature, we should eat our flesh warm and bleeding and quivering—as do the other carnivora—there is this additional objection, that, even if

[1] " Logic of Vegetarianism," p. 27.

this were not the case, we must ever entail the duty to others of killing the animal for us—so disgusting is the very idea of dipping our hands and mouths in blood before and during each meal !

Granting, then, that fruits and nuts can supply us with all the essentials for the upbuilding of a healthy body, and that this is man's natural diet—the question arises : How would it be best to break away from the old foods, and adopt this simpler dietary ? Certainly this should not be done at once, in the majority of cases. Many persons can pass from one diet to another instantaneously, with no harm, but with decided benefit. My own case is an example of this. Once I was thoroughly persuaded that this was the ideal diet, I dropped meat at one meal, and lived upon fruits and nuts the next, and thenceforward from that day. I never experienced any ill effects from such an abrupt change, but only benefit. Though, at the present time, I pay no attention, practically, to exercise, to breathing, or to any of the other thought-to-be-essentials of the physical culture life (I claim that all of these measures can be practically dispensed with, if only the diet be regulated carefully) I am always more or less in condition, and I may fairly say that I never knew anyone who could work more continuously and steadily for so many hours at a stretch, and for so many days together, as can I. Of course this is only one person's testimony, and hence my own method might not be suited to all equally well. But I have introduced this personal item to show that the old dogma that one cannot make abrupt changes in the diet without detriment to oneself is all pure nonsense. I never experienced any ill effects whatever—and no more have numerous other persons of my acquaintance, who have adopted the fruitarian diet as abruptly as I did.

But, granting that this abrupt change is not desired,

what then ?   In that case, I should advise the patient to leave off meat at one of his meals (if he has been in the habit of eating it more than once a day) and sub-stitute eggs for it—in the morning or evening—or beans, peas, cheese, etc., at noon.   Let him get accustomed to this change before another step is taken.   Then, abolish meat altogether from the bill of fare, and live on the ordinary vegetarian foods for a few days.   Next, decrease the amount of cooked vegetables, and increase the quantity of the fruits.   Remember the advice previously given regarding food combinations here. It will soon be found that an egg or two, and a couple of slices of bread, or a simple vegetarian dish, will supply all the wants, for the first half of the meal ; and this should be followed by an abundant allowance of fruits. Keep this up until the patient has grown thoroughly accustomed to the change, and then (preferably in hot weather) let him try his first meal of fruits, nuts and whole-wheat bread and nut-butter.   Later on, these last articles may be abolished, if desired ; but most persons find it almost harder to give up their bread and butter than they do their meat !   The patient is now fairly on the diet, and additional alterations and restrictions are merely a matter of time.   Doubtless by this time he is sufficiently interested in the question himself, and sufficiently delighted in his altered physical condition, to need but little persuasion, and will gladly adopt and follow the diet himself.

XIII

FOOD COMBINATIONS

THERE are very few foods which, if eaten singly, would be found to disagree. Most of the trouble arises when we combine the various foods which do not suit or harmonise ; and the result is, distress and a complication of disorders, due to the bad combination of such foods. Such foods disagree with one another, so to speak, rather than with us. This question of food combinations is one which has been very largely overlooked, but it is a highly important one, nevertheless. Most people have never paid any attention to the relative proportion of their foods, or thought how each would combine with the other ; and it is largely due to this lack of foresight that so much dyspepsia is present, and that so many digestive troubles are active throughout the world. The motto of the average individual would seem to be, " Out of sight, out of mind " ; but it must be remembered that, while the stomach *receives* the food, the body has to *retain* it ; and long digestive processes, involving an enormous outlay of energy, and many and complicated chemical changes, have to be gone through, before food is appropriable by the system. Of course, the tendency among civilised peoples is in the direction of increasing the number of articles of food at each meal, instead of decreasing it. They like to see the table spread with a litter of dishes, while a fifteen-course dinner is supposed to be the height of luxury ! Were the processes of living considered a little more from the physiological, and a little less from the gormandising point of view, such would not be the case. The tendency would then be (at least among all intelligent people), to *reduce* the number of dishes, as much as possible—limiting them at each meal to three or two, or even one.

Food should be solid. The digestive juices are fluids, and an excess of liquid, with the food, tends to dilute these gastric juices, and consequently to interfere with their converting action. If fluids be drunk with any meal they will dilute the power of concentrated action of the gastric juice, and other digestive juices ; and will, further, have a tendency to wash the food through the stomach into the intestines before it has undergone proper stomach-digestion. Water, therefore, should not be drunk *at* meals, but shortly before, or an hour or so afterwards. In this way the requisite amount of fluid is supplied to the system, without interfering with digestion in the manner indicated.

Another result of drinking at meals is to prevent thorough mastication of the foods. When these are dry, they should be thoroughly insalivated before being swallowed, for any liquid taken at the time softens these foods artificially, and will also cause more food to be eaten than would be the case, were it eaten dry.

Dr Latson, in his " Food Value of Meat," says :

" Fresh fruits all combine well with one another. As a rule fruits, fresh or cooked, combine well with bread or cooked cereals, and with nuts or nuts foods. Fruits do not, as a rule, combine well with cooked vegetables, nor with meat, eggs, cheese, milk, or cream. Milk and cream are so liable to decomposition that, if only for that reason, they are not desirable foods. Milk or cream with cereals, fruit, sugar, or cooked vegetables is apt to cause difficulty. . . . In arranging meals in which flesh-meat is not to be included, it is only necessary to remember that the nuts and the legumes (peas, beans and lentils) contain the same food elements as flesh-meat, and may always be eaten in its place with advantage. . . . The best breakfast is one that consists of fresh ripe fruit, and nothing else. To this may be added, if desired, whole-wheat bread, or some cereal. The cereal may be served with fruit juice."

The following are a few sample meals arranged, according to merit—only those foods being taken which will combine well together.

Breakfast No. 1.—Raw fruit, cereal with fruit juice, whole-wheat bread.

Breakfast No. 2.—Stewed apples, whole-wheat bread.

Breakfast No. 3.—Cereal with fruit juice, soft boiled eggs, whole-wheat bread.

The following are one or two sample luncheons :—

Luncheon No. 1.—Stewed fruit, nuts or nut-butter, whole-wheat bread.

Luncheon No. 2.—Pea-nut purée, boiled rice (or baked potatoes), stewed fruit, whole-wheat bread.

Luncheon No. 3.—Salad of any kind, garnished with olive oil and lemon juice ; fresh fruit and whole-wheat bread.

The following are a few sample dinners :—

Dinner No. 1.—Fresh fruit, salad, macaroni, whole-wheat bread.

Dinner No. 2.—Peas, beans or lentils, browned rice, baked potatoes, stewed fruit, whole-wheat bread.

Dinner No. 3.—Soup, eggs, cooked vegetables, whole-wheat bread.

Dinner No. 4.—Bean soup, or pea soup, boiled rice, baked potatoes, stewed fruit, whole-wheat bread.

Dr William S. Sadler [1] gives the following directions as to food combinations :—

GOOD COMBINATIONS

Fruits and grains	Grains and milk
Grains and meat or eggs	Grains and vegetables
Grains and nuts	Grains and legumes

[1] "The Science of Living," p. 145.

Q

FAIR COMBINATIONS

Grains with sweet fruits and milk
Meat or eggs with vegetables
Nuts and vegetables

BAD COMBINATIONS

Fruits and vegetables　　　·　　Sour fruits and milk
Milk and vegetables　　　　　　　Milk and meat

Mr and Mrs Christian, in their " Uncooked Foods "
(p. 68), give three elaborate meals, composed of uncooked foods entirely, though it will be seen that their
grouping of combinations is not so strict as that formulated above. The meals are as follows :—

" *Breakfast*.—One ripe apple, two ounces pecan meats,
six or eight black dates, one very ripe banana, sliced
with thick cream, one glass milk.

" *Luncheon*.—Two bartlett pears, one ounce pecan
meats, three Turkish pulled figs, one ounce pignolias,
cold slaw with olive oil, one cake of unfired bread, four
prunes with thick cream, sweet butter, egg-nog.

" *Dinner*.—Half pound of grapes, two ounces mixed
nut meats, vegetable salad with dressing, one cake unfired bread, cream cheese, six or eight black dates, one
very ripe red banana, with thick cream, pint of whole
milk."

Personally, I think that the above combinations are
by no means ideal, and in addition to that, far too much
in bulk has been prescribed for each meal. Were the
breakfast omitted, and but two meals daily eaten, the
amount prescribed would be more proportionate, but
even then I feel certain that the amount is greatly
in excess of bodily needs. The authors, however, have
made an extended study of food combinations, and,
in fact, are almost the only writers who have paid much
attention to this subject. In their chapter on food
combinations, they say :

" The following combinations have been found by

experience to be chemically harmonious, healthful, and very nutritious :—

" Flaked wheat, with nuts, dates and cream.

" Flaked wheat, nuts, honey, milk and cream.

" Egg-nog, pecan meats, dates, banana and cream.

" Cold slaw with olive oil, pecan meats, unfired bread, sweet apple with thick cream.

" All foods composed largely of starch, such as cereals, potatoes, and nearly all legumes, should not be eaten at the same meal with sweets, especially cane sugar. All foods, whether fluids or solids, that contain starch or sugar, such as rice, potatoes, corn, oats, in fact all the cereal class may be eaten with safety at the same meal. Milk can also be taken with all the carbo-hydrate family of foods.[1] All foods containing gluten, albumen, or gelatine, such as meat, eggs and a few kinds of nuts, are classed as protein, and require an acid solvent to be digested. Therefore, they can be eaten with safety with all kinds of fruits. Milk, one of the best foods known, can be taken with all kinds of fruits, provided no cereal starch be eaten at the same meal. All foods that contain both carbohydrates and protein compose healthful combinations." [2]

In balancing any dietary, care must be taken, of course, to keep the relative proportion of proteids, fats and carbohydrates, equal ; and to see, also, that the proper amount of mineral salts is contained in all the foods ; also that a due supply of water is furnished to the system. One of the chief causes of failure on the part of those who leave off meat, and attempt to take up vegetarianism, is that they do not rightly balance their diet, and do not supply to the system the proper amount of proteid food, to take the place of that which the meat supplied. Vegetarians, as a rule, eat far *too much* food. Under the impression that they must eat

[1] It will be seen that the authors are here in disagreement with Dr Latson. See his advice above.

[2] A number of very good recipes of uncooked foods may be found in an otherwise very odd book, entitled " Unfired Food : and Tro-photherapy," by George J. Drews (Chicago).

more, in order to offset the supposed greater "nutri-tive" value of the meat which they have given up, they eat far more than they should : while as a matter of fact, the vegetarian foods are richer and far more nutritious than the ordinary mixed diet. Consequently, less, instead of more, should be eaten. Anyone leaving off his meat must expect to feel a certain de-pression for a few days, as before pointed out—owing to the fact that the stimulating quality of the meat is withdrawn ; but, those few days once past, a general invigoration of the system will be noted. Due attention should be paid to all hygienic auxiliaries, and an excess of food should by all means be avoided. Substitute eggs, cheese, peas, beans, lentils and nuts for the meat formerly eaten ; in other ways pay attention to the balancing of the diet, and no inconvenience will be experienced, as a result of leaving off meat and adopting the newer dietary.

Dr Susana Dodds, in her " Health in the Household, or Hygienic Cookery," says, in writing of food combina-tions :

" It is folly to overlook the fact that there is a certain fitness or adaptation to be observed both in the selec-tion and classification of foods which enhances their value as a whole ; it will not do to huddle them together indiscriminately, either on one's palate or on the stomach ; baked beans and grape-juice are both very satisfactory in themselves ; but they have so little in common that no one would think of eating them together ; though the harm resulting from so injurious a combination would be more apparent in some cases than in others. Nearly half a century of close contact with invalids has placed before the hygienic physician certain *facts* which cannot be ignored ; and whether the signs behind them are fully understood or not, the facts themselves remain. For example, if we have a nervous dyspeptic to treat, we know better than to set before him at one and the same meal strawberries, and beets, or strawberries and cabbage, or apples (raw or cooked) and sweet potatoes, or apples and beans. These are only examples of at least fifty combinations which could be made, any one of which would give a weak stomach indigestion. . . . Sweet potatoes and tomatoes make a good combination and one very acceptable to most persons—the one being sweet the other acid, the one highly nutritious, the other decidedly juicy."

To those who have not made this subject a study the following hints may be of practical use, though in many things it is next to impossible to lay down definite rules.[1]

1. Fruits and vegetables should not, as a rule, be eaten together—that is, at the same meal. If they are so eaten, persons with feeble digestive organs will suffer.

2. If vegetables are eaten, the noonday meal is the best time to take them, two or three varieties being quite sufficient. Tomatoes do well with vegetables, grains, or meats; but they should not, as a rule, be eaten with fruits.

8. The Irish potato seems to be an exception among vegetables; it is so unaggressive in its nature that it seldom quarrels with anything. It may therefore be eaten (by most persons) with *either* fruits or vegetables; and it always does well with grains.

4. Fruits and cereals are particularly suited to the morning and evening meals; and very little other food is required.

5. A good rule, when suppers are eaten, is to make the meal of bread and fruit only, these being taken in limited quantities and at an early hour.

6. Fruits, if eaten raw, should be ripe, and of good quality; and persons with feeble stomachs digest them

---

[1] In the following suggestions it will be assumed that the diet is vegetarian, and not yet fruitarian—these suggestions being offered as a help toward that diet, by breaking away, gradually, from the ordinary "mixed" diet.

more easily at the beginning of the meal; this is particularly true when warm fruits make a part of the repast.

7. Fruits, raw or cooked, may be eaten at dinner, provided no vegetable (unless it be the potato) be taken. But if raw, they should be eaten *first*, particularly if there are warm foods to follow.

8. Some persons cannot digest certain kinds of raw fruits for supper, or late in the day; let them take these on sitting down to the breakfast-table; or the first thing at dinner, unless there are *vegetables* at this meal.

9. If meats "must be" eaten—take them at the noonday meal, with or without vegetables; and in cold weather, rather than warm.

10. The grains digest well with all other foods; though some persons cannot eat them in the form of mushes. They should always be thoroughly cooked.

11. Persons with feeble digestions should as a rule confine themselves to a *single kind* of fruit at a meal; they can make the changes from one meal to another.

12. Those who find it difficult to digest vegetables should not attempt more than one kind at a given meal, until the digestion is improved. And often it is best to leave them off entirely for a time.

13. In selecting vegetables for a single meal, do not, if there are several varieties, have all of them of the watery or juicy kinds, as cabbage, asparagus, white turnips, etc.; nor all of the drier sorts, such as baked beans, winter squashes, sweet potatoes, etc.; but blend the more and less nutritious kinds in a judicious manner. Or if you have only the watery ones at hand, be content with not more than two varieties; prepare a side dish of something *rather* nutritious, and then add a dish of warm corn bread, as an accompaniment, particularly if it be a cold day.

14. If you have for dinner a thin vegetable soup,

follow with something more substantial, as baked beans, baked potatoes (sweet or Irish) or corn bread; but if you have bean or split-pea soup, let the other vegetables be of a kind less hearty.

15. On a very cold day have a warm dinner of good nutritious articles; select mainly solid foods with grains, rather than thin soups and watery vegetables.

16. On a warm day make the breakfast largely of fruits, with a moderate supply of cereals. The dinner may be of young vegetables (or fruits), a dish of grains, if you like, and a little bread. Eat lightly, and you will suffer less from heat—particularly if no seasonings are taken. For supper, a glass of cold grape juice, and a slice of loaf bread, is excellent in hot weather.

17. In very cold weather take the chill off your stewed fruit, fruit pies, or other dishes, before serving them. Pastries, if used, are best at the noonday meal—and so are puddings.

18. If there are invalids at the table, they should eat nothing that is very cold; food not much below blood heat is best, particularly in cold weather; and the dining-room should be comfortably warm.

19. Never have too great a variety at a single meal; have few dishes well prepared, and make the changes from one meal to another; this will please better on the whole, and it will not too rapidly exhaust your limited supplies.

20. If one meal happens to fall a little below the average in either quality or variety, see that the next is fully up to the mark.

The evil results which follow bad food combinations may be summed up in a very few words. We know that certain chemical elements, acting upon one another, will form resultant gases. Various food substances that do not properly combine, will form such gases in precisely the same way; and these will be largely absorbed by the blood, and carried to the cells throughout the body, which they poison, more or less, in consequence. The harmful results of these poisonous gases, absorbed in this manner, are particularly noticeable in their effect upon the various nerve centres—producing an inhibitory effect upon them, and inducing that general condition of weariness and debility experienced and noticed under the host of symptoms known to us as nervous exhaustion, fatigue, lassitude, etc., etc. The simple and obvious method that should be followed in all such cases, in order to eliminate these poisons from the system, is to abstain from food until the system has had a chance to eliminate such toxic substances. This once accomplished, the system being freed from the ashes of previously mal-assimilated food material, and a fresh supply of oxygen being furnished, by continued breathing, in the interval, the system will soon return to its normal condition of health, and will enjoy a higher standard of energy and vitality than has been the case for some considerable time in the past.

XIV

HYGIENIC FOODS AND HYGIENIC COOKERY

In discussing this question of foods and food values and constituents, we must be very careful to keep clear in the mind the distinction between *proximate* elements, or foods proper, and *chemical* or *ultimate* elements. This is very important. All alimentary substances are composed of certain constituent parts, which may be properly called alimentary principles. These are formed by certain combinations of elementary constituents, which are denominated chemical elements. Thus wheat, beef, potato, apple, etc., are aliments, or foods proper ; and starch, sugar, rum, fibrin, albumen, gelatin, etc.—their constituents—are proximate elements. Proximate elements of food are compounds of the simple or chemical elements ; and aliments or foods proper are compounds of the proximate principles.

It is important to keep these distinctions in mind, because the human body can be nourished and retain its health upon organic combinations of proximate elements, while it would starve to death on the ultimate elements administered in exactly the same proportions. Dogs have been fed on sugar, gum, starch, butter, fat, fibrin, albumen, etc., exclusively, and with the uniform result that they sooner or later starved to death ! No animal can sustain prolonged nutrition on any single alimentary principle, though all of them may on a single aliment.

Other things being equal, a food is nutritious, and capable of sustaining life, in proportion to its complexity. The more simple the food, the less it is capable of sustaining life and health. This does not mean that a large *number of foods* should be eaten at one meal—in order to supply this lack—since nearly all foods, or a reasonable admixture of them—contain all the essentials for sustaining life in a state of health and vigour. Certain foods—nuts, *e.g.*—seem to contain about all the essentials and in exactly the right proportions. I have discussed this aspect of the question in the chapter on the fruitarian diet.

One very important fact may be mentioned here. Animals cannot appropriate mineral or inorganic elements *directly*; they must obtain all these substances through or by means of the vegetable world. Vegetables have the power of utilising these inorganic materials, and build them into their bodies ; but animals have to obtain all such substances in an organised form —*i.e.* organic materials—and cannot possibly utilise the *in*organic elements. Thus, if an animal requires iron, it cannot eat iron filings, to supply this need, but must take it in the form of spinach, and cabbage, and fruits containing large quantities of iron ; he cannot possibly eat it in its mineral form. The vegetable world, on the contrary, has the power of building these mineral elements into its structure. Vegetables feed upon minerals, and animals upon vegetables ; and this order cannot be reversed. It will thus be seen that the vegetable world is that designed for man's food ; and from it he should derive all his nourishment. Certainly he can derive no part of it from the *mineral* world.

Hints on Hygienic Cookery.—While I believe that the ideal diet is that which is uncooked—or sun-cooked— nevertheless some foods are best cooked, if the ordinary vegetarian diet is to be adhered to. Thus, grains when uncooked are but slightly nutritious, a large portion of their starch remaining unconverted ; but when cooked this is converted into dextrine, and thus rendered more appropriable by the system. Cooking is therefore justified, if vegetable foods and grains are to be eaten ; and I propose, accordingly, to jot down a few notes and instructions which will, I believe, be found useful to all those who wish to reform their food habits, to a certain extent, and cook as hygienically as possible. I shall not attempt any elaborate outline of hygienic cookery in this place ; several of the vegetarian cook-books on the market go into great detail on these questions, and I shall therefore confine myself to a few brief notes.

Bread should be well cooked, and the crusts thoroughly baked brown. It had best be baked in a *closed* pan. Bread should, of course, always be made from whole-wheat flour—never white flour. Salt is never necessary. Trall has given numerous receipes for wholesome bread-making—in some of them no other ingredients are used but flour, water, and air ! And they are sweet, excellent breads too.

All pastries should be made quickly, and with very little kneading. Have the oven ready before this kneading is commenced. Roll the crust thin, and see that the bottom crust of a pie is browned before adding the fruit and the top crust.

Vegetables—nearly all of them—should be dropped into boiling, not cold, water, and should be cooked rapidly. The purpose of this is to coagulate and con-dense the outer rind or layer of the vegetable, and thus prevent the juices and valuable food properties from boiling out, into the water. The same is true of all meats, when these are fried or grilled.

If fruits are cooked at all, green fruits should be selected in preference to over-ripe fruits—which should be cooked but little. Unripe fruits should be started in *cold* water, and cooked slowly. All grains are best steamed.

Sugar added to fruits renders them sweet-tasting, but liable to fermentation. The ordinary sugar on the market is open to many objections. Numerous hygienists will not use it at all, and if fruits are found to be a trifle sour, or need sweetening, they use dates instead.

See that all currants, raisins and dried fruits are thoroughly clean before cooking them. In the summer months especially they are liable to contain insects, and these should be washed off before the fruits are placed on the fire to cook—otherwise they will be cooked with them !

If soda is put into bread, etc., use it sparingly. Salt need never be used. One can soon get accustomed to food without a particle of salt or other dressing ; and, once the normal taste is acquired, salt, pepper, etc., will never again be desired or craved.

Meat as an Article of Diet.—I have advanced reasons, throughout this book, for thinking that meat is by no means a suitable article of food, but is, on the contrary, extremely pernicious in its effects upon the system. The reasons for this are given in full elsewhere. At the same time, I am disposed to think that a *limited* amount of meat is not so harmful, frequently, as a larger amount of other foods—fine flour, cake, pickles, sauces, etc. A large quantity of any of these, long continued, will tend to ruin the body more effectually than a limited quantity of meat, and hence are to be more strictly avoided. Nevertheless, I consider meat a highly stimulating and unwholesome article of diet, for the reasons given above, and should strongly advise other foods in its place, whenever possible.

If the reader feels that he *must* eat meat, however, let him be sure (or as sure as he can be) that the meat is fresh, and is not diseased. Two great dangers are avoided in this way. The animals which are to be eaten should be fed on the cleanest of food, and should have plenty of pure water to drink; they should never be kept in confined places, in a vitiated atmosphere, or in filthy surroundings. They need plenty of exercise. The animal should be killed in a sanitary manner, and kept clean and free from contamination after it is killed. The meat should be put on ice at once, and, needless to say, no chemicals or other drugs injected into the tissues.

Beef and mutton are doubtless two of the best meats which can be eaten. The diet of these animals is the cleanest; and their tissues should be the "cleanest," in consequence. Beef is, of course, the most widely eaten of all meats; and, more than that, we feed upon or utilise almost every conceivable part of the animal. As Dr Brush so well said [1]:

"We are veritable parasites on this animal. We milk her as long as she will give milk, and we drink it; then we kill her, and eat her flesh, blood, and most of the viscera; we skin her, and clothe ourselves with her skin; we comb our hair with her horns, and fertilise our fields with her dung, while her calf furnishes us with vaccine virus for the prevention of smallpox!"

Is it any wonder that we manage to contract some of the diseases from which this animal suffers? The only wonder is that we escape at all! The same thing may be said in a lesser degree of mutton, veal, pork, and, in fact, all the animal substances. They all contain, along with a small amount of nutritive material, a large amount of poisons and excreta.

When we come to pork, bacon, ham, etc., there is no longer any excuse for the practice at all. If it is felt that meat *must* be eaten, let it be clean meat, such as beef or mutton, without turning to the pig for our supply! Nothing so lacks excuse as this. Writing

[1] "Human and Bovine Tuberculosis," pp. 6-7.

upon the practice of pork-eating, in her "Diet Question," Dr Dodds says :

"The hog is a scavenger by nature, and by practice ; it is his proper mission on this earth, not to be eaten, but to eat up that which the nobler animals disdain to touch. Indeed, he adapts himself to circumstances, devouring whatever comes in his way. He is equally well pleased with the clean ears of corn, or with the seething contents of the swill pail ; he will dine on live chickens or devour carrion. Nothing is too fine or too foul to suit his undiscriminating palate : he has been called 'the scavenger-in-chief of all the back-boned animals.' Truly he is omnivorous. . . .

"Will anyone give an intelligent reason why people should eat him, and from choice ? If we must dine on our fellow-creatures below us, are there not decent, clean-feeding animals, as the ox, and the sheep, that we could take in preference ?

"From a sanitary point of view, the condition of the hog, in his best estate, is not flattering. His scurvy hide (which is perhaps the cleanest part of him), his foul breath, and his filthy feeding habits—are not these enough to bar him from our tables ? Or must we wait for such logical sequence as is sure to follow the violation of physiological law ? Wait till diseases are multiplied in kind, and intensified in character, till we are fairly driven from the no-longer questionable provender? Wait till our nearest friend is stricken with supposed typhoid fever, and dead of veritable trichinosis ? There can be no doubt that a number of persons have sickened and a number died, of what was thought to be typhoid fever, when really the disease was due to the presence of these parasites (the trichinæ) in the system ; for the symptoms in the two diseases are quite similar.

"As stated in the last chapter, one of the principal objections to the use of animal flesh as food, is the fact that it is filled with the debris of the vital organism, working its way through the capillaries into the various excretions, and out of the domain of life. Now, if this effete matter is objectionable, even in clean-feeding animals, what must be its condition as it is thrown off from the tissues of scavengers ? And what the nature of the tissues themselves, when they are not only made out of, and nourished by a diet of garbage, but are thoroughly saturated with the almost putrescent matters with which the venous blood is laden ? It is a fact that we seem rather slow to recognise, that the quality of all animal tissues partakes of the character of the materials out of which they are made. In other words, if we expect sound bodies, with good firm tissues, we must look to the nature of the food we eat. . . .

" Nor is it enough that we devour the several parts of the animal, even to his liver and kidneys ; we strip the intestines of their fat, melt it down, and use it in the form of lard ! This latter is the very quintessence of the swine ; it is the diseased product of all his filthy feeding ; and it is the article that forms a staple in almost every American family. It shortens the biscuits, the plain cakes, and the pastries ; and it even finds its way into the loaf bread. It oils the bake-pans, it fries the drop-cakes, the doughnuts, the Saratoga potatoes, and all the other ' fried things,' or nearly all. In short, there is neither breakfast, dinner, nor supper without it, in some form or other.

" Do the people wonder that they are afflicted with scrofula ; and that it crops out, full-fledged, in a single generation ? Oh, for a Moses among the Gentiles, to forbid them, by legal enactment, the use of this vile thing, swine's flesh ! "

Birds and game of all kinds are to be avoided. The flesh of the goose, duck, etc., is very oily, greasy and unwholesome. Chicken, turkey, etc., are somewhat better. but their flesh is not nearly so nutritious as beef and mutton, while the amount of poisons they contain is certainly equal to the latter. It must be remembered that these animals are frequently confined and artificially fed, in order to " fatten " them for the market ; and even when this has not been done, the birds have very rarely sufficient room to exercise as they ought to, and their food and water supply is by no means what it should be. Of course, when artificial feeding has been employed, their flesh is little short of poisonous. The " fat " noticed and so highly praised is merely retained filth and excreta, and should be outside the animal's body, and not in it. Needless to say, the flesh of all such birds should be eschewed.

Fish is considered by some to be a very fine article of diet—being nutritious and easily digested. For that reason, it is often given to invalids ! Where such a curious hallucination could have arisen it is hard to see. Its flesh is exceedingly gross, tough, fibrous, and contains but little nutriment. The flesh of all animals partakes more or less of the nature of their diet; and fish and fowl are certainly not the cleanest of feeders ! Their flesh is in no sense superior to that of the cow or sheep; but is, on the contrary, distinctly *inferior*. All shellfish are unclean articles of diet—they being merely the scavengers of the sea; and should be avoided most carefully. They are exceedingly indigestible, and frequently the cause of skin disease, on the one hand, and of ptomaine poisoning, on the other.

It seems hardly necessary to say that all internal organs of animals are to be avoided ! Not only for the reason that a large number of the animals found on the market are diseased; but also because all these organs are merely *depurating* organs, should they be eschewed. If any person were to consider for one minute the *function* of the liver or the kidneys, it is more than probable that he would not touch them ! During the whole of the animal's life, they have been merely *filters* for the filth and excreta which passed through its body; they were the great reservoirs of poisons and toxins of all sorts ! The idea of eating such offal should be repellant to any sensitive, even sensible, mind.

Soups.—But little need be said of soups. As a whole, they may be said to be lacking in every essential which is necessary in order to recommend them as suitable articles for human diet. Meat soups, broths, beef teas, etc., we have already discussed. They are practically stimulants, and consist of water, and poisonous excreta in solution! They contain no fats, carbohydrates or salts of value, and but very little proteid. Vegetable soups have somewhat more to recommend them, but *all* soups are open to the prime objection that they are invariably eaten without mastication, and hence are taken into the stomach in a condition totally unsuited for the initial stages of digestion—which the stomach is called upon to perform. It must be remembered, in this connection, that mastication is not only for the purpose of dividing the food into small particles, so that the gastric and intestinal juices may act upon them, but also, that important *chemical changes* take place in the mouth—starch being converted into dextrine, etc. Soups are always swallowed without this initial process. Further, the large amount of water they contain renders them unsuitable food for the adult—whose food should be less in quantity and more solid in quality ; and any liquid which is supplied during the process of digestion by way of solvent and dilutent should be the digestive juices only. *Jellies* are of very low nutritive value, and should never be administered to invalids. Animals fed on jelly die as soon as if they were not fed at all. In her " Notes on Nursing," Miss Florence Nightingale contends very strongly against the use of jellies of any kind, and finds it difficult to select words strong enough to suit her antipathy to jellies.

Puddings, Pies, etc.—It is now all but universally admitted that these articles of diet are indigestible —rich, greasy, and objectionable in many ways.

R

The usual crust which is bought is made of white flour, in the first place, while the grease contained is a poor quality of lard. As animal food, this is certainly objectionable; lard being a filthy article of diet in any case. The sugar, flour, grease, and all the other ingredients used are generally harmful, and exceedingly indigestible. All the constituents can be supplied in a pure form in other foods. The fruit is the best thing contained in such pies, etc.; and this is spoiled by being cooked, and is also covered with spices and nutmeg, etc., which offset all its original value, and spoil its flavour to all educated palates. As usually presented, such foods have nothing to recommend them.

Still, as Dr Trall said[1]: "the crust for pies and tarts may be made comparatively wholesome in a variety of ways. Any kind of flour or meal, or various admixtures of them, may be wet with water and shortened with sweet cream, or the flour or meal may be wet with milk and shortened with olive oil." In this book, and in various others. may be found a number of recipes for making bread, pies, puddings, etc., in the hygienic style. I shall not discuss this aspect of the question in the present work, which is devoted more to the philosophy of diet than the details of cooking—especially since I am recommending no cooking at all! However, there is doubtless a right and a wrong way to do everything; and if people continue to feel that they *must* have breads and pies, they might as well have them made as hygienically as possible. There is no reason why such foods should be indigestible or innutritious, if properly made. It need hardly be said that all hot breads, buckwheat cakes, etc., should be sedulously avoided.

Sugar.—Hygienists have no objection to the use of saccharine matter, provided it is taken in the natural way—that is, in organic combination with other food

[1] " Hydropathic Cook Book," p. 177.

principles—not separated as a proximate element. Sugar contained in fruits, grains, vegetables, etc., are thoroughly wholesome; but an excess of sugar of the ordinary sort, as bought upon the market, is very detrimental. Particularly is this the case when the sugar is not rightly combined with other articles of food. We have discussed this at greater length, however, when considering "food combinations." Miss Mary H. Abel, in her pamphlet, "Sugar as Food," published by the U.S. Department of Agriculture, says:

"Within certain limits we can look upon sugar as the equivalent of starch that has been digested and made ready for absorption, A mealy, boiled potato, or a lump of laundry starch, is, in fact, very akin to a lump of sugar; and the potato, like all forms of starchy food, must be turned into a kind of sugar by the digestive juices before it can be absorbed as food by the system. . . . The main function of sugar, as found in the blood, whether resulting from the digestion of sugar or of starch, is believed to be the production of heat and energy. The proof has been amply furnished by experiment. By ingenious devices, the blood going to and from the muscle of a living animal, may be analysed, and it is thus shown that more blood traverses an active or working muscle, and more sugar disappears from it than is the case with the muscle at rest."

While the system needs sugar, this should not be supplied in the form of the common beet sugar upon the market—since this is adulterated in various ways, and contains, in addition to the saccharine elements, much inert, mineral matter. Sugar in its pure form, however, is a very important article of diet—far more important, probably, than has hitherto been acknowledged: Not only are starches, etc., converted into sugar in the process of digestion, but it has frequently been noted that when a lesser amount of proteid is consumed, a proportionately larger amount of sugar is craved.

Mr Horace Fletcher noticed this in his diet experiments, and stated that, as the appetite for meat decreased, that for sugar increased—which is a very significant remark. If the saccharine elements in the food-supply were increased, there can be little doubt that there would be a decreased consumption of meat and all proteid matters. The craving of children for sweets is to be looked upon, *not* as a morbid appetite, but as a physiological craving of the organism. In saying that this appetite should be gratified, however, I do not mean that unlimited quantities of sweets and sweet-stuffs, as found upon the market, are to be allowed the child, but a greater proportion of sweet-stuffs should be allowed in the form of sweet fruits—such as dates, figs, etc. Administered in this way, sugar will be found a highly valuable article of diet.

Tea, Coffee and Other Stimulants.—Most persons know, I should imagine, that none of these drinks are suitable for the human stomach. In the first place, no drink at all should be taken at meals, but only between meals ; the reason for this being that the digestive juices are unduly diluted and the food is washed through the stomach, and into the bowels, before it is properly digested, when water or any liquid is drunk at meal-times. All drinks should, therefore, be between meals, and not for at least an hour after a meal, if we wish to ensure the best digestion of the foods eaten.

If this is true of water, the best of all drinks, it is certainly far more true of tea, coffee, and all other stimulants taken at meals. Not only are the effects detrimental (in that they are liquids), but they are of themselves more or less direct poisons also. Tea contains a poison known as *theine*, which corresponds to a similar poison contained in coffee, and known as *caffeine*. Both are strong poisons. Half a gram causes a quick pulse, nervous excitement, slight delusions, and lastly a desire for sleep. Small doses cause sleeplessness, irritability of the bladder and bowels, trembling of the extremities, and other signs of cerebral and nervous distress. Both these poisons work havoc with the system, ruining the nervous and mental life, and creating a dependence on stimulants, which may lead to alcoholic and other excesses. These poisons ruin the taste buds, retard proper digestion, cause constipation, and in many ways tend to ruin the constitution. They cannot be too strongly deprecated. Even *cocoa* contains injurious alkaloids, analogous to those contained in tea and coffee, and for that reason is to be avoided. Like all hot drinks, it tends to ruin the taste buds and induce a desire for more food than is needed, physiologically, and more than the system really requires. For that reason, also, all such drinks are to be avoided.

The injurious effects of *alcohol*, and all other similar stimulants are now so widely known that it is unnecessary to do more than refer to the fact here. Alcohol is *never* necessitated, and is detrimental at all times—more so at some times than at others. The widespread delusion that alcohol is a food ; and, on the other hand, the idea that it actually furnishes " force " to the body, is responsible for much of the abuse which exists. Alcohol imparts no force and no energy to the system, but on the contrary wastes and expends both. Were this once thoroughly realised there would be no excuse whatever for the administration of alcohol, or its use in any form. But the injurious effects of alcohol have been discussed so frequently that I shall not do more than refer to it. (See the discussion of " Stimulants," in my " Vitality, Fasting and Nutrition," pp. 84-44.)

Water.—This is the beverage supplied by nature to furnish all the liquid the body requires ; and water in a pure distilled state is contained in all vegetables, etc., and particularly in fruits. Fruitarians have often found that they can live in good health for weeks and months at a time without a drop of water—while keeping closely to their fruitarian diet. Nevertheless, water is very essential for the majority, and especially so upon an ordinary " mixed " diet. It will be found as a general rule that the more stimulating the food, the more water is required ; and the same is true of all greasy foods. It is well known that all foods containing a large amount of *salt* call for water—this being due to the demand of the system for extra fluids, to wash out the offending and irritating substance. This fact alone should show us how harmful common salt is. The system clearly tries to wash it out of the tissues as soon as possible. Water containing any mineral substance in solution should be avoided. It is never beneficial, but always detrimental to the system. The mineral salts contained are just as injurious as if they were procured from the drug-shop, and taken in the usual way. Pure water is the best at all times—there is but one simple rule to follow in this connection : the purer, the better ! Water should never be drunk at meals, but always between meals. It should be cool, but not ice cold. Hot water may occasionally be of benefit. A plentiful supply of water should be indulged in at all times. The secretions will thereby be increased in volume, the kidneys and liver stimulated into action, the blood rendered less thick, and the general system invigorated. I cannot speak too strongly in favour of large quantities of water each day—say from one to two quarts—if health is to be maintained. (This is of course on the ordinary " mixed " diet.) In all diseased conditions, the necessity for water is greatly increased, and the body is frequently rendered sick because of the very lack of it.

It is an interesting fact that water is the only article

which is taken into the system that is not digested—in one sense of the term. All foods are digested, of course ; and even air goes through a process which might well be called digestion. But water is not digested. It passes through the stomach, and into the bowels unchanged ; it enters the system *as water*, and it leaves it *as water*, and any changes which are noted are simply due to the added salts and excreta which the water has washed through the body along with it. Of itself, it has undergone no change. This is a remarkable fact, and would serve to indicate the tremendous cleansing and flushing properties of water. Next to air, it is doubtless the most necessary article which the body can appropriate. A man can live sixty or more days on water (and air) without solid food ; but he can live only ten or twelve days on solid food (and air) without water. It will thus be seen that water is far *more* essential to life than is solid food ! It is of interest to note, also, that, in all hard manual labour, water is invariably craved long before solid food is called for by the tissues—*i.e.* thirst invariably returns before hunger.

Air and Breathing.—It is not generally known that all air taken into the lungs is *digested*—in one sense of the word—and that next to the last stage of all digestive processes is carried on in the lungs. For that reason a plentiful supply of fresh, pure air is so necessary. Every book we pick up upon the question of health and hygiene is most emphatic upon the value of fresh air ; but few tell us *why* it is so necessary. The majority of persons know that a certain amount of oxygen is needed by the system, and that the blood is purified as it passes through the lungs, but they do not know that these processes are only the first crude outlines of what takes place, and that the processes carried on are both detailed and complicated. Further, as I have said, one of the stages of digestion is carried on in the lungs. The blood

stream carries the food material to the lungs, and there
it meets the oxygen of the atmospheric air, and becomes
oxidised, and rendered appropriable by the system.
It is important to bear in mind this important fact,
that, no matter how much food we may eat, if it is not
oxidised in this manner in the lungs, it cannot be
appropriated by the system, and for that reason remains little better than refuse matter—floating at large
in the system. That is, suppose we eat two pounds of
food during the day, and breathe only enough (correspondingly) to oxidise one pound, only one pound will
be utilised by the system, which will derive no benefit
whatever from the other pound—no matter how good
and nutritious the food may be ! In fact, it will harm
it, by floating about, as mal-assimilated food material.
That is why deep breathing, and breathing fresh air
is so essential. Without this supply of air, food would
never nourish us, or be of any use whatever to the
system.

XV

THE QUESTION OF QUANTITY

I HAVE discussed this question of the quantity of food necessary for the human body so exhaustively in my former book, " Vitality, Fasting and Nutrition," that I need say but little in this place, beyond re-emphasising what I there said. I may, however, add one or two further reflections that have arisen in my mind since the publication of that book, and which may be of interest to those who think about their food at all. This book is devoted to the *quality* of the various foods, as my last was devoted to the *quantity* ; and the disproportionate size of the two volumes rightly indicates what I conceive to be the relative value or place of the two—viz. errors in quality and errors in quantity. I believe that, although errors in quality are tremendously important, errors in quantity are vastly more so, and that, as Dr Graham so well said, many years ago : " It is as a general rule strictly true that a correct quantity of a less wholesome aliment is better for man than an excessively small or an excessively large quantity of a more wholesome aliment." So far as health and longevity are concerned, therefore, it is incomparably better for man to subsist on a correct quantity of vegetable and animal food, properly prepared, than habitually to indulge in an excessive quantity of pure vegetable food of the best kind, and prepared in the best manner ; and the difference is still greater if the vegetable food be badly prepared. And it is solely from the want of a proper regard for this important truth, that many have been unsuccessful in their attempts to live exclusively upon a vegetarian diet.

I have previously pointed out the harm that may result to the body from an excess of food—showing how food in excess chokes and blocks the system throughout —impeding its proper functions, and rendering the perfect manifestation of life impossible. During the healthy growth of the body, the great process of up-building and the functions of nutrition are necessarily somewhat in excess of the processes of destruction ; but even here a great excess of food is invariably eaten ; and, while the growing child may be adding (say) half-an-ounce a day to its weight, it is urged and even forced to eat a pound of food a day, and even more ! And the natural result is that the child becomes sick, and has colds and fever and other troubles, and no one can account for it ! The same false notions are carried into adult life. Nearly everyone eats far too much—I mean by this very much too much. I believe that most persons could reduce their three. daily meals to one, and curtail the amount eaten at that one meal, and still be ingesting too much food for the bodily needs. This will at all events show us how enormously we do overeat, and the only reason that we do not get ill immediately is, that the body is constantly getting rid of the excess of food material and poisons that are formed, as the result of this constant over-ingestion of food. It is generally believed that, as long as an individual is in health, or apparently so, he is not injured by habitually eating more than is really necessary for the healthy nourishment of his body, but this opinion is utterly and dangerously false. It is, indeed, one of the most mischievous errors entertained by the human mind. For there is nothing in nature more true, more certain, than these propositions : that all vital action is necessarily attended with some expenditure of vital power, and draws something from the ultimate fund of life ; and therefore all excessive vital action, all intensity of vital action, increases the expenditure of vital power, and necessarily abbreviates the duration of human life ; and consequently, however long the vital economy of any human body may be able to preserve the general balance of action, between the composing and decomposing elements, and maintain a general health of the system under excessive alimentation, yet nothing is more certain than that, just in proportion as the alimentation has exceeded the real healthy wants of the vital economy, and thus caused an unnecessary expenditure of vital power, life has been abbreviated—even though the individual die from what is called old age, without a single violent symptom of disease. The error of opinion on this subject is common and mischievous ; and the truth should be presented in its strongest light.

But we have as yet only presented the subject and contemplated it in its most favourable aspect. The case I have presented is a very extraordinary one. As a matter of fact, very few indeed who have constantly over-nourished their bodies *do* die from old age, but as a rule they die from painful and exhausting diseases long before that period is reached. Millions of human beings perish by disease, in all periods of life, from excessive alimentation or overeating. Generally, they are cut off by disease long before they have lived out their lives, and often prematurely. And the chief cause of all such death is, I must insist, overeating. This can readily be proved ; and I have endeavoured to show why it should be the case in my previous work. Overeating is the chief cause of all diseases ; and disease shortens and destroys life. Of that there can be no question. But even if no adventitious cause comes in to induce sudden and violent death, either local or general, the continued overworking of the system will almost inevitably exhaust, debilitate and relax some particular organ, and so destroy the balance of action in the vital economy, and thus gradually lead to chronic disease. Adipose tissue is deposited in various parts of the body—causing ruptures of the heart and the blood-vessels, and hence premature death.

It is therefore true, beyond all question, that in all countries where human aliment is abundant and easily procured, gluttony or excessive alimentation is decidedly the greatest source of disease and suffering and premature death known to man. " Excess in drinking," said Hippocrates, more than two thousand years ago, " is almost as bad as excess in eating ! " And the statement has remained true from that day to the present.

How much food should be eaten, then, in order to remain in the best of health, and to preserve that " just balance we term health " ?   I have no hesitation whatever in laying down one general rule, which it is always safe to follow. Every individual should restrict himself to the *smallest* quantity that he finds, from careful investigation and experiment, will meet the wants of his system—knowing that whatever is more than this is harmful.

Physiologists have got into a vicious circle when discussing the question of the amount of food that the system really requires. They have measured the income and the outgo of the food values and co-efficients, and have calculated the supposedly necessary quantities of food that the body needs from these figures—a practice open to many objections, and proved erroneous, in certain directions already—as *e.g.*, by the Chittenden experiments on low proteid intake. It never seems to have struck these men that the more food that is ingested into the system, the more must necessarily be eliminated—for otherwise the body would choke up and die. The fact that more N. is excreted because more is ingested does not prove that the body has utilised all this N., because it needs it, but shows merely that it was enabled to convert it, by the expenditure of a great amount of nervous energy, in the processes of digestion. The experiment of mankind should be, *not* to see how much food they can eat and live, but how little they can eat, and yet live : for the *minimum* quantity of food is doubtless the best for the system, and that indicated by nature. But many physiologists do not see the matter in this light. For them the amount of waste determines everything ! [1]

"But," as Dr Nichols pointed out, "what determines the amount of waste ? A man must get rid of all he eats and drinks, or he must retain it in his system. If he keep at the same average weight, the daily waste will depend upon the daily consumption. He who eats and drinks two pounds will lose two pounds ; he who eats and drinks six or eight pounds must get rid of that quantity. How, then, are we to get at the normal waste, and therefore at the requisite quantity of food ? "

Dr Nichols says further :

" It is my experience—and I believe of many others who work as I do—that the less I eat the better I feel. I do not vary much in weight through months and years from 160 pounds. In solid, dry weight, my food, day by day, would not exceed ten or twelve ounces, and often, for days together, it would not exceed six ounces. I am satisfied by my experience and what I have seen of the effects of diet upon others, that most persons can be perfectly well nourished in full health and activity on from four to eight ounces of food, excluding liquids, and that the amount of water may safely be left to the demands of thirst."

This is even a more conservative estimate than mine and Dr Rabagliati's—since we both agree that twelve

[1] " The Diet Cure," p. 19.

ounces is the amount that is needed by the average man, for an average day's work. But then our calculated allowance was not strictly " dry " diet ; and the difference may not be so great after all, when this is allowed for.

The quantity of food eaten has so little relation to strength and weight that we see men eating ravenously and at the same time wasting to skeletons, and growing weaker and weaker ; and we have strong men living on a spare and simple diet and increasing in weight. Indeed, we see many patients increase in health and strength during a *fast* of many days, when no food at all is eaten ! The truth is, that the amount of food said to be eaten by navvies and other strong men is not the cause of their strength, but it is their strength which enables them to digest and dispose of such quantities of food. Weak men would break down under the strain. And indeed both weak and strong men do, when the resistance of the body is lowered by disease.

To economise life, which is the great secret of health, we must find just the quantity of food we require—that which will supply (indirectly) the force we need, and will not uselessly take from what we have. Of course, we must keep within the limits of our digestive power ; but we must do better than that. A man may be able to digest and dispose of three times as much food as he really requires. One ounce more than he requires is a waste of force, a waste of life. We waste life in eating more food than we need, in digesting it, and then in getting rid of it. Here is a triple waste. " We have other work to do in this world than eating unnecessary food, and spending our strength for nought."

In an excellent little book entitled " The Stomach and its Difficulties," by Sir James Eyre, M.D., there is to be found some very good advice on this question of diet, and particularly the quantity of food that man requires. Speaking of this, Sir James says :

" John Hunter, it is recorded, fed an eagle entirely on vegetable, and a sheep on animal food ; and yet life and apparent health were sustained. Rabbits, if kept fasting a long time, will eat meat greedily. The teeth, however, were no doubt intended by our Creator to be our main guide on this point. . . . Eating in excess is the vice of the present day, and so well managed is it that even religious persons will not see its sinfulness— *sinful*, as absorbing and wasting so much more life and food than the body requires, and which so many absolutely need. Is drunkenness a sin and gluttony not ? . . . Gout, rheumatism and various other disorders are often produced by the injudicious supplies given to the stomach, both in quantity and quality. . . . We too often charge cold and wet with being the cause of attacks of disease, but these attacks would not have occurred unless the blood had been infected with particles of depraved matter resulting from over-indulgence, or other irregularity of the organs of digestion—first and foremost, from our injudicious supplies to the stomach. . . . Perhaps we might lay it down as a rule that the majority of men eat twice as much as is really required for the support of health and strength. . . . No doubt as life advances we really require less food. . . . According to our mental and bodily employment, so should we eat. . . . Nature herself often gives notice of over-indulgence, by destroying appetite. Children take the warning and refuse food altogether ; but it is so common a notion that we cannot go on without regular meals, that many adults aggravate stomach and liver derangements by persisting in taking food of some sort, but which affords no nourishment at all, because it cannot be digested, and thus acts as any other extraneous substance, by increasing the already deranged powers of the organ. We may rest assured that mischief rarely happens in disease from want of food, although much mischief is often caused by the ignorant in pressing it, against the warnings of nature in depriving us of any desire for it. In the incipient stage of many diseases, abstinence at first, and then a very strict attention to judicious nourishment, will alone cure them."

After such a simple and clear statement of facts, it seems to me little remains to be said. I cannot emphasise too strongly the importance of limiting the amount of the food supply ; and particularly is this warning applicable to vegetarians who are apt to overeat, under the erroneous impression that they must eat more, in order to offset the greater nutritive value of the meat (supposedly) ! The fact of the matter is that they should eat *less* ; and the more nourishing and concentrated the food is, the less of it should they eat. Most of the vegetarian dishes are highly concentrated, and exceedingly rich in nutritive values. For that reason they should be eaten sparingly. Nuts are especially rich, and contain a large amount of proteid in a small compass. In his pamphlet " Nuts and their Uses as Food " (Yearbook, U.S. Dept. of Agr.), Professor Jaffa says of such foods :

" The digestibility of protein in 28 experiments with mixed diets, to which were added fruits and nuts, averaged 90 per cent. [see pp. 86-88] . . . The digestibility of the carbohydrates in nuts, so far as the available *data* show, is about equal to that of the same ingredients in other foods. . . . It would appear that, while it is not possible to state the exact digestion coefficients for all nuts, enough has been done to indicate their high nutritive value and digestibility. . . . The distress sometimes experienced when nuts are eaten is undoubtedly often due to improper mastication or to over-indulgence. The investigations made at the California station indicate clearly that considerable quantities of nuts properly eaten do not cause distress. . . . A fruit and nut diet may be arranged to furnish sufficient protein. mainly from nuts, to satisfy the requirements of the body. . . . When considering nuts, it is readily observed that 10 cents will buy about the same amount of nut protein as of animal protein, except in the case of cheese and skim milk (which furnishes less). If spent for peanuts, it will purchase more than twice the protein and six times the energy that could be bought for the same expenditiure for porterhouse steak. . . . It is of more than passing interest to note that 10 cents' worth of peanuts will contain about 4 ounces of protein and 2767 calories of energy, which is more protein and energy than is furnished by many rations regarded as adequate for a day. . . . As a whole, nuts may be classed among the *staple foods*, and not simply as food accessories."

I desire only to show in this place that nuts are a very concentrated article of diet, and should be eaten sparingly. The idea that more food should be eaten, when going on to a vegetarian diet, is grossly erroneous, and is the reason why many vegetarians fail. Less, not more, food, should be eaten ; and as soon as the stomach has shrunk to its right proportions, and the customary reaction from the stimulation of the meat has worn off, a general feeling of invigoration and well-being will be experienced—and retained, if the diet be properly managed thenceforth. Too great care cannot be taken not to overeat ; everyone would be better for a few days' fast—particularly if they have been in the habit of eating meat !

XVI

GENERAL CONCLUSIONS

I THINK I have shown, in the preceding pages, that fruits and nuts are man's best, natural, and original food—the food best suited to his organism—capable of sustaining it in the highest state of health. If I have merely induced a number of persons to experiment upon themselves I shall at all events feel that this book has performed its mission, as there can be no question that wherever the fruitarian diet is tried, it is adopted and finds its adherents. I have frequently known persons go back to a mixed diet, after having tried vegetarianism for a time, but I have never known of *one*, who after once having tried the fruitarian diet, gave it up permanently. Of course everyone may relapse once in a while ; and go on to another diet for a few days, but invariably the fruitarian diet is again resumed at the end of that time, with added appreciation of its worth. The fruitarian diet is as far superior to the ordinary vegetarian diet as that diet is superior to the " mixed diet "—including meat. There is no comparison between the two. Far more energy is experienced, while living upon fruits and nuts ; the necessity for so much sleep is done away with—persons living upon this diet manage very nicely on about six hours of sleep, generally speaking ; a feeling of cleanness and lightness is experienced throughout the body ; and in many other ways the effects of the diet are noticeable. The fact that man is intended by Nature to live upon such a diet is very clearly indicated by his structure ; and it is safe to say that the nearer we live to Nature, the healthier and the happier we are.

I shall conclude with a few practical health hints, in relation to diet, which I have omitted to mention in the preceding pages.

Let us consider first of all mastication.

The importance of thorough *mastication* is now becoming generally recognised. The experiments and researches of Horace Fletcher, Professor Chittenden, etc., have done much towards calling the attention of the public to the importance of this subject, and its great advantages—not only in ensuring health, but in rendering the life longer and happier—are now generally recognised. This subject has been so ably handled by the two authors whose books I have mentioned, however, that it would be unnecessary for me to go into this question in greater detail here. To anyone who has not made a study of this subject, I can but recommend Fletcher's " New Glutton or Epicure " and " The A.B-Z. of our Nutrition " ; also Professor Chittenden's " Physiological Economy in Nutrition," and " The Nutrition of Man." Now for a few practical hints.

Never eat when mentally excited or very tired. It is best to lie down a few minutes before each meal, if possible, and take a short rest after it. Never take exercise soon after a meal, or take a bath, or a swim. All these have a tendency to draw the blood away from the stomach—to the surface, or the parts exercised. This is to be avoided, if possible. It is best to make the meals somewhat regular, but never eat if you are not hungry—go without any solid food until the next meal. Drink water plentifully, meanwhile. In this way, an appetite will be gained, and sickness prevented.

Take a few deep-breathing exercises each day. In this way the requisite oxygen is supplied, and the food ingested is utilised, instead of remaining more or less mal-assimilated and unused by the system. Do not take very hot or very cold foods or drinks. The best temperature is that of the surrounding atmosphere, in a comfortably warm room. Great care should be taken of the teeth, as, when these are once gone, no false teeth can ever take their place, and the standard of health is almost invariably lowered, on account of the fact that insufficient mastication is practised.

Finally—and this is a factor of great importance—the *mental condition* should be one free from worry or care. I have been contending very strongly throughout this book for the superiority of certain foods over others ; and the value of a hygienic diet ; and I still think that this question is one of the most important before the world to-day—alike for the individual and the race. Nevertheless, I am persuaded that much, if not all, of the value of a reformed diet may be offset by constant fretting and worrying about the food eaten. I believe that it would be better to eat a moderate amount of any food upon the market and think nothing about it, than to eat the best of foods—the most wholesome and the most nutritious—and keep worrying about them all the time. The hygienist should supply his body with good food, and then forget it. He should not think or worry about his food or himself in the least. Some individuals spend almost the whole of their lives in thinking about their food ; and the consequence is that they constantly have dyspepsia, and get no benefit from any of it. One can dwell upon this food question far too much—to the point of becoming morbid about it. I went through that transition stage myself—one which I am glad to say I have experienced, because it enables me to appreciate the mental condition of others in a like state. I am also glad I have passed through that stage, and have emerged into what I consider a more sane and normal view of these matters. At one time in my life, the foods I ate formed a large part of my mental occupation and interest : I thought between meals what I should have for the next. I balanced up my every article of diet, and even went so far as to discriminate between the various kinds of nuts, because of the different percentages of proteid they contained! In those days I should as soon have thought of killing my dearest friend as eating a piece of meat!—so monstrous did the idea seem to me. I sided with all those individuals who stated with glee that " they had not touched a piece of meat for twenty-two years "—and so on. When I went out to dinner, I informed my hostess that I was a vegetarian, and asked to be excused from being helped to meat. But now I have emerged from that state of narrowness. Now, while I live upon the fruitarian diet, and that pretty strictly, when alone, I do not think I am being poisoned if I taste a piece of meat, when dining out, knowing that my system can well take care of the poisons generated, so long as I live all the rest of the time upon a normal diet; and I do not at all worry about my food, but eat a little of most of the things that are upon the table, and make up for it by slightly added care in my diet during the next day or two. Thus, though I consider the diet question one of the most important—if not *the* most important—before the civilised world to-day, I must warn all diet reformers against this tendency to get into a rut, on account of their food habits, and would advise them to be careful to preserve a sane balance of mind on these questions, and a just proportion in their viewpoint. Most diet reformers are too deadly in earnest. They should cultivate a sense of humour !

APPENDIX

IT is with pleasure that I present a photograph of my
friend Max Unger (" Lionel Strongfort "), doubtless the
strongest man in the world to-day, and one of the most
beautifully and perfectly proportioned. He is a strict
vegetarian—at times a fruitarian—and a strong advocate of this diet.   His statue in marble is in the National
Art Gallery at Berlin.   It was made at the request of
the German Government, by Prof. Louis Tuaillon, of
Rome.   The famous artist, Max Klinger, also considers
him the ideal of symmetrical athletic beauty, and found
in him the inspiration of several of his masterpieces.

Mr Unger has doubtless performed feats of strength
never equalled in the history of the world.   With one
hand he has lifted a bar-bell above his head weighing
312 pounds.   Even the far-famed Eugene Sandow
never lifted more than 250 pounds in this way.   He is
the only man who has ever torn five packs of playing
cards in halves, at one time—a thickness of 260 cards.
He has lifted a weight (using his entire body) of more
than 8000 pounds—a sixty horse-power automobile,
containing several men, together with a heavy bridge,
over which the machine passed.   In view of this, how
absurd the contention that strong men "must eat meat";
that " they are strong because of the meat they eat,"
etc. !   And how doubly absurd the contention that the
average man, who takes but little exercise, cannot perform his daily duties without the use of this article of
diet !

INDEX